Commentary on the Book of Job
Bible Study Notes and Comments

by David E. Pratte

Available in print at
www.gospelway.com/sales

Commentary on the Book of Job:
Bible Study Notes and Comments

© Copyright David E. Pratte, 2010, 2014
Minor revisions 2016
All rights reserved

ISBN-13: 978-1495909535
ISBN-10: 1495909530

Note carefully: No teaching in any of our materials is intended or should ever be construed to justify or to in any way incite or encourage personal vengeance or physical violence against any person.

Front page photo
Statue with artist's conception of Job

Photo credit: Jörg Syrlin the Younger distributed under GNU free documentation license, via Wikimedia Commons

Other Acknowledgements
Unless otherwise indicated, Scripture quotations are generally from the New King James Version (NKJV), copyright 1982, 1988 by Thomas Nelson, Inc. used by permission. All rights reserved.

Scripture quotations marked (NASB) are from *Holy Bible, New American Standard* La Habra, CA: The Lockman Foundation, 1995.

Scripture quotations marked (ESV) are from *The Holy Bible, English Standard Version*, copyright ©2001 by Crossway Bibles, a publishing ministry of Good News Publishers. Used by permission. All rights reserved.

Scripture quotations marked (MLV) are from Modern Literal Version of The New Testament, Copyright 1999 by G. Allen Walker.

Scripture quotations marked (RSV) are from the Revised Standard Version of the Bible, copyright 1952 by the Division of Christian Education, National Council of the Churches of Christ in the United States of America.

Scripture quotations marked (NIV) are from the New International Version of the Holy Bible, copyright 1978 by Zondervan Bible publishers, Grand Rapids, Michigan.

Other Books by the Author

Topical Bible Studies

Growing a Godly Marriage & Raising Godly Children
Why Believe in God, Jesus, and the Bible? (evidences)
The God of the Bible (study of the Father, Son, and Holy Spirit)
Grace, Faith, and Obedience: The Gospel or Calvinism?
Kingdom of Christ: Future Millennium or Present Spiritual Reign?
Do Not Sin Against the Child: Abortion, Unborn Life, & the Bible
True Words of God: Bible Inspiration and Preservation

Commentaries on Bible Books

Genesis
Joshua and Ruth
Judges
1 Samuel
2 Samuel
1 Kings
Ezra, Nehemiah, and Esther
Job
Proverbs
Ecclesiastes
Gospel of Matthew
Gospel of Mark
Gospel of John
Acts
Romans
Galatians
Ephesians
Philippians and Colossians
Hebrews
James and Jude
1 and 2 Peter
1,2,3 John

Bible Question Class Books

Genesis
Joshua and Ruth
Judges
1 Samuel
2 Samuel
1 Kings
Ezra, Nehemiah, and Esther
Job
Proverbs
Ecclesiastes
Isaiah
Daniel
Gospel of Matthew
Gospel of Mark
Gospel of Luke
Gospel of John
Acts
Romans
1 Corinthians
2 Corinthians and Galatians
Ephesians and Philippians
Colossians, 1&2 Thessalonians
1 & 2 Timothy, Titus, Philemon
Hebrews
General Epistles (James – Jude)
Revelation

Workbooks with Study Notes

Jesus Is Lord: Workbook on the Fundamentals of the Gospel of Christ
Following Jesus: Workbook on Discipleship
God's Eternal Purpose in Christ: Workbook on the Theme of the Bible
Family Reading Booklist

Visit our website at <u>www.gospelway.com/sales</u> to see a current list of books in print.

Other Resources from the Author

Printed books, booklets, and tracts available at
www.gospelway.com/sales
Free Bible study articles online at
www.gospelway.com
Free Bible courses online at
www.biblestudylessons.com
Free class books at
www.biblestudylessons.com/classbooks
Free commentaries on Bible books at
www.biblestudylessons.com/commentary
Contact the author at
www.gospelway.com/comments

Table of Contents

Job 1 9
Job 2 23
Job 3 29
Job 4 33
Job 5 38
Job 6 44
Job 7 48
Job 8 52
Job 9 56
Job 10 62
Job 11 65
Job 12 69
Job 13 74
Job 14 80
Job 15 84
Job 16 90
Job 17 93
Job 18 96
Job 19 99
Job 20 104
Job 21 108
Job 22 114
Job 23 120
Job 24 123
Job 25 128
Job 26 130
Job 27 133
Job 28 137
Job 29 141
Job 30 145
Job 31 150
Job 32 156
Job 33 160
Job 34 166
Job 35 172
Job 36 175
Job 37 181
Job 38 186
Job 39 191
Job 40 194
Job 41 197
Job 42 202

(Due to printer reformatting, the above numbers may be off a page or two.)

Notes to the Reader

To save space and for other reasons, I have chosen not to include the Bible text in these notes (please use your Bible to follow along). When I do quote a Scripture, I generally quote the New King James Version, unless otherwise indicated. Often – especially when I do not use quotations marks – I am not quoting any translation but simply paraphrasing the passage in my own words. Also, when I ask the reader to refer to a map, please consult the maps at the back of your Bible or in a Bible dictionary.

You can find study questions to accompany these notes at www.gospelway.com/sales

To join our mailing list to be informed of new books or special sales, contact the author at www.gospelway.com/comments

Introductory Thoughts about Commentaries

Only the Scriptures provide an infallible, authoritatively inspired revelation of God's will for man (2 Timothy 3:16,17). It follows that this commentary, like all commentaries, was written by an uninspired, fallible human. It is the author's effort to share his insights about God's word for the purpose of instructing and edifying others in the knowledge and wisdom found in Scripture. It is simply another form of teaching, like public preaching, Bible class teaching, etc., except in written form (like tracts, Bible class literature, etc.). Nehemiah 8:8; Ephesians 4:15,16; Romans 15:14; 1 Thessalonians 5:11; Hebrews 3:12-14; 5:12-14; 10:23-25; Romans 10:17; Mark 16:15,16; Acts 8:4; 2 Timothy 2:2,24-26; 4:2-4; 1 Peter 3:15.

It follows that the student must read any commentary with discernment, realizing that any fallible teacher may err, whether he is teaching orally or in writing. So, the student must compare all spiritual teaching to the truth of God's word (Acts 17:11). It may be wise to read several commentaries to consider alternative views on difficult points. But it is especially important to consider the *reasons or evidence* each author gives for his views, then compare them to the Bible.

For these reasons, the author urges the reader to always consider my comments in light of Scripture. Accept what I say only if you find that it harmonizes with God's word. And please do not cite my writings as authority, as though people should accept anything I say as authoritative. Always let the Bible be your authority.

"He who glories, let him glory in the Lord" – 1 Corinthians 1:31

Abbreviations Used in These Notes

ASV – American Standard Version
b/c/v –– book, chapter, and verse
ESV – English Standard Version
f – the following verse
ff – the following verses
KJV – King James Version
NASB – New American Standard Bible
NEB – New English Bible
NIV – New International Version
NKJV – New King James Version
RSV – Revised Standard Version

Job 1

Introduction

Basic Information

Author and date

Other Bible references confirm the historical truth of the story of Job, showing that he lived and his story was well known: Ezek. 14:14,20; James 5:11. He was a real man, his story actually occurred, and he was a faithful servant of God, just as surely were Noah, Daniel, etc. Further, the inspiration of the book is confirmed by the apostle Paul in 1 Corinthians 3:19, where he quotes directly from Job 5:13 saying, "it is written." This expression is used repeatedly to refer to inspired Scripture.

However, the date when the book was **written** and by whom it was written are so uncertain as to be unworthy of any in-depth discussion. Various commentators have speculated upon nearly every imaginable Old Testament author and every imaginable Old Testament time period. Nor do we know for certain the exact location of the land of Uz where these events occurred. Horne argues, on the basis of Lamentations 4:21, that Uz refers to Edom or Idumaea, the area south of the Dead Sea. He adds, "...there seems to be no good reason for supposing that it was not written by Job himself." However, he grants that it is possible that, even if Job wrote the original record, it may have been edited and revised by some later inspired writer. So it is possible that the events themselves occurred long before they were recorded in the inspired book that we have now received.

The time period when the events of the story **occurred** historically, however, is much easier to determine. The evidence shows almost certainly that the events occurred during the period of the patriarchs. This is demonstrated by the following facts:

* The lifestyle of Job and his family is described much like that of Abraham and other patriarchs. They are keepers of flocks and herds, whose wealth is indicated by the extent of their flocks. They have a large household of servants who assist in this work. Having many children was considered a sign of blessing and greatness, etc. The Chaldeans lived a similar wandering lifestyle – 1:17.

* Since this is an Old Testament story, if it did not occur during the period of the patriarchs, then it must have occurred during the Mosaic age. But virtually every story that occurred during the Mosaic age directly or indirectly involves Israelites. Yet there is no reference of any kind in the book of Job to the Israelites, either to the nation or to their worship, etc. There are no references to the Law of Moses, the tabernacle, the priesthood, the judges or kings, etc.

On the contrary, God speaks directly to Job, just as He does in the patriarchal age with Noah, Abraham, Isaac, Jacob, and other heads of households (see Job 38-42). Furthermore, Job offers his own sacrifices and sacrifices for his friends, rather than bringing them to the Levitical priests at the tabernacle or temple, etc. (1:5; 42:5-8).

If these events happened after the giving of the Law, it must be one of the only Old Testament books written then that makes no reference whatever to the history, nation, or religion of the Israelites or Jews. This strongly implies that it occurred before the giving of the law.

* We are not told Job's tribe, which would be a very unusual omission if this were under the Mosaic Law.

* The most conclusive evidence, however, is Job's age. When the story begins, he already has ten grown children (1:2-5), as well as great wealth and notoriety. This would imply significant age. However, he lived another 140 years after the main events of the story, having another ten children, etc. (42:16). Such ages are most common during the period of the patriarchs, but are unheard of even shortly after the giving of the law. Abraham, Isaac, and Jacob each lived about 150-180 years. While Moses lived to be 120, neither he nor any of his contemporaries approached Job's age. By the time of David, ages over 70 were unusual.

This evidence, taken together, indicates strongly that the story of Job occurred during the age of the patriarchs, before the giving of the Law of Moses.

Theme

The issue of suffering is used to demonstrate the authority of God in His universe. Does God have the right to control events according to His will, and should we trust Him to do right even when it does not make sense to us?

Main characters

Job and his friends (Eliphaz, Bildad, Zophar, and Elihu)

Divisions of the book
* Description of Job's trials (ch. 1,2)
* False comfort from his friends — debates over why people suffer (ch. 3-31)
* Speech of Elihu (ch. 32-37)
* God's response to Job and his friends (ch. 38-42)

Observations about inspiration

Like all Scripture, the book of Job was inspired by the Holy Spirit (2 Timothy 3:16,17; 2 Peter 1:20,21). But while inspiration guarantees that the book gives an accurate historical account of the events that happened, it does not guarantee that the uninspired speakers in the story spoke the truth. In other words, when uninspired people spoke error or committed sins, the Bible writer may still record what was said; the record would show what the person really did say or do, but that would not mean the things said or done were pleasing to God. It may be an accurate record of things that displeased God.

This should be an obvious conclusion, since the Bible records all kinds of sinful acts. The acts really occurred and there are lessons we can learn from them, so the Bible records them, from the sin of Adam and Eve to the crucifixion of Jesus, etc. The fact they are recorded in Scripture does not mean that God was pleased by the acts or that we should imitate them. The Scripture records that the events happened, but we are expected by context or other passages to realize that the conduct was wrong and we should not practice it.

Likewise, the Bible writers may record when people in error spoke falsehood. Many examples can be cited. The serpent told Eve, "You will not surely die" (Genesis 3:4). The fool says there is no God (Psalms 14:1). The Jews said Jesus cast out demons by the power of Beelzebub (Matthew 12:24). Peter denied Jesus saying He did not know Him, etc. And in the book of Job, Job's wife says, "Curse God and die" (2:9). All these statements are accurately recorded in the Bible, because they really were said. But they were said by people who sinned in saying them. The result is that the Bible accurately records these false statements. But we are expected to know by context or other passages that they are false, and that we should not believe them to be truth.

This is especially of concern in the book of Job, because we have chapter after chapter spoken by Job's friends, yet they are clearly in error, speaking many things that are not true. At the end God rebukes them for not speaking truth (42:7,8). This tells us that there are many things they say that we must not believe as truth, yet the book accurately records that they said them. Of course, like all people in sin, they do say some things that are true. So we must face the challenge of determining which is true and which is error.

And even Job at times says things he should not. He too repents at the end and admits that he said things that he did not understand and did not know. He repented in dust and ashes (42:1-6). He spoke more truth than his friends did (42:7,8). But still he spoke some things that we should not believe to be true.

Observations about the manner of speaking in the book

Not only do the speeches of the friends and even of Job contain both truth and error, but their speeches are highly poetic. Perhaps they spoke this way at the time, or perhaps the author reworded the meaning of their speeches into poetic form, like poets often do today (if so, of course, he did so by inspiration, so the results accurately express the thoughts of the speakers). But poetry is often highly symbolic and figurative. Much of the language in the book is not meant to be taken literally.

Furthermore, the speakers use a number of words that are not used in other books, making translation difficult. It may be that their manner of speaking is unique to their age and society. In any case it is highly repetitious. The same thoughts are expressed over and over. This is typical in any confrontation in which people are defending opposing views. But it is especially so in Job. Hailey makes the interesting observation that perhaps the repetition of the book is a tool used by the author to help us appreciate how tedious, tiring, and seemingly endless suffering is to those who endure it.

In any case, the result that cannot be denied is that specifics of the book are at times difficult to understand. Nevertheless, the main points of the story are clear and extremely practical.

For all these reasons, we will approach the book by trying to understand the main point of the speakers, without always analyzing every detail. We will consider details as needed. But this book should not be treated as a highly doctrinal statement to be carefully analyzed as, for example, New Testament epistles. We will try to understand the overall thrust of the speeches, without getting overly bogged down in difficulties.

Lessons from the Story

The story of Job

Job 1:1-3,8-12,22; 2:1-10 – Job was a godly, upright man who feared God. Yet God allowed him to suffer, not because he was guilty of sin, but because Satan was trying to tempt him to commit sin. Job's suffering included the loss of his children and all his wealth in a single day, then the loss of his health, and finally his wife and friends turned against him (1:13-19; 2:7-9).

Job 1:20-22; 2:10 – Job reacted to his suffering by maintaining his faith in God.

Job 4:7-9; 8:3-6; 22:5-11 – Like many people today, the friends believed that only the wicked should suffer (compare 11:4-6; 18:5-10). So when Job suffered so grievously, they mistakenly concluded that he was guilty of grievous sins.

In Job's responses throughout the book, he maintained that he did not know why he was suffering, but he knew he was not guilty as they were accusing him. Yet, Hailey makes another interesting observation, that Job's view is mistaken in a way that is similar to that of his friends. He often expresses the view that suffering **ought** to be reserved to the wicked! He knew it apparently was not reserved for the wicked, since he was convinced he did nothing to deserve what he was suffering. But he thought God should not allow the righteous to suffer, so he complained against the justice of God in allowing such suffering for the righteous. (9:22-24; chapter 12)

Job 38:4-7; 40:7-9; 42:1-9 – In the end, God never does explain to Job the reasons why he suffered; rather, God proves that He is wiser than men, so we often do not understand Him. Job then realized that he had no right to criticize God. Job's friends had to offer sacrifice for having said false things about God and about Job, but God rewarded Job by giving him even more blessings than he had at the beginning – 42:10-17.

Conclusions regarding suffering

* Suffering is not always a punishment for evil we have personally done.

* Suffering is sometimes a temptation from the devil to get us to sin.

* Just as man cannot understand God's power in creation, so we do not (and sometimes cannot) understand His affairs in the world. Specifically, even when we do not know why certain people suffer, nevertheless we should trust God to do right, instead of criticizing or doubting Him.

* We can endure suffering faithfully, just as Job did, even when we do not understand all God's affairs – James 5:10,11; 1 Cor. 10:13.

Chapter 1-3 – Description of Job's Trials

Chapter 1 - Satan's First Temptation of Job

1:1 – Job was upright, feared God, and shunned evil.

We are told that these events occurred in the land of Uz, but we do not know for sure where that was. It is said to be in the east (verse 3). It was in an area where Chaldeans and Sabeans might raid (1:14,17). And obviously it was an area suitable for maintaining large flocks and herds. Hailey thinks this would place it east or northeast from Palestine. Horne argues, on the basis of Lamentations 4:21, that Uz refers to Edom or Idumaea, the area South of the Dead Sea.

Much more important to the story than its location, however, is the character of Job. He was a blameless and upright man who feared God and avoided evil. This is confirmed throughout the book, especially in these first two chapters (1:8,22; 2:3,10). Compare the description of Job to the description of Noah in Genesis 6:9 and Abraham in Genesis 22:12.

So, at the very outset one of the basic issues of the book is resolved. The book discusses at length the subject of suffering and why men suffer. Job himself is used as a case history to prove that people do suffer even when they are righteous, and that suffering is not always the direct result of evils we personally have committed. To establish this, we are told right off that Job was a good man, not an evil man. Whatever happens to him in this book, it is not because of sins he has committed.

1:2,3 – Job had seven sons, three daughters, great flocks and herds, and a large household.

Next we are told about Job's prosperity and blessings. He had a large family: 7 sons and 3 daughters. And he had great flocks and herds of sheep, camels, oxen, and donkeys. He had a large household, which implies, not just children, but also many servants (like Abraham) to help in caring for such large herds (compare 1:15,16,17).

All this describes a man of great prosperity, richly blessed both in goods and family. Wealth was apparently measured or indicated by great flocks of animals. And a large family with many children indicated rich blessings from God. Job was richly blessed.

In fact he was the greatest man among the people of the East (compare 29:25; 31:37). This could imply great and important position as well as prosperity. Job was not just a good man, he was important, wealthy, and influential. No one in that area was greater.

This helps us understand how completely his eventual suffering would contrast to what he was accustomed to. When people live in poverty and deprivation all their lives, they may become resigned to suffering. But one who is so richly blessed would experience a great shock when his great blessings are replaced by equally great suffering. The very contrast of his suffering as compared to his former prosperity would make additional temptation for Job.

1:4,5 – *In case his children had sinned, Job would make sacrifice for them when they had their feasts.*

Job's sons had feasts from time to time. Each of the seven of them, on their appointed day, would invite the other brothers and sisters to come and feast with them. Note that this describes a close family. Though they are apparently grown and married, or at least living in their own houses, yet they still enjoyed one another's companionship. They acted as though they were good friends. (It would be interesting to know if the reference to each brother's day refers to his birthday, so they took turns celebrating one another's birthday as many families do today. Note that Job's "day" refers to the day of his birth in 3:1,3. But the language may simply mean that each had accepted a time in the year to hold a feast.)

When each feast had ended, Job would rise early in the morning and offer sacrifices for each one of his children. Nothing implies the feasts were riotous or lascivious, but he was concerned that maybe they may have said or done something sinful, perhaps even cursing God during their feasting. The passage says Job regularly did this. The fact he arose early shows his diligent dedication.

This illustrates the patriarchal concept of that day. The father, as the head of the extended family, was a spiritual leader. He was responsible to teach the family about God, lead them in serving Him, and rebuke them when they erred. And he would offer sacrifice on behalf of those who sinned.

It appears that he offered sacrifices even for unknown sins: "It may be that..." Can we learn a lesson in this? Of course, God would not forgive the children if they stubbornly refused to repent. Yet, could this relate to that fact that sometimes we may sin unknowingly and so should confess and seek forgiveness for things we may have done that we don't yet realize to be sinful or that we have forgotten about?

In any case, Job was clearly concerned for his children's spiritual well-being. Just because children leave home, that does not mean their parents no longer have a sense of concern for them. Godly parents continue to pray and seek God's favor for the salvation of their children.

1:6,7 – Satan presented himself before the Lord.

On a certain day or time, the sons of God presented themselves before God. 2:1 shows that other such times occur. We are not told why this meeting occurred or how often such meetings occurred. Perhaps it is implied that God calls His angels before Him at times to report or give an account or to be given assigned tasks. Since we are dealing with God and spirit beings, it is difficult to know the full implications.

The "sons of God" here are surely not humans, so are most likely angels (compare 38:7). But Satan was among them. The Bible does not say much about Satan's origin or about how he communicates with God or other spirit beings. But Job 1,2 describe him as personally speaking with God. On this occasion he joined other spirit beings in an audience before God. It seems likely that he did not always come on such occasions, but he did this time perhaps because he had a plan in mind.

Note that Satan is a real spirit being, just as real as God, Job, etc. His name means "adversary." He most certainly proved himself to be Job's adversary, but he is just as much the adversary of all humans. He does not seek our good, no matter what he may pretend. Since he works by deception (2 Corinthians 11:13-15), many people do not see his real evil. And even more likely, we do not know when he is working in any given situation to mislead us. But we can be sure that he is always working to cause our spiritual downfall, just as God is working for our good. (1 Chronicles 21:1; Zechariah 3:1)

When God asked Satan where he had been, Satan said he had been going to and fro, walking back and forth on the earth (compare Job 2:2). Indeed, 1 Peter 5:8 says he prowls about like a lion seeking whom he may devour. He did not here tell God the intent for which he travels around the world. It is like he says vaguely, "Oh, I've been here and there." But of course God knew, as we should, that he travels everywhere seeking opportunity to lead men to sin. Satan's presence is real. We do not understand the nature of spirit beings and how they travel. Whereas God is omnipresent, able to see everywhere at once, Satan must be more limited. But it seems that he can appear at any place at any time, and he also has his demons who work for him to achieve his will.

1:8 – God upheld Job before Satan as an example of a blameless man.

God challenged Satan to consider the case of Job. God from his own speech confirmed that Job was truly a blameless and upright man; he feared God and avoided evil. This is how we were introduced to Job in 1:1 (see notes there). God directly confirmed this to be His view of Job, and He repeats it in 2:3.

In calling Job His "servant," God is not insulting Job but praising him. Some today consider it to be beneath their dignity to be a servant. But Jesus taught that service is the greatest of honors – Matthew

20:25-28. Servants in that day were often highly honored, serving in roles of great responsibility. To be a trusted and respected servant in a great house was a great honor. How much more then should we rejoice in the role of servants of God?

God almost appears to be reminding Satan that not all people will submit to Satan's temptations and deceits. Surely they both knew that many people fail to serve God, yet there are some who are faithful (Matthew 7:13,14). God appears to hold Job's case forth as a victory for His work on earth, as if He said, "If you have been walking back and forth on the earth, Satan, then you must know that you have been unsuccessful in seducing Job."

1:9-11 – Satan claimed that Job would turn from God if he were to suffer enough.

Satan argued that people serve God only for the blessings they hope to receive in this life. They expect that serving God will lead to material benefit, so they serve so long as the blessings continue. But they will turn from God if the blessings cease.

At least he challenges God that this was so in Job's case. He says Job fears God because God has protected him (built a hedge around him) on every side. He has blessed his work and given him great possessions. But Satan affirms that, if God were to touch all that Job has – i.e., destroy it – Job would curse God to His very face. Satan discounts that any man would serve God out of love for God or out of true respect to God as the Creator and proper Ruler of the universe.

There are many reasons given in Scripture why we should serve God, but material prosperity in this life is not one of them – at least not in the New Testament. The Old Testament seems to put greater emphasis on material blessings in this life for God's people, but even so the greatest reward comes after this life. Many people, even in the Old Testament, made great sacrifice to honor God (see Hebrews 11).

The New Testament especially emphasizes that we have a spiritual reward after this life. Our reward is not temporal (2 Corinthians 4:8-18). This life is a testing ground to honor God and receive a reward after this life. Christians must remember this.

But there are other reasons to serve God. God deserves our service simply because of who He is. He made us. He rightly rules the universe. He is all-wise, all-powerful, and infinitely good and holy. Therefore, He deserves our service. However, as the story of Job reveals, we may not always see His wisdom and goodness revealed in any given event or series of events in our lives. We may not understand His ways. Nevertheless, the Bible assures us that He is good and deserves our service. Scripture gives us the evidence of miracles, fulfilled prophecy, Jesus' resurrection, etc., to prove this to be true. Then God expects us to serve Him based on this truth.

But Satan denies all this and argues, in effect, that every man has his price. If he suffers enough, he will give up serving God. This becomes a major theme of the book. It follows that, if we sin against God because we suffer, then we are allowing Satan to be victorious in our lives. He wins. We lose and God loses (in this specific case). We can win the victory over Satan only if we remain true to God. All of this, however, is here revealed to us in Job's case, but is unknown to Job at this point.

Yet Satan knows his own arguments are often invalid.

I believe it is worth remembering that suffering is just one means Satan uses to lead men to sin. Interestingly enough, sometimes Satan just as effectively uses the opposite approach. Many people sin against God when they ***prosper***. Great physical blessings and wealth become a temptation that leads them to trust in self instead of God and to fail to give God credit and fail to use their blessings to serve God. Riches can be as great a temptation as suffering (1 Timothy 6:6-19; Luke 12:15-21; Matthew 6:19-34; etc.).

And conversely, suffering can often cause people to turn ***to*** God. There are many people who enjoy a pleasant life, refusing to give God credit or submit to Him, but if they lose these benefits and begin to truly suffer, they humble themselves and see their need for God. Consider the prodigal son in Luke 15. So, whereas Satan claims that suffering will lead Job to sin, in truth suffering is often a means that leads people to turn ***from*** sin.

And Satan knows all this. He often uses wealth and prosperity to tempt people and keep them from turning to God. So it appears that he is being two-faced here with God. In Job's case, he was richly blessed but was faithful. OK, well, let's try a different approach. Let's make him suffer greatly and see if that leads him to sin. But if riches had led Job to become proud and disobey God, Satan would gladly have sought to continue those riches and would have opposed any suffering that might lead him to repent! But Job gave God the credit for his blessings and remained faithful, so Satan claimed that he was serving just for temporal gain.

Satan does not mind contradicting himself, if it works. Evil people are often self-contradictory. No matter what happens, they have an excuse why people should not serve God. No matter which way things go, there is always an explanation to justify their sin. Note Matthew 11:18,19.

1:12 – *God granted Satan permission to test Job but not to harm him personally.*

Satan had challenged God that Job would lose his faith if he suffered sufficiently. This was, in effect, a slander against Job's faith. The temptation that resulted gave Job the chance to demonstrate his

Study Notes on Job

faith. Job became the test case. God granted Satan power to test Job, but limited how far Satan could go: he could not bring physical harm on Job.

Note that Satan, not God, is the one who brings temptation into our lives (James 1:13-15). And in particular, Satan, not God, is the ultimate cause of suffering on earth. God originally created a world that was "very good," blessing man with an ideal garden in which to live (Genesis 1,2). He warned man what he must do to avoid suffering. But Satan, through the serpent, tempted Eve and Adam. They gave in, resulting in suffering of all kinds being introduced into the world (Genesis 3:1-19).

But it is Satan who initiates temptation, as in this case. God allows Satan to use suffering to tempt us, even as he uses other means to tempt us. God allows it in order that we might demonstrate our faithfulness and willingness to serve Him. He hopes we will remain faithful. But Satan is the one who initiates and carries out the temptation. He hopes we will sin and be lost. The resulting temptation, terrible as it may be, becomes an opportunity for His people to prove their faith and grow stronger (James 1:3-5,12; 1 Peter 1:6,7). As in the case of Paul in 2 Corinthians 12:7-10, Satan brings the temptation, but God uses it for the ultimate good of those who are faithful. We may suffer in the process, but God will bless us in the end. See Romans 8:28-39.

God also limits what Satan is permitted to do in tempting us. He is not permitted to bring into the life of any individual a temptation beyond that person's ability to handle. See 1 Corinthians 10:13. Hailey points out that this may be one reason why Satan came before God (verse 6) – perhaps he came to find out how far he could go in tempting Job.

In Job's case, God refused to allow Satan to physically harm Job. So, while God does allow Satan to tempt us, His motives are different from those of Satan, and He makes sure that we have the means to endure every temptation faithfully without sinning. If we sin, then, it is because we have failed to take the way of escape.

1:13-17 – *Calamities began as Job's flocks and herds were destroyed or stolen.*

Having received permission to test Job, Satan began bringing one calamity after another on Job, all in the same day. This was one of the days when his sons and daughters were having a feast in the house of the oldest brother.

First, a messenger came saying the Sabeans had made a raid and had captured all Job's oxen and donkeys. The servants who were tending them were all killed by the sword, and the messenger was the only one who escaped.

Even as he spoke, another messenger came saying fire had fallen from heaven (lightning?) and burned up all Job's sheep and the servants who were tending them. Only the one servant remained, and he came to tell Job.

Then even as he spoke, another messenger came saying three bands of Chaldeans had come upon the camels and captured them, killing all the servants who had been tending them with the sword. And only the one remained to take a message to Job.

The hardships caused by such suffering

We know from the context that Satan intended Job to turn against God because of the loss of these material possessions. When we lose what we value, we may tend to blame God. Some may think God Himself has caused the harm, though we know from the context that this was not the case. Others may think that, if they serve God, then God ought to reward them in this life or at least should protect them from harm. So they view such tragedies as Job suffered as an indication that God has failed to keep His word or that He cannot be a good God if he allows such suffering. All such views imply that God is somehow obligated to reward us in this life for our service. It fails to consider the long-run consequences, including the possibility that God will give us an even greater reward in the end if we are willing to suffer for Him.

The effect of such suffering is multiplied when several tragedies happen in succession. A single tragedy we may be able to handle or may adjust to. But a series becomes especially troubling. The series of events Job faced was so unlikely and such great loss that it could not be explained away as coincidence. Some supernatural power must be at work here.

Remember, again, that we know why this was happening and who is responsible, but Job did not know. Likewise, today, we cannot know specifically why we are suffering.

We observe here also the power of Satan. We may not know what all he is able to do, but this case shows he had power above normal human power, and he can use that power to work us harm.

Finally, it follows that we should not view suffering as a sign God is trying to reveal a message to us. When problems come, some people argue that God is giving us a sign we are traveling a wrong or mistaken path; God is trying to hinder us by placing roadblocks in our way. But if things go well, that is a sign that God wants us to do as we are doing. This is just a variation of the theory of Job's friends. It converts hardship or ease into a means of revelation from God. But Job's suffering was not a message from God, nor was it an indication he had been traveling the wrong road. On the contrary it was an effort by Satan to discourage Job because he was on the right road.

1:18,19 – Then all Job's children were slain.

The final messenger, who likewise arrived as the previous messenger was still speaking, brought news that Job's children had all been slain. They were feasting at the home of the older brother, when a great wind struck the house (like a tornado). The house collapsed, killing all of Job's children at the same time. Only the messenger escaped to bring word to Job.

Only a parent who has lost a child can begin to appreciate such a tragedy. Parents naturally expect to die before their children do. You expect them to have to bury you, not vice-versa. When a child dies an early death, it is a special tragedy that seems to be out of the natural order.

To have ten children, and they all die prematurely would be an unbelievable tragedy. And to have them all die at the same time would be unthinkable. And then to have it follow on the very same day that one loses all his other possessions, the grief would be unimaginable. Yet that is what Satan did to Job.

This series of events demonstrates Satan's power to work through nature to bring about events that he uses for his purposes. None of these events were miraculous in nature – that is, they were not impossible by natural law, but all worked through natural processes. Nevertheless, they demonstrate that Satan can use natural events for his purposes. We do not understand how such powers work, but we must acknowledge, from this and other Bible accounts, that Satan does have such power. God also has power to work through natural means to answer prayer and work His providence, but surely God's power must be greater than that of Satan. As already discussed, God limits what Satan can do in bringing harm into our lives. And Bible examples of miracles prove that God has power to do acts that are truly impossible by natural law, which Satan cannot duplicate.

1:20-22 – Job reacted to such horrible suffering by worshiping and refusing to blame God.

Satan had anticipated that Job would be so discouraged or grieved by such losses that he would turn against God. And Job surely was deeply grieved, as we would expect. He tore his robe and shaved his head, both of which were ancient ways of expressing great grief. See Genesis 37:29,34; Joshua 7:6; Job 2:12; Isaiah 15:2; Micah 1:16. It is proper to sorrow when we face financial reverses and even more so when we suffer death of loved ones. Even Jesus wept at Lazarus' tomb (John 11:35). But we must not allow our grief to lead us to turn against God or otherwise sin.

But in his grief, Job did not turn against God. Instead, he fell to the ground and worshiped God. Though he did not understand why these tragedies had befallen him, he did not see it as reason to turn from God. Instead, he turned to God for strength. Too often, in time of suffering, people tend to feel so bad they think they cannot worship God or do not want to worship. Instead, however, times of sorrow and hardship are times when worship is especially needed. Instead of neglecting or rejecting worship, we should view it as a source of strength and help that we need more than ever.

Further, Job recognized that all that he had lost were just temporary things anyway. He had none of them when he entered the world, and he would take none of it with him when he left. So why should he blame God if he must live without them between birth and death? See also Ecc. 5:15; 1 Timothy 6:7. A proper understanding of the temporary, passing nature of material things is essential to proper service to God. Too often we become so attached to them that we let them hinder or prevent our service. See Matthew 6:19-33; 10:34- 39; 16:24-27; Romans 8:5-8; 12:1,2; John 6:27,63; Luke 12:15-21; 1 Timothy 4:8; 6:6-19; 2 Corinthians 4:16-18; 8:5; 10:3,4; Colossians 3:1,2; 1 John 2:15-17.

He also expressed trust in God's wisdom and goodness. God had given him all these blessings anyway. If God saw fit to remove them, then God had the right to do so. Job did not understand why this was happening, but he left it in God's hands and accepted the result.

In all this he did not sin by blaming God as though God had done him wrong. Had he blamed God, he would have done exactly what Satan wanted. Instead, he maintained his spiritual integrity.

Hailey points out, however, that Job's statement may express some misconception of what was happening. While he did not turn from God, he did place the responsibility for the loss of his blessings on God: "The Lord has taken away." This concept may have been a germ that led to some of his later problems in which Job did criticize God unjustly. In truth, God had not taken Job's possessions and children. Satan had taken them.

There may be times when God justly does bring suffering into our lives as punishment for sin or as consequence of natural law. And it is true that God brought death and suffering into the world as a consequence of sin (Genesis 3). But specific acts of suffering, especially the suffering brought upon the righteous who serve God faithfully, must be blamed on Satan. See 2 Corinthians 12:7-10; Luke 13:16; Acts 10:38.

Many people today make the same mistake that Job did, sometimes having good intent like he did. They say, "God took my loved one to be in heaven with Him." "My loved one was too good for this earth, so God took her." Other such statements imply that God is responsible for death of suffering of a loved one. Generally speaking, such is simply not taught in Scripture. And the effect of it, like Job's statement, is to make God responsible for suffering which He has not caused. Death is an enemy. Satan has the power of death – Hebrews

2:14. Let us take care, even in good intent, that we do not accept false concepts that can lead to spiritual danger.

But Job's trials have just begun. Yet to come is the full force of Satan's temptations, as the subsequent story reveals.

Job 2

Chapter 2 - Satan's Second Temptation of Job

2:1-3 – When Satan again presented himself, God reminded him that Job had not sinned despite his hardships.

The scene of 1:6-12 is here repeated with Satan coming before God on the day when the sons of God presented themselves before God. God asked Satan again where he came from, and again he said he had been going to and fro, walking back and forth on the earth (see notes on 1:6-8).

God again asked Satan about Job, again affirming that there was none like him on earth, a blameless and upright man who feared God and shunned evil. But this time He added that Job continued to hold fast his integrity, even though Satan had incited God against Job to destroy him without cause. Again, we have proof that Job was a good man and was not suffering because of any evil he had done. In fact, God specifically stated that Job had suffered "without cause" (compare 1:1,8).

God acknowledged that He had some responsibility in Job's suffering. He had been moved against Job. But He placed the blame for the problem where it belonged: on Satan. Satan incited God against Job. And God made plain that neither He nor Satan had any just reason to destroy Job. Note that God expressly acknowledged that Job did not deserve what he suffered. Remember this throughout the subsequent discussions.

The word "destroy" is interesting here, since Job not only still existed but was even alive. Yet God said he had been "destroyed": his life had been ruined. One can be destroyed even as he continues to consciously exist.

2:4-6 – Satan insisted that Job would yet turn against God if he were personally harmed. God granted this permission, but said he must spare Job's life.

Satan abandons his argument that people are motivated by desire for personal gain (1:9-11). That approach had failed. So now he takes up a new and related approach. He says a man will do anything to preserve

Study Notes on Job

his own life and health: his "skin." To this point, God had not allowed Satan to attack Job himself physically. Only his possessions and children had been harmed. Satan claimed then that, if Job's own health were destroyed ("touch his bone and his flesh"), he would turn against God and curse Him to His face. He would give all that he had (including his relationship to God) for the sake of his life.

God granted Satan permission once again to test Job. He again gave Job the opportunity to prove his integrity. However, again he limited what Satan could do. He said he must spare his life: he could not kill Job.

Note that Satan does not mind contradicting himself. In 1:9-11 he had said that Job would curse God if his possessions ("all that he has") were attacked. But it did not happen that way. Satan failed. He was wrong. But instead of admitting defeat and error, he just modified the argument somewhat and continued on. His servants are amazingly like him. Watch people in religious discussions. Time and again they can be shown by Scripture to be in error, but rarely will they confess they are wrong. No matter how clearly they have been proved wrong, they just shift ground and maintain their conclusion.

In particular, Satan still views man as basically selfish. He thinks Job will turn from God if he suffers enough. He does not view Job's devotion to God as genuine, but something Job maintains only so long as it is not too inconvenient. We must learn that, when we turn from God in time of hardship, we simply prove Satan to be right, and he is victorious in our lives.

Satan is persistent. He does not give up. We need to learn this. Don't think that, just because he has been beaten once or even a few times, we don't need to remain on guard. In some ways, he becomes even more determined when he has been beaten. When he has people in his control, he can leave them alone. He may even give them prosperity to encourage them to stay in his service. But when people like Job resist him, he redoubles his efforts against them.

2:7,8 – Satan struck Job with boils from the soul of his foot to the crown of his head.

Satan then attacked Job's health. He struck him with boils from the sole of his foot to the crown of his head (compare Exodus 9:9; Deuteronomy 28:35). He took a potsherd to scrape the wounds as he sat in the ash heap. A potsherd is a shard of pottery, a broken fragment. Presumably he used it to scrape off the secretions from the boils. Sitting among ashes was a sign of great grief – Jeremiah 6:26; Ezekiel 27:30 Jonah 3:6. Some suggest that perhaps the ashes had (or Job maybe thought they might have) a medicinal or painkilling effect.

There is some doubt as to exactly what kind of sore is meant by the word for "boil." Some suspect it was a form of leprosy. But English translations generally use "boil," and that is surely sufficient to convey to our minds the agony Job faced. The point is that he had "painful" sores or infections all over his body. If you have ever had even one boil, you have just a slight concept of what it might be like to have them all over your body. Any position you choose – whether sitting, standing, or lying – puts your weight on the sores, multiplying the pain they already cause.

Note that physical pain and loss of health can be temptations from Satan. They can be extremely difficult to tolerate and very discouraging spiritually. As one deals with the physical pain itself, he has increasingly less emotional and mental strength. It becomes increasingly difficult to think clearly, to understand what is happening and how to deal with it. Maintaining faith in God and understanding His will also becomes far more difficult. Physical, mental, and spiritual well-being are often closely intertwined. Add this to the deep grief and emotional distress Job had already experienced from the loss of his possessions and his children, and we can hardly imagine the depth of his suffering.

2:9,10 – *Job's wife urged him to curse God and die, but he said that we must accept harm as well as good from God.*

Job's wife has not been mentioned before, though of course he obviously was married since he had ten children. Here she reached the point of such discouragement that she urged Job to give up his integrity, renounce God and die. Of course, this is exactly what Satan said Job would do. Job's wife, at least, had reached the point Satan hoped would come.

It is easy for us, seeing Job's strength, to view his wife as some kind of unspiritual, even wicked woman. But it must be remembered that she too had suffered greatly in all his sufferings. She was not isolated from his problems. All his possessions were her possessions, and she had suffered financial catastrophe right alongside him. And all his children were doubtless her children. Hard as it is for a man to lose his children, it is if anything harder for the wife who gave them birth. She carried those children within her, gave them birth at great pain, and raised them to adulthood with a mother's love and devotion. To lose one's children is a great grief to a mother. I have seen such grief in my own mother when my sister died at age 25. Job's wife too had suffered greatly in Job's loss.

And now Job was in great physical pain. There is no indication that his wife was physically attacked, but a woman who is devoted to her husband will suffer along with him. Seeing him suffer, she would undergo deep agony and would want him relieved. She had reached the point that she would welcome his death. But her greatest error was in blaming God for it all, or at least concluding that God had somehow failed them in allowing all this. In any case, she saw no reason to maintain faith in God. In this she took exactly the course Satan hoped she would.

But her conduct simply added immeasurable hardship to Job. A man can stand much hardship if he has the strength and encouragement of a devoted wife. Her faith in God and her courage in hardship make a major contribution to his faith and courage. Woman was given to man by God to be his helper (Genesis 2:18-24). She needs to realize how important she is to his ability to be strong.

But contrariwise, when she loses faith and strength – and worse yet when she attacks and criticizes the man for his stand – she can add an unbelievable burden. I suspect many women have little understanding of what a burden they can be to their husbands when they criticize and carp at him at the very time he most needs their help and support. After all Job had suffered, he had to bear with a wife who, not only failed to support him, but worse yet criticized him for maintaining integrity and urged him to turn against God. What a crowning blow such unfaithfulness on her part would have been to Job!

Job rebuked her, saying she was speaking like a foolish woman. Perhaps this implies that she was not usually so foolish, but in this case she had placed herself among those who are foolish.

He says that, if God gives us good, should we not likewise accept adversity from His hand. See notes on 1:21. It is good to appreciate God as the giver of good. And surely God does not owe it to us to give or even to continue such riches as Job had. But again I wonder if attributing the adversity to God wasn't more of a weakness than a strength in Job. Such thinking may have been a precursor of his later errors. The fact is that God had not caused the adversity, though he had allowed it.

Nevertheless, the passage says Job did not sin in his speech in all this. If his understanding was weak, it was definitely not sinful. God approved his integrity, even in the face of his wife's opposition.

2:11 – Job's three friends came to mourn and comfort him.

Next we are introduced to three other men who become major players in the subsequent story. These were Job's three friends: Eliphaz the Temanite, Bildad the Shuhite, and Zophar the Naamathite (not listed here is Elihu, who joins in the discussion later – chapter 32). We know nothing of these men except what is recorded in this book. While some have speculated about the places where they came from, we really know nothing with certainty about that either. And of course, that is of no great consequence.

These men had heard of Job's suffering and had agreed upon an appointed time to meet and visit with him. They came with the intent of mourning with him and comforting him. This is surely a good intent. Friends ought to offer comfort and weep with those who weep. See Galatians 6:2; 2 Corinthians 1:3-11; Romans 12:15. Christians can be a great source of strength and comfort to one another. We should never allow a brother or sister in Christ to suffer alone without offering what strength and encouragement we can.

But the fact is that the men actually came to accuse Job of sin. Their view was that he was suffering because he had committed sin. So the end result of their visit was anything but comforting to Job. In their own minds, no doubt, they thought they could help by accusing him of sin. If they were right, then he could just repent of the sin and his problems would be solved. In that sense, when people are really guilty of sin, it is right for God's people to rebuke them and warn them to repent. See Revelation 3:19; Galatians 6:1,2; James 5:19,20; 1 Thessalonians 5:14; Ephesians 5:11; 2 Timothy 4:2-4; 1 Timothy 5:20; Titus 1:10-13.

But despite their good intentions, the men ended up committing a grievous sin for which God in the end severely rebuked them. While rebuke may be beneficial when it is properly administered, we must take care to be sure we rebuke those who are really guilty. In this case we have been repeatedly told that Job was innocent. So in their attempts to help Job, these men actually became still one more burden for Job to bear. In fact, though Job had endured all his other hardships without sin, it was the harping, repeated false accusations by his friends that finally provoked him to say things for which he later had to repent.

As with our comments regarding Job's wife (verses 9,10), friends can be a great source of strength when they say what is true to God's word and what is needed to those who are weak or erring. But false accusation is a great burden and discouragement to those who are not guilty. False accusation, when it comes, usually comes from those who are already enemies. But when it comes from those who ought to be friends, the burden can be almost unbearable, especially when it comes at a time when people are already suffering greatly. We must take care to speak the truth in love (Ephesians 4:15).

On false accusation see Proverbs 17:15; Isaiah 5:20; 1 Peter 2:12; 3:16; 4:4; 1 Kings 18:17,18; Matthew 5:10-12; Luke 6:22,23,26; 3 John 9,10; Luke 3:14; John 7:24; 2 Timothy 3:3; 1 Corinthians 5:11; 6:9-11 (revilers); 1 Timothy 6:4; Titus 3:2; 1 Peter 2:1; Ephesians 4:31.

2:12,13 – *The friends expressed their grief, sitting speechless for seven days.*

When the friends arrived, they did not even recognize Job at first, presumably because his appearance was so altered by the disease, the ashes, the shaved head (1:20), and the effects of his suffering. They expressed their own sympathy by weeping, tearing their clothes, and sprinkling dust to the sky. These were common expressions of grief in those days (Joshua 7:6; Lamentations 2:10; Ezekiel 27:30).

They were so moved that they simply sat down with him for seven days and seven nights, saying nothing because they realized his great grief. Sometimes the best thing we can do for people in grief is just to be there and express sympathy. What matters is not so much what we say as just the fact we show we care by our presence.

Some commentators suppose that the friends remained silent, not so much as an expression of grief, but because they knew they were going to accuse Job of sin. They could not express sympathy, because they thought he was suffering as a result of his sins. So they said nothing till enough time had passed to show their respect for their friend before they began their criticisms. In any case, silence was the best thing they did during their whole visit! They would have been better off had they remained silent. It was when they started speaking that they got themselves in trouble.

The very fact these men lived in a society where they were able to sit for seven days saying nothing, let alone however long their conversations with Job lasted, shows they lived in a different society from ours. They lived much longer lives at a much slower pace. Doubtless, even for them this was a long time to go without speaking, or it would not have been noteworthy. But this is another indication that these events occurred in the Patriarchal age.

The scene is now set for the discussions and debates between Job and his friends that are the core of the story. Remember that we understand why Job is suffering, but neither he nor his friends understood. Their discussions expressed their attempts to state their views apart from Divine revelation.

Job 3

Chapter 3 - Job Mourns for His Troubles.

The friends had not spoken since they arrived. They apparently waited till Job was ready to speak. When he finally spoke, he poetically described his grief for his suffering. He was so troubled that he repeatedly says he would rather not have been born.

3:1-3 – Job began his first speech, asking for the day to perish on which he was born.

Job begins his speech by cursing the day on which he was born. He states his wish that the day of his birth would perish as would the night of his conception. The meaning is that he wishes neither had ever occurred.

He contrasts the day of his birth to the night of his conception, but the effect is simply poetic repetition. This form of poetry is common in Old Testament writing. The speaker emphasizes his point by saying essentially the same thing in a variety of ways.

Note that, on the night of his conception it could have been said, "A **male-child** is **conceived.**" That which was conceived was a "male-child" ("man child" — ASV) on the very night of its conception. The word for "male-child" (Heb. GEBER) elsewhere means "man," i.e., a human individual. See examples in Job 3:23; 4:17; 10:5; Psalms 127:5; 128:4; etc. (or consult a concordance). This word inherently, without exception, refers to a human individual.

So, Job is affirming that **he was a human individual from the very night he was conceived.** This may not seem significant at first, but such concepts become important in the modern discussion of abortion. This shows that human reproduction produces a new human individual – a male-child – at the very moment of conception.

3:4-7 – Job views his origin as a time of darkness and blackness, not a time of joy.

Job continues to speak of the day of his birth and the night of his conception. He says the day of his birth should be viewed as a dark day that God does not respect and the sun does not shine. It should be characterized by darkness, terrifying blackness, clouds, and the shadow of death.

Likewise, the night of his conception should be seized by darkness, a barren, lifeless night, with no expressions of joy. It was unworthy of being counted even among the days of the year or counted on the calendar. Just skip it and eliminate it from existence.

Of course, all this is just a way of expressing his grief that he was ever born. He birth is a sad, sad day in his eyes. If he was going to suffer like this, why should he ever have been born?

3:8-10 – The day of his birth should be cursed. It should not have dawned; his mother should not have given birth.

Job said that people who pronounce curses should pronounce one on the day of his birth. The stars that shine in the early morning (just prior to sunrise) should be dark and the first rays of dawn should not come when the day expects it.

All these consequences, he said, should come on the day because it allowed him to be born. It should have shut up his mother's womb so he could not be born, rather than to allow him to come into the world to see such sorrow.

Of course, the day itself had no real control over any of this, and Job knew that. It was all a poetic way of expressing his grief that he had ever been born, if it was going to lead to such suffering as he was experiencing.

Leviathan is described later in 41:1. It is creature such as a crocodile or dinosaur. Hailey says that, in ancient mythology, Leviathan was thought to swallow the sun and heavenly bodies. So Job was saying men should rouse it up, so it could swallow the heavenly bodies on the day of his birth, leaving it a dark, cheerless day. Again, no doubt Job knew it did not really happen that way, just as he knew it was not really the fault of the day that he was born. But he referred to the myth as a way of saying that he wished something had swallowed that day so that he had not been born.

3:11-15 – Job wished he could have died from the womb.

Rather than being born to suffer so, Job would have preferred death in the womb. He asked why he did not die at birth, perishing when he came from the womb. Why was he received to sit on his parents' knees or nurse at his mother's breasts? All these are just poetic ways of expressing that he would rather have died instead of living.

Had he died, he could have lain quietly and slept at rest. His life would be over just like kings and princes and rulers who possessed gold and silver and built great houses and monuments for themselves. These men may now be dead and their buildings left in ruins, but there would be no difference between him and them if he had died from the womb. When one dies, all differences from life cease. Whether you die in the womb or live a great life, people are all the same when it is over. So Job wondered why he could not have avoided all the suffering by just dying from the womb.

Job did not seem to have a clear conception of afterlife (remember that we have already established the fact that he is not speaking as an inspired man). Perhaps at this early point in the patriarchal age not much had been revealed, at least not to him. In any case, he expressed the idea that death would lead simply to quiet sleep and rest. That is true physically for the body, but not for the spirit (Luke 16:19-31). One who died from the womb, nevertheless, would need have no fear even after death.

3:16-19 – *If he had died from the womb, he could be at rest like those whose problems have ended.*

Again Job asked why he could not have been stillborn like an infant who died from the womb and so never saw light. He describes the grave as a place where all who had trouble in this life cease their troubles. The wicked cease causing and experiencing trouble as a result of their evil. The weary experience rest. Captives and slaves do not suffer from the commands of their oppressors but can rest. Servants are free from their masters. Small and great are all the same in the grave.

Again, this is true only regards the body. But even so, no matter how much one has suffered in this life, that suffering at least ends at the grave. So the great kings and rulers of verses 14,15 are no different in death from the slaves and prisoners of verses 17-19. All are equal, at least physically. And it can be true spiritually as well, that all are at rest if they die in a right relationship with God. Even the wicked cease to suffer the consequences of their sins, if they are forgiven before they die. So Job would rather have died from birth than to be born to suffer as he was.

Note here again that Job speaks of babies that die before birth (a "stillborn child" — NKJV) as "***infants***" who never saw light. This is exactly like babies that are aborted, but the passage refers to them as "infants" (Heb. OLEL). This word always and without exception refers to human individuals (compare Hosea 13:16; Psalm 8:2 — "babes"). Joel 2:16 lists "children" (OLEL) as "people." So, babies that die in their mother's womb, like aborted babies, are "infants" — human individuals separate and distinct from other human beings. (See notes on verse 3.)

3:20-22 – *So Job asked why life was given to one who would suffer such misery and would rather not be alive.*

Having eloquently expressed his wish never to have been born, Job concludes by asking why a person would be given the light of life if he was destined to face such misery and bitterness of soul. He longed for death, searching for it like hidden treasure, but it eluded him. He

Study Notes on Job

would have rejoiced exceedingly if he could simply have died and gone to the grave.

Having not escaped life from the womb, Job said even at this point in his life he would have delighted to just die and end his suffering. When people seek hidden treasure, they are obsessed with the quest. They seek it fervently with zeal and commitment. That is how Job sought death.

Yet, interestingly, for all his desire to avoid life, at no point does Job even mention the concept of suicide. His wife had told him to curse God and die (2:9). He refused to curse God, but he dearly sought death. Yet nowhere in the record does he suggest that he would ever do anything to cause his own death.

All Bible examples of suicide are people who had no true faith in God. No faithful servant of God ever deliberately caused his own death out of desire for death or for the purpose of ending his own life. All who trust God will rely on Him to care for them. They may call on Him to let them die, but they will not cause the death themselves. Death will come when it does, but it is not up to us to cause our own death any more than to murder someone else.

Yet, even so, Job's statements appear to show cracks in his faith. No doubt, if we were in his place, we would all be as shaken as he was and most likely much worse. Yet it seems that we see the beginnings of his questions that later develop into actual accusations against God for allowing Job to suffer as he has.

3:23-26 – Job concluded with a statement of the great distress and groaning of his soul.

Job then asked why light was given to a man whose way is hidden, whom God has hedged in. Verse 20 shows that the giving of light refers to being born or given life. So he seems to be questioning why life would be given to a person who would be so troubled that he was trapped and could see no solution to his problem. Why not allow him to die before he was born, as he earlier asked, rather than allow him to continue to live, if he is to suffer with no recourse. One of the most troubling aspects of serious problems is when we see no solution. We feel hopeless and helpless because there is no way out.

He then describes further his grief. Even before he eats, he is sighing. Hailey explains that the translation here is uncertain, so of course the meaning is uncertain. Perhaps the idea is that grief is more fundamentally a part of his life than even eating. Eating is basic to human life, but weariness and trouble are an even greater part of Job's life. He pours our groaning like pouring out water.

He has experienced the thing he feared and dreaded would happen. Exactly when or how he dreaded this, he does not explain. Perhaps the idea is that, after the problems began, he feared and dreaded that there would be no relief but that problems would only continue and even grow worse.

He has no ease, quiet, or rest. All he has is trouble. So Job ends his complaint to his friends describing his grief for his suffering.

Job 4

Chapter 4-14 – First Round of Speeches

Chapter 4,5 - Eliphaz' First Speech

4:1,2 – Eliphaz began the debate, saying he could not withhold from speaking.

Remember that the friends came to comfort Job and sorrow with him (2:11). And the record has stated repeatedly that Job is upright and without sin before God. This of itself will disprove the basic approach of the friends. Their intentions may be good, but they end up accomplishing everything except what would be comforting to someone in Job's position.

Remember also that we know the reasons for Job's suffering as a temptation from Satan, but neither Job nor his friends have been informed of this. So the debate centers around the cause of Job's suffering.

Eliphaz began by asking if Job would be wearied if someone tries to speak with him, but he says he cannot withhold from speaking. The very first words he speaks imply that he intends to say things he knows will be upsetting to Job. He anticipates that Job will be grieved (ASV) – offended or angered. But he cannot avoid speaking. So the very first recorded words of the very first speech to Job reveal that conflict will result. It seems a strange way to begin to comfort a friend.

Nevertheless, the format is not that of a formal debate, as we might think of one. Rather, each speaker poetically expresses his view of life and of suffering and of God's rule in the universe. Much of what is said is true or not especially relevant to Job's suffering. But included in the speeches from time to time are statements of viewpoint regarding suffering.

4:3-5 – Eliphaz claimed Job had assisted others in time of trouble, but now he had difficulty facing it in his own life.

He says that Job had instructed others in time of trouble, strengthening those who are weak or feeble and upholding those who stumble. But then Job was incapable of dealing with his own suffering. When trouble touched his life, he was wearied (faint – ASV) and troubled.

The implication was that Job himself could not handle the things he had advised others to handle. Implied might be that his understanding of suffering was flawed, since it was incapable of sustaining him through his own troubles.

4:6-9 – Eliphaz stated the friends' proposition: suffering always results from guilt.

He states that Job has placed his confidence and hope in his integrity and his respect for God. This implies that the reason Job is confident that he does not deserve to suffer is that he has done right, not wrong. In a sense, this is what Job thought, and it was part of Job's mistaken concept that led to his misunderstanding of his troubles.

But Eliphaz ignores the possibility that this view may be inadequate – i.e., the possibility that people who walk in integrity may still suffer in this life. Instead, he chooses another conclusion, arguing the no one ever perished if he was innocent. The upright are never cut off.

He argues from his own experience ("I have seen") that people reap trouble because they have sown and plowed iniquity and trouble. They perish and are consumed by the blast of the anger of God.

Here is the fundamental proposition for debate. It is the statement that the friends will defend as the reason why people suffer: People suffer because they sin. It is a simple matter of sowing and reaping. The kind of crop you reap is determined entirely by the kind of seed you sow. The unstated conclusion is that Job is suffering, so he must be guilty of sin. No one perishes being innocent; Job is perishing, therefore Job is not innocent. People reap trouble because they sow iniquity. Job has reaped trouble, therefore he must have sown iniquity. Compare 8:20; 36:6,7; 15:31,35.

This fundamental view is held by many today. Hindus call it "karma" – every good thing that happens to a person is the consequence of something good he did earlier, and every bad thing that happens is the consequence of something bad he did earlier. The only significant difference is that karma might result from good or bad done in a previous incarnation – a previous life lived as another person or animal before the current reincarnation. Whereas, Job's friends argue that suffering or blessings occur as a consequence of conduct in the same lifetime.

Other people defend similar viewpoints. Some preachers defend a gospel of health and wealth: Serve God faithfully, pray for a miracle, (and send the preacher a donation), and God will give whatever you asked for – including a new house, fancy new car, money, etc. If you don't receive it, then you aren't living right or don't have enough faith. Some call this concept "seed-faith." When your faith leads you to plant a seed by doing some good deed (especially sending money to the preacher), then you will reap the crop of blessings that you desire. The concept is even based on the same illustration Eliphaz used: sowing and reaping.

We can agree that ultimately people will suffer or be rewarded according to the way they lived; but the ultimate reward comes *after life*, not during life. Job's friends believe the reward comes during life. This is their fundamental error. It *may* be that people suffer or are rewarded in this life for their deeds, but often they are not rewarded in this life. Often the reward must wait for eternity after death. Note Luke 16:25. See Matthew 25:31-46; John 12:48; Acts 1:9-11; 10:42; 17:30,31; Romans 2:4-11; 14:10-12; 2 Corinthians 5:10; 1 Thessalonians 4:13-18; 2 Thessalonians 1:5-9; 2 Timothy 4:1; Hebrews 9:27; 10:26-31; Revelation 20:11-15; Ecclesiastes 12:13,14.

Note the source of Elphaz' authority for his statement: "I have seen." He has no Divine revelation, only personal experience and observation. This is the "authority" many people appeal to, but human experience is never infallible. It amounts merely to human wisdom, whereas the only sure source of truth is Divine revelation. See Matthew 15:9,13; Galatians 1:8,9; 2 John 9-11; Colossians 3:17; Jeremiah 10:23; Proverbs 14:12; 3:5,6; Revelation 22:18,19; 1 Timothy 1:3; 2 Timothy 1:13; John 5:43.

4:10,11 – Lions illustrate the point.

Eliphaz then uses lions to illustrate his view, applying it to lions in general, fierce lions, young lions, old lions, and even cubs. Lions will eventually suffer. Their teeth are broken, they lack prey, they are scattered. Perhaps the point is that Eliphaz is comparing lions to evil people, who suffer because they are evil.

If this is applied to Job's case, the point would be that he was once great and respected like a lion. But every lion will sooner or later come to a bad end, because it is a fierce beast who preys upon other animals. So likewise Job has come to a bad end because he has mistreated others or otherwise lived in sin.

The extent to which the illustration is true even of lions is doubtful. Some lions live pretty well till they die. True, they do die, but all animals and all people die eventually, good or bad. And lions have no soul to punish after death as people do. So the illustration does not seem valid.

4:12-15 – Eliphaz claimed to have received a vision in the night as evidence for his view.

The next evidence Eliphaz introduces is a vision he had during the night. It came secretly and whispered in his ear. It disquieted or troubled his thoughts at the time when men are usually in deep sleep. It caused him fear and trembling, so all his bones shook. A spirit passed before him, making the hair of his body stand on end!

It is true that sometimes, before the Bible was completed, God did use dreams or visions to reveal His will. But not all dreams or visions come from God. Some are natural and prove nothing whatever. Some are nightmares that are best disregarded. What proof is there that this vision demonstrates the truth, even if it ever really occurred?

Lots of false teachers today likewise claim to have visions or dreams in which God spoke to them. But there is no proof the message is from God. I would hate to use dreams that cause me fear and trembling as proof of anything – mostly they just prove I have an upset tummy!

Once again Eliphaz attempts to support his conclusions but he uses evidence that proves nothing. There is no reason to believe his conclusions are true or valid, let alone that the message came fro God.

4:16-19 – The spirit informed Eliphaz that man cannot be more righteous than God.

Eliphaz says the spirit that passed before his face (verse 15), then stood still before him. He could not discern its appearance. Everything was silent for a time, then the spirit spoke to him.

The spirit said (in rhetorical question) that no man can be more righteous than God or more pure than his maker. God does not trust His servants and even finds errors in His angels; so how could a man be sure he was right before God? Man is so frail that he dwells in a temporary corruptible house of clay, that is founded or based on dust and can be crushed before a moth.

This seems to be saying that God is infallible, but man is fallible. So how can man be right and make God appear to be wrong? God discerns errors in every one of his servants, even his angels. Man himself will die and leave his body made of dust and clay. He can lose his life as quickly and easily as a moth that is crushed. If man is so weak and God is so great, how can man possibly be right and make God appear to be wrong?

It appears to me that Eliphaz' statements, as applied to men, are true (I doubt their validity as applied to angels – see below). If so, then it is true that man has no right to criticize God or imply that God has done something wrong. However, it is not clear to me that Job is guilty at this point, though he does become guilty of this later.

But it seems that Eliphaz was saying that Job had already impugned God simply by saying that he was suffering though he had done nothing wrong. From Eliphaz' view, that alone would be an accusation against God. Eliphaz believed that no one who was righteous or innocent was ever cut off; only the wicked reap troubles (verses 7ff). Job was suffering, so Job must have sinned. In which case, if Job denied he has sinned, then Job was accusing God of making him suffer even though he is innocent. From Eliphaz' view, that is accusing God of error and injustice. So, Eliphaz instead said that man has no right to accuse God of error, since God is infallible and man is always the one in the wrong. I can agree with Eliphaz view of God's greatness without agreeing that Job was yet in error.

Incidentally, I question Eliphaz' statements about God finding fault with His angels. Some claim that Satan and his demons are fallen angels. That is as good an explanation as any, though I don't know it to be correct. If it is correct, then angels can be wrong. But that does not prove that all of them have sinned. If some are holy and righteous, that would seem to disprove Eliphaz' point. His argument appears to be valid only if all men are sinners like all angels are sinners. Of course, we agree that all men are sinners (Romans 3:23), but I question the conclusion that all angels have sinned. [Perhaps "angels" refers to messengers (human), such as those God uses to convey His messages to others. If so, then it would be true that humans all err, even those whom God uses to convey His word to others. But the contrast appears to me to imply that he is talking about spirit angels, not to human messengers.]

4:20,21 – *So men die and perish.*

The conclusion of Eliphaz' dream just further emphasizes man's frailty and corruptibility. Just as the moth is crushed, so men are broken in pieces all day long – men are always dying. They perish, and this is so commonplace that other people make no great deal about it. When they die, whatever excellence they have achieved is gone. They die especially because they have not achieved the wisdom that comes from God.

This just seems to continue the point of the vision from verses 17-19. True, man is frail and will surely die. But this does not prove that all suffering is direct result of the sins committed by the man who suffers. And it surely does not prove that Job was suffering for that reason, since we already know that is not the reason for his suffering.

Job 5

Eliphaz' First Speech (cont.)

5:1-3 – Eliphaz claimed men die and are cursed because they are foolish and guilty of sin.

Eliphaz continued his speech begun in chapter 4. He asked Job who would answer if he called out. To what holy one could he turn? The point is not obvious. Eliphaz seems to be implying that no one on God's side would agree with Job or defend his view. No holy one (angel?) could he turn to for help, because he was in error.

A man suffers because he does foolish things. This expresses again Eliphaz' approach to suffering. A man dies or is slain because he is guilty of wrath and envy, demonstrating that he is foolish or simple. The application is that Job is suffering because he has been foolish before God – he has not served obediently.

Eliphaz acknowledges that such a foolish man might take root for a while – he might appear to be established and bear some good fruit. It might seem that he is living a useful, profitable life. But then Eliphaz says that such a man's dwelling place is accursed. He and all that belongs to him will suffer for his misdeeds. He may appear to prosper for a time, but it cannot last. Again, Eliphaz argues here from experience; this is what he has seen, but it is not revelation from God.

Again, these statements are true if one includes spiritual and eternal consequences in the discussion. It is not necessarily true if one looks only at this life, as Eliphaz was.

5:4,5 – The family of the evil man also suffers.

Eliphaz continued describing the curse on the foolish man who does not serve God. He said that his children will suffer too. They are far removed from safety or from one who would deliver them. They are crushed in the gate. Official business and civil judgments were often rendered in those days at the gates of the city, where people met with city officials and other people of influence. But no one there would deliver the foolish man's children; instead, they would be crushed, oppressed on defeated (justly or unjustly) because of their father's evil.

Hungry people eat the foolish man's harvest – he and his family do not receive the benefit of it. Perhaps this means his harvest will grow thorns and thistles; it will not be a good harvest, because of his sins. But even what he grows will benefit others, not his family. Or perhaps the meaning is that, even if he plants a hedge of thorns around his fields, others will still take his crops from among the thorns. His substance will be snatched away by snares. Again, the meaning of each specific term is not certain, but the overall point is clear.

The point is that a man's sins bring harm on his family as well as on him. This may be a reference to the fact that Job's children had been slain and his prosperity lost to others. Like Eliphaz' other claims, this may be true if one includes spiritual consequences in the discussion. The children of a wicked man may suffer because he does not lead them to serve God properly. However, it is not necessarily true even in spiritual matters, since a wicked man's sons may obey God and be saved (Ezekiel 18). In physical matters, as Eliphaz meant the application, it may also be true, but not necessarily. It surely does not explain the troubles of Job's family.

5:6,7 – *Eliphaz claimed that people are born to trouble, but they suffer for a reason.*

Afflictions and troubles do not just spring from the dust or the ground (note the obvious parallelism). He has returned to the illustration of sowing and reaping (4:8). A crop does not grow from the ground for no reason; it is the result of seed that has been sown. So man is born to suffer trouble and problems (compare 14:1). This will happen as surely as sparks fly upward. But there is a reason why the sparks go up, instead of down. And so there is a reason why men suffer.

Eliphaz does not here repeat the reason which he believes is the cause of trouble, but it is clear from the argument he has made through his speech. He believes each man suffers trouble because he himself has committed some sin that led to the suffering as a consequence. Troubles are not just random occurrences that enter men's lives for no reason. They are not just the common lot of mankind for which there is no assignable reason. Man does suffer, as sure as he is born, but it is because he himself is guilty of sin. He may mean that all men suffer because all men sin. But in any case, the solution when one is suffering is to admit one's guilt and turn from it (as in verses 8ff).

This view again is sometimes true, but not always. It does not fit Job's case. In fact, we often do reap in this life what we have not sown. Weeds may grow where we sowed good seed. So suffering often is simply the common lot of mankind, not just the result of some specific sin we have committed. We suffer because we live in a world cursed by sin (Genesis 3:16-19). Sometimes the suffering comes to us specifically because we committed some sin, but sometimes it comes for no fault of our own as in Job's case.

5:8,9 – Eliphaz stated his solution: a man should commit his cause to God who does marvelous things.

Having stated that a man suffers because he has committed some sin, Eliphaz then stated the obvious conclusion. If one is suffering, he should turn to God to forgive him and remove the trouble. Correct the wrong before God, and the trouble will cease because the cause is gone. It appears to me that this is implied in these verses.

He urges Job that, if he were in Job's situation, he would seek God and commit his cause to God. God is great, doing numberless great and marvelous things. We do not understand His wisdom and power.

From Eliphaz' viewpoint, this is an obvious conclusion, and he appears to mean it for Job's good. He thinks he knows why Job is suffering, so as a friend he is advising Job how to relieve his troubles. Perhaps he speaks sincerely and with good intent. The problem is that he is wrong in his beliefs about the cause of suffering and specifically about why Job is suffering. So his conclusion does not follow.

5:10,11 – Eliphaz' described God as one who sends rain, exalts the humble, and protects those who mourn.

Eliphaz breaks out into a description of God, most of which is accurate and informative (properly understood), but which has little to do with Job's case.

He says God gives rain on earth, sending water on the fields. Giving of rain is often attributed to God (compare 36:27-29; 37:6-11; 38:26). He made the world with its natural laws. In particular, the principles that control the weather and the rain appear to have been established at the flood (Genesis 6-9). But God sends rain and sunshine on the just and on the unjust (Matthew 5:45); so true as Eliphaz' statement is, it gives no information of help regarding Job's case.

He exalts the lowly and brings to safety those who mourn. This is also true in the sense that God gives spiritual blessings to those who humbly submit to Him. And when His children pray to Him, He may choose to lift the burdens that grieve them (Psalms 113:7). Every blessing that so comes is a gift from God (James 1:17). Nevertheless, this does not mean that God always removes all physical problems from His faithful children, for many of them like Job have suffered in this life.

5:12-14 – God defeats the plans of the crafty and wicked.

Eliphaz describes how God overthrows the devices and plans of the crafty. This would include those who plot to commit evil and harm to others. This again is true and is repeated in various forms elsewhere in Scripture (Nehemiah 4:15; 1 Corinthians 3:19; compare 2 Samuel 17:7-14). Various Psalms and Proverbs call upon God or describe how He can defeat the plans of the wicked (Ecclesiastes 10:8). Sometimes they are caught in their own wicked plans. Haman, for example, suffered the very fate that he had plotted for Mordecai (Esther 7). The result is that their plans are frustrated like a blind man who walks in darkness even though it is broad daylight.

Again, it is not clear what application Eliphaz would make of this. If he is directing this toward Job as though he is one whom God has defeated because of his craftiness, then he has missed the point. God has not promised to always defeat all wicked people in this life; sometimes they prosper here. Nor has he promised to give prosperity on earth to all good people; sometimes they suffer here. However, God can and often has defeated the crafty in this life, and He definitely will do so in the judgment.

5:15,16 – God saves the needy and gives the poor hope.

In contrast to His defeat of the crafty, God aids and helps those in need. He saves the needy from the sword and from the words and deeds of those in power (who would seek to harm the needy). This gives hope to the poor and defeats (shuts the mouth) of those who would practice injustice against the poor and needy.

Again, it is true that God can and sometimes does do this, as is also stated elsewhere in Scripture (Psalms 35:10; 1 Samuel 2:8; Psalms 107:41,42). He has often demonstrated His care for the poor and needy, and has instructed His people to show concern for those in need. (Compare Psalms 64:3.)

However, again, if the point is that Job is not prospering because he is not trusting in God to take care of Him, the point does not fit Job's case. It is not true that God has promised to always relieve the poor and needy of their suffering in this life, not even when they are righteous. Often good people do suffer need and injustice. Lazarus was godly but lived as a poor beggar, where the rich man fared sumptuously despite his sins – Luke 16:19-31. The ultimate correction for such injustice will be after death and especially in eternity.

So, while God does care for the poor and needy, and He sometimes does protect and provide for them in this life, such is not a promise and does not always happen. But those who are righteous will be rewarded in eternity and those who are wicked will be defeated.

5:17,18 – Do not despise God's chastening, because He heals after wounding.

Eliphaz' conclusion is that God is chastising Job for his sins. So instead of feeling sorry and confused, Job should recognize his problems as a lesson from God. He should not despise the chastisement but appreciate it and, by implication, should repent and correct his life.

God not only bruises and wounds, but He binds up the wounds and heals. This implies, as shown in the following verses, that God will remove the problems Job has and will heal him from his troubles, if he will repent and correct his life and his relationship with God.

These verses clearly state the problem as Eliphaz and Job's friends see it. Job is suffering as punishment for his sins. God is chastising Job. The solution is simple: repent and return to God's favor, and God will remove the problems.

The Bible does teach that God sometimes chastises us in this life for our sins – see Hebrews 12:5-11 (compare Proverbs 3:11,12). When this is the case, exactly as Eliphaz says here, we should not despise that chastening but learn the proper lessons. And it surely follows that, when we suffer, we should examine our lives and see whether or not we have committed any sin for which God may be chastising us.

However, we must again realize that this is not the case with all suffering. As in Job's case, sometimes we suffer when we have committed no sin. We should not necessarily conclude that people are suffering for sins they committed. When an honest examination of God's word convicts a person of no sin, then we should not condemn him when he is innocent.

5:19-21 – *Eliphaz gave examples of troubles from which God will deliver.*

Eliphaz then waxes eloquent describing various problems men might have as chastisement from God, but from which God would deliver them. The point is that people have these problems because they sin, but they will be delivered from the problems if they heed the chastisement and repent.

He says God will deliver men from six troubles, even in seven of them no evil will touch them. This six, yes even seven, approach appears to be a poetical expression using numbers to emphasize a point. The method was used also by Solomon in the Proverbs involving various numbers (six, yes even seven – compare Proverbs 6:16-19; etc.). Here Eliphaz uses it to list things that cannot harm one who will heed God's chastisement.

Included is famine, from which God will redeem or buy you back from death. In war, you will escape the power of the sword. You can be hidden from the scourge of the tongue. A scourge involved a whip lashing, but in this case it is administered by speech. One who will need God's chastisement need not be afraid of any destruction.

Obviously, Job had not escaped these problems. So the point is that he must not be right with God.

5:22-24 – *Heeding God's discipline avoids catastrophe.*

Eliphaz lists other problems the faithful can avoid. He repeats again destruction and famine, saying those who heed God's chastisement can laugh at them – i.e., he does not need to take them seriously, since they are no threat to harm him.

Even the beasts of the field cause him no fear, for they shall be at peace with him. This may mean wild animals cause him no personal harm, but also they do not harm his crops. He will have a covenant of peace with the stones of the field – perhaps meaning they will not hinder his work of growing crops. In any case, even the forces of nature that normally frustrate men would actually cooperate with the righteous man.

As a result, his dwelling place will have peace. Nothing will be found amiss anywhere in it. And again, this was not the case with Job. Everything in nature seemed against him. There was much amiss in his dwelling place. So he must not be listening to God.

5:25-27 – The man who heeds God will have many descendants and will live to a ripe old age.

Finally, Eliphaz claims God will bless the family and health of the righteous man. He will have many descendants and offspring numerous as the grass. Like a ripened sheaf of grain, he will live to a good old age, having no fear of an early death.

Eliphaz claims that he and his friends know all this to be true, because they have searched it out. They have studied the matter thoroughly. It is right. And if Job will listen carefully, he too can know it to be true.

He offers no proof. He just affirms it based on his personal conclusion and claims Job will know it too if he will think about it. Note how, throughout the discussions, the friends appeal to all kinds of sources, but none of them real evidence.

And again, the application to Job is so obvious as to be almost cruel. Job had just lost all his children and his own health. So Eliphaz tries to "comfort" him by saying that righteous people will have no such problem. They will have many children and will live long lives. So of course, Job must not be righteous.

And again, there is some truth is these statements. God often blesses good people with children (compare Abraham). And faithfulness to God helps us avoid problems that may cause early death (alcoholism, drug addiction, etc.). But it is not always true that good people have many children and live long lives. Many are childless or die young.

But note how Eliphaz' emphasis is entirely physical. Physical harm will be avoided and physical blessings enjoyed if one will heed God's chastisement. It simply is not always true physically, but it is true spiritually in that the righteous will please God and be assured of eternal life where none of the problems of earth can enter.

Job 6

Chap 6,7 - Job's Response to Eliphaz

6:1-3 – Job exclaimed again over the weight of his calamity.

Job responded to Eliphaz' speech by describing again the depth of his hardship. He stated he had been so oppressed that, if his grief and calamity could be weighed on a scale, it would outweigh the sand of the sea. He continued to emphasize the terrible burden he has experienced.

He does acknowledge that his speech has been rash. It could be that he is acknowledging that he overstated his case in expressing his desire to die, or perhaps he is saying that his rashness was justified by the terrible circumstances he faced. In any case, he will say considerably worse things before the speeches end.

6:4-7 – Job believed God had brought this calamity on him.

He said he felt like a target for poisoned arrows shot at him by God; not only did the arrows find their target in him, but the poison has reached his spirit as though he drank in the poison. It seemed to him that God had arrayed His terrors against him, like an army arraying itself for battle against an enemy. Shooting of arrows is a common Old Testament illustration for God's punishment against His enemies: Job 16:13; Psalms 38:2; 18:14; 144:6; Habakkuk 3:8-12.

This seems to be part of the problem for Job as well as his friends; they all assume that God is the one who has brought these problems. The friends assume God did it as punishment for Job's sins. Job does not know why it has happened, but still thinks God is responsible. It never seems to occur to any of them that Satan may be responsible, or even that there may be no specific reason but could be the common lot of mankind to suffer since sin entered the world. We know the reason from chapter 1,2, but they do not know. In any case, Job is not as far mistaken as the friends, yet he is mistaken.

He explained his complaints by comparing himself to a mule or ox. He asked if such an animal would complain (bray or low) if it had received its food. If the owner meets the animal's needs, it will be content. But it would complain if it is neglected. His point is that he has a reason to complain. If he had not been mistreated, he would not speak out so.

He then asked if anyone could eat tasteless food without salt. Or could they find any flavor in the white of an egg (the translation here may be uncertain). He said they are loathsome food to him, which he would refuse to eat if he had a choice. What is the application? Perhaps he refers to the speech of Eliphaz: it is meaningless and unhelpful like the tasteless food and the egg white. Given his choice, Job would refuse it as something loathsome.

6:8-10 – Job still hoped God would just let him die.

In his opening speech, Job had repeatedly stated his desire to just die and be done with the suffering (chapter 3). Here, despite the rebuke of Eliphaz, he repeated the request. If God was going to torment him so, he wished God would just go ahead and finish the matter by killing him so it would be over. Once again we note that, for all the horror of his suffering, he never even suggested taking his own life. Suicide was not an option, but if God would take his life then his suffering would end.

Yet he maintained that, through all his suffering, he had spoken nothing false against God (compare 1:22; 2:10). He took comfort in his confidence that, despite his anguish and the fact God did not spare him from suffering, yet he had not concealed (denied – ASV) God's words. He believed he had still spoken the truth.

6:11-13 – He was at the end of his strength.

Job saw no reason for his life to be continued. He felt that he had no strength to continue, no hope for the future. In order to resist such hardship as he was facing, he would need strength like stones and flesh like bronze. Perhaps then he could be able to endure, but he had no such strength. There was no help in him to endure; success had been driven from him.

The point seems to be that he had reached the limit of his ability to endure such hardship. What was the point of continuing to endure? He appeared destined to die from his hardship anyway, so why not just get it over with?

6:14-18 – Job rebuked his friends for being unhelpful like a deceitful brook.

He claimed that, when a person is so afflicted as he was, his friends should show him kindness. He had not shown disrespect for God; but even if he had, he says they should treat him better than Eliphaz had treated him. Whether or not Eliphaz speech would have been out of line if Job had been in sin, it surely was true that he had not shown proper understanding and kindness under Job's circumstances.

Job compared his friends to a deceitful brook or stream that passes away. In cold weather, it freezes with ice and snow. What water there is accomplishes no good for anyone. Then when heat and warm weather comes, the brook dries up and ceases to flow. It wanders off and perishes, accomplishing no good for the land, people, and animals that need the water. Such brooks are common in the Middle East. They are called "wadis."

This is how he viewed the "help" offered him by his friends. They may seem to be friends, but were no more helpful than the deceitful brook. When he really needed their help, they deserted him or were not useful.

6:19-21 – The brook provides no good for travelers.

Job here applied his illustration of the brook. Caravans and travelers would arrive looking and hoping to find water in the brook. But their confidence would be misplaced and their hopes would be disappointed. They would be confused, not finding the help they needed from the brook.

This was how Job felt regarding his friends. They were of no help at all. They saw his problems, but instead of offering help, they offered nothing but fear. They did not comfort him and meet his needs, but like the deceitful brook, they came up empty when he needed them.

6:22,23 – Job had not asked his friends for anything.

Job then asked his friends whether he had asked for their help. Had he asked them to bring him anything or to use their wealth on his behalf? Had he asked them to deliver him from his enemy or his oppressors? The point seems to be that he had not imposed on them in any way nor made any requests of them, so why don't they just leave him alone? If he had asked for their help, it might make sense for them to say what they thought, but he had not asked.

6:24-27 – Job was willing to consider any real evidence against him, but Eliphaz had proved nothing.

Job stated his willingness to be taught. He would listen if they could prove to him wherein he had done wrong. Truth has power, but their arguments had no power because they proved nothing. If they had produced evidence to support their accusations against him, that would have been worth listening to. But they had no proof, so their statements had no force. This is true in all cases, and is something we should remember: we have no right to accuse people of sin unless we can offer valid evidence of their guilt.

He asked them if they intended to rebuke his words. If so, he is willing to admit that he spoke from desperation words that are like the wind – he apparently grants (as in verse 3) that his speech was rash. He wants them to take his initial speech "with a grain of salt." (Or instead, perhaps he meant that their speeches were desperate speeches consisting of no value, only of wind.)

If they plan to rebuke him and speak of him as one who is in error, then they are like people who overwhelm an orphan. Rather than helping a helpless person in need, they attack and harm him. So they were undermining a friend. They should have taken pity on him and tried to really help. Instead, they offered no valid help but simply attacked and overwhelmed him with unfounded accusations.

6:28-30 – *Job assured them that he would not lie to them but would be fair.*

Eliphaz had accused Job of sin as the cause of his suffering. Job had denied his guilt. He here assured them that he would not lie to their face. He called on them to "look him in the eye" and see that he is telling the truth. He still defended his righteousness and calls on them to concede that he is righteous.

He affirmed that he is able to discern what is improper (unsavory), but he knows of no guilt to confess to them. He is not speaking unjustly and calls on them to yield and acknowledge that there is no injustice (this could mean they should admit he is not practicing injustice in denying his guilt or that they should not practice injustice by claiming without proof that he is guilty).

Eliphaz had produced no proof of guilt in Job. The only one present who could witness against Job was Job himself. He knew right from wrong but was denying his guilt. They should therefore acknowledge that justice required them to yield to his conclusions and acknowledge his righteousness.

Job 7

Job's Response to Eliphaz (cont.)

7:1,2 – Job compared himself to a hired servant awaiting his wages.

Having responded in chapter 6 to Eliphaz' theory that Job suffers because of his sins, Job returned to describing his complaint. He compared life – presumably especially his own life – to a hired servant who faces hard service. So man's life is a time of difficult service all the while he is on earth.

But the servant desires the shade (evening) when he will receive his wages. Men then were generally paid for each day they served (Matthew 20:1-16). So as the man labored all day, he looked forward to the end of day when he would receive his wages.

Job compared his own life to the hardships faced by a hired servant: all of life is full of hardship and labor. But man looks for the reward when life is over, like the servant looks for his wages. In Job's case, he was looking for his life to end. Perhaps he thought that would give him some rest from his suffering, or perhaps he looked for a Divine reward after life.

7:3-5 – Job's nights were troublesome and his flesh diseased.

Job described his life as months of futility or vain emptiness. His nights were wearisome. When he lay down at night, he would hope for the night to end so the day would come. He tossed until dawn, because of his suffering. Imagine trying to lie down to sleep, when one's body is covered with sores!

He described his flesh as caked with dust and worms. His sores were caked with dust, perhaps because of the ashes that he sat in (2:8). Worms and insects would be attracted to the festering sores. Then his skin would crack and break out with new sores or the sores would open and seep.

Surely such a life would be miserable, yet that is what Job lived with. No wonder he could not sleep at night but simply wished for the day.

Study Notes on Job

7:6,7 – Yet life is swift and short like a breath.

Despite the suffering, Job said life is short. He compared it to a weaver's shuttle. We are not much familiar with the weaving process today, since it is done in factories. But people in those days would often weave their own cloth, or at least they could visit people who wove the cloth. The shuttle holds a strand of thread that a skilled weaver would pass rapidly back and forth from side to side, weaving it into the other threads. That is how the days seemed to Job to pass. He compared his life to a breath, because it passed away so quickly.

Many other passages likewise describe the brevity of life. Job 14:1,2; 8:9; 9:25; 16:22; 7:16; Psalms 78:39; 89:47; 90:5,6,9; 102:11; 103:15,16; 144:4; Isaiah 38:12; 40:6,7; James 4:13-15;

Yet Job said his life passed without hope and he despaired of ever seeing good again. What a discouraging way to live, having life without hope of rest or good health. Each day itself would seem unending, but when one looked back on life, it would seem to have flown past. Commentators are of the opinion that this verse begins a section addressed to God.

7:8-10 – Job compared his life to a cloud that vanishes away. He will leave and not return.

Job said that people could see him now, but soon his life would end and no one would be able to see him again. He said "your eyes" (God's eyes?) would be on Him, but he would no longer be – i.e., no longer be living on earth.

He compared his life, much like James 4:14, to a cloud that appears but then disappears and vanishes. It is very brief, then gone forever. This is what a man's life is like when he goes to the grave. His brief life has ended, never to return. He will never come back to his house, nor shall anything that belonged to him ever know him again.

The word for "grave" here is Sheol (ASV). It can refer to the grave where the body goes or to the place where the spirit goes when a person dies, equivalent to Hades as in Luke 16:19-31.

7:11,12 – Job refused to keep quiet about his anguish.

Because of all that he was suffering, Job said he would not restrain himself from speaking about it. He felt anguish and bitterness that compelled him to complain. He thought he had a right to complain.

He asked if he needed to have a guard watch him as if he were a sea or a sea serpent. The meaning is hard for me to understand. Perhaps his point is that men (such as sailors) watch the sea for signs of danger: storms, enemies, etc. They watch for animals that may endanger them, illustrated here by a sea serpent. So maybe Job was asking whether God considered Job to be a source of danger like sailors watch for danger at sea. If that is the meaning, then the implication would be that Job was no threat, so why restrain him by such suffering?

7:13,14 – *Job's dreams at night terrified him.*

Job had earlier stated that, at night, he tossed and turned hoping for day to come (verse 4). In these verses he said that, during the day, he hoped for the night, thinking he may be more comfortable in bed. But then when he lay down, he had terrifying dreams and visions.

He blamed these on God, though of course they could have been the natural consequence of his condition. People who are so seriously ill and in pain may tend not to sleep well or dose in and out of sleep. That is when people tend to dream. And they tend to fear further tragedy, so their dreams are nightmares.

7:15,16 – *Job would choose to die, rather than to live.*

Job has stated several times that he would rather die than to continue to suffer so (see chapter 3). He repeated that sentiment here. He loathed his life and would prefer to strangle and die than to continue living in his body. People who are suffering a long-term illness know that it will end someday, but it seems like it will go on forever. So Job said he did not want to live like this forever.

He called on God to leave him alone. His days are short like a breath (see notes on verses 6,7). He would not live long in any case, so he called upon God to leave him alone and let him have some peace for the short time he had left on earth.

7:17,18 – *Job asks why God had chosen to so test him.*

Job asked what motivated God to view men as He does. Why choose one man to focus His trials on (this is the only sense I can make from "exalt" in this context – not exalt in the sense of honor, but choose one person from among others to focus on).

So he asked why God would visit a man every day to bring trials and tests into his life. Of course, God would not answer such a question, and perhaps Job did not expect an answer. He is just voicing his troubles and griefs. He is asking, as some do today, "Why me?" Why should he be the one singled out for such problems?

7:19-21 – *Job continued to question God about his suffering. He asked, if he had sinned, why did God not forgive him?*

He asked how long this would continue, and when he would get some relief. When would God look away: "go pick on someone else"? He felt like he did not even have time to swallow. This was an obvious exaggeration to make the point that the problems never let up. We today may say, "I didn't have time to breathe!" It was just constant suffering with no let up.

He then asked God to let him know if he had sinned. What had he done that God would use him as a target for such suffering? We know the answer is that he had done nothing. It was his very goodness that made him the object of this test case. But he did not know that. He called God the "watcher of men," showing that he knew God was aware of His life and conduct. So what fault had God found? His whole being was like a terrible burden that he struggled to carry.

If he had sinned and that was the cause of his suffering, then he asked why God would not forgive the sin and end the suffering. Why not take away the iniquity he had committed, if iniquity was the problem. Evidently he had been praying to God for forgiveness. He knew of no guilt in his life; but if there was sin, why wouldn't God forgive it and then relieve his suffering?

Death was inevitable. He would lie down (be buried) in the dust and lie down in the grave. Then no one would find him to cause further problems for him. If this still is addressed to God, then perhaps the point is that, when Job died, God would no longer be able to cause him to suffer then.

Job 8

Chap 8 - Bildad's First Speech

8:1,2 – Bildad the Shuhite began his speech by accusing Job of speaking wind.

Eliphaz had tried and failed to convince Job that he was suffering because he was guilty of sin. Here the second of Job's friend tries his hand at convincing Job. His view is that same as that of Eliphaz.

Bildad began by dismissing Job's response to Eliphaz as a strong wind. We would say it was a lot of "hot air": lots of talk but no substance or value. So he asked how long Job would continue to speak since he had nothing worthwhile to say.

8:3,4 – Bildad said God is just, so Job's children must have died for their sins.

Bildad first asked if God subverted judgment or perverted justice. Of course, the answer must be that He does not. God is a righteous, just, and good God, so He must be just. This much is true, but Bildad's conclusion does not follow.

He says that Job's sons must have died – God cast them away – for their transgressions, because they had sinned against God. The point must be that God would be unjust to cause innocent people to suffer. Job's sons suffered, so they must be guilty!

This is a clear, concise statement of the friends' view. They can only see one reason why a person would suffer: because he has sinned and God is punishing him for his sins. As Bildad states, it would be unjust of God to punish innocent people, so all who suffer must be guilty of sin. This view allows no possible alternative reason for suffering: the righteous must never suffer, else God is unjust!

Of course, many Scriptures disprove this, including the clear record of chapter 1,2. Job is suffering, not because he is guilty of sin, but because he is righteous and Satan is tempting him to sin. This being true, Bildad's accusation is a horrible thing to say. Great as Job is suffering, Bildad adds to his agony by arguing that his sons got just what they deserved, so they must have been wicked men! Other passages show that the innocent may suffer for other reasons too,

Study Notes on Job

including simply because suffering is in the world since Adam and Eve's sin.

It seems that many people today still hold Bildad's view. If God allows innocent people to suffer, then God would be unjust. Atheists and skeptics use this as evidence God does not exist: innocent people suffer, a good God would never allow that, therefore there is no God. Others acknowledge God's existence, but claim He is not just. This is the view Job comes dangerously close to defending. This faulty reasoning leads many to turn away from God when they or they loved ones suffer.

All such errors are based on the same false foundation: that only the guilty should be allowed to suffer, so good people should never suffer.

8:5-7 – Job would prosper if he would be pure and upright.

Since Bildad assumed that Job and his family were suffering for their sin, then as Eliphaz had stated, the solution would be to turn and practice what is pure and upright. Seek God and pray earnestly to Him. If Job were upright before God, God would listen to him (awake to him) and prosper him properly in his dwelling place. The necessary implication is that God was not prospering Job because Job was not pure and upright.

He stated that, not only would Job prosper, but the end result would increase him so that he would be better off than he had been at the beginning. He had started out small compared to his latter end. Of course, Job's end does turn out to be greater than his beginning, but not for the reason Bildad assigned. Job was not suffering for sin, so repentance was not the solution. One does not necessarily suffer in this life for sin or prosper in this life for righteousness. The reward for our lives comes after life.

8:8-10 – Bildad urged Job to listen to the wisdom of previous generations.

The friends sought authority for their assertions. Eliphaz had appealed to personal experience and a dream he claimed to have had. Bildad appealed to human tradition: the wisdom of former ages. He said to consider the things discovered by their fathers.

Compared to those of the past, Bildad asserted that they were "born yesterday" and knew nothing (an interesting use for that expression). Their days on earth were but a shadow (though they lived long compared to us). So, whereas Eliphaz had appealed to his experience, Bildad tried to strengthen the argument by appealing to the accumulated wisdom of past generations. He said they would teach Job the truth in such matters, uttering words from their heart.

Note how then, as now, people sought evidence to add the weight of authority to their conclusions. Many today still appeal to human tradition as authority for their religious beliefs, but Jesus completely opposed such a view when the teaching was not found in God's word (Matthew 15:1-9,13). People still make errors by appealing to human wisdom (Jeremiah 10:23; Proverbs 14:12; 3:5,6; 1 Corinthians 1:18-25).

The friends sought many authorities, but never did cite any evidence from God. The truth from God, had they known it as in chapter 1,2, would have refuted them, and eventually God so states.

8:11-15 – Bildad compared the godless man to a papyrus plant that grows up and withers.

The verses that follow explain what Bildad claimed he had learned from the wisdom of the ancients. They appear in the form of proverbs or ancient sayings.

First, he asked if a papyrus reed could grow without a marsh or reeds flourish without water. Of course, reeds grow in marshy areas by ponds and rivers, such as along the Nile. Growing without water is impossible. They will wither more quickly than other plants, even when they are green, if they don't have water.

Bildad compares this to the destiny of those who forget God or are hypocrites. Their hope perishes and their confidence is cut off. What they trust for strength will disappoint them like living in a spider web for a house. When he leans on it for support, it collapses. No matter how he holds to it, it cannot last.

The point of all this is that Job was suffering because he had forgotten God. Like the reed without water, he was perishing. His confidence is cut off like a man who trusts in a spider web for protection.

These illustrations are appropriate if one applies them to eternal rewards and ultimate destinies. But Bildad missed the point by assuming this would apply to material prosperity in this life.

8:16-19 – So a godless man is trusting in things that do not endure.

Bildad continued illustrating the way of one who is ungodly. He may be like a plant that spouts up and grows green in the sun, spreading out its branches as in a garden. It sends out its roots for nourishment, but wraps the roots around rock and finds only stones. There is no adequate nourishment because it cannot find good soil.

The result is that the plant is destroyed. The earth denies what it needs as though it said the plant did not even exist. Destruction is the extent of his joy. He dies and others take his place.

Again, this is how Bildad viewed what had happened to Job. He was withering like the plant without nourishment, because he was not righteous before God.

8:20-22 – Bildad claimed that, just as God will not uphold evildoers, so He would not cast off those who are upright.

Having showed at length how God would allow the wicked to suffer without a solution, Bildad contrasted this to how God would treat the blameless. God would not uphold those who are evil, which is why Job is suffering. But likewise, God would not reject one who was righteous. But Job had been cast off, so he must not be righteous.

But Bildad assured Job that God would restore his well-being if he would turn. God would fill his mouth and lips with laughter and joy. And whereas now his enemies were rejoicing over Job, they would then become ashamed. The dwelling place of the wicked will come to nothing. This would apply to Job as long as he remained in sin. But it would apply to his enemies if he would repent.

We may hope that the friends sincerely thought they were helping Job by showing him the solution to his problem. But again, their continual error was the assumption that God settles all his accounts by means of material prosperity or hardship during this life. What Bildad said is true in the long run. But the final outcome is postponed till after this life. So one who is righteous may suffer like Job in this life.

Job 9

Chap 9,10 - Job's Response to Bildad

9:1-3 – Job acknowledged the greatness of God.

Job began his response to Bildad by acknowledging that some of Bildad's speech was correct. This probably refers especially to Bildad's descriptions of God's greatness. Perhaps he also agreed that God would reward the righteous and punish the wicked.

But he asked how a man could be righteous before God. This may refer to Bildad's appeal to Job that God will not cast off the blameless (8:20). If a man has to be upright to receive God's blessings, why isn't Job good enough? He knew of nothing specific for which he needed to repent, and the introduction showed that in fact he was upright before God. Does Job mean that, if he is not good enough to receive God's blessings, he does not know how he could be good enough?

If a man were to try to have a discussion with God, the man would not be able to answer even one of a thousand of God's questions or arguments. This becomes literally true in chapter 38,39, when God does begin to question Job. But perhaps Job here meant that, if he is suffering because God is set against him, Job does not know what he could say that would convince God otherwise.

Note that Job still appears to be accepting the view, held by the friends, that he is suffering because God is opposed to him. Unlike the friends, he cannot understand what he has done that has turned God against him.

9:4-6 – God is wise and powerful, so no one can successfully defy Him.

Job then begins another of the sections, found commonly in both his speeches and those of the friends, in which they magnify God's character. Job began by praising God for His wisdom and His strength. Because of these qualities of God, no one can successfully resist Him. If one tried to stubbornly oppose God, he could never prosper. (Compare Psalms 95:8; 2 Kings 17:14.)

Job then gives examples that demonstrate God's greatness. God removes mountains and shakes the earth so that it trembles to its very pillars (Isaiah 2:19,21; 13:13; Joel 3:16; Hebrews 12:26). Of course, this is all symbolic language. Job does not know of specific pillars in the earth, but refers to the foundations of the earth (compare Job 26:11; Psalms 75:3). We would say that an earthquake or volcano had shaken the earth to its very core, even overturning mountains.

9:7-9 – Job described God's wonders in the heavens and the sea.

Job's description of God's greatness continued as he said that God would command the sun and it would not rise. He would seal off the stars – i.e., keep them from shining. He alone spreads out the heavens and treads on the waves of the sea. He made the constellations of the heavens and the chambers of the south (the context would indicate this may refer to another constellation unknown to us).

These expressions must involve some symbolism as in other similar Old Testament passages (compare Habakkuk 3:15). God could literally prevent the sun from rising and the stars from shining. This might be by appearance as in an eclipse or even heavy cloud cover. But He has also caused the sun to stand still as in the long day of Joshua. He created the sky. Jesus literally walked on the water. But these appear to me to have more reference to symbolic expressions of what He can do – not necessarily what He often does or has done.

9:10-12 – God does wondrous things without number, so who can question Him?

Job said that God did great things beyond man's comprehension. This is true of many things in nature that even after thousands of years of study men do not understand. But more specifically, He does wonders without number: miracles throughout history. We have difficulty even understanding how things work by nature. So surely comprehending how God does great miracles is, by definition, beyond man's understanding. That is the point of them!

Yet for all His great power and wonder, He is invisible. We cannot see Him, so He could walk right past us without our knowledge. He is, in fact, constantly around us in the sense of seeing everything we do, yet we do not see Him. This is also amazing since all the intelligent beings that we know in nature are visible. We can find them, confront them, and talk with them.

So with such great power that God has, what human being can withstand Him? Who can stop or hinder Him from His purposes, even when He destroys what He has made? What right would we even have to call in question His deeds? (Isaiah 45:9; Daniel 4:35)

This relates to Job's problem in that he has and will yet call God in question. He does not understand why God (in his view) causes Job to suffer, when Job knows of no reason for it. He wants answers from

God, yet knows in a sense that He has no right to question God, and would not know where to find Him anyway.

9:13,14 – *God does as He wants and no one can stand in judgment on Him.*

When God becomes angry and brings penalties on men, no one can convince Him to withdraw His anger. The proud man can find no ally that will effectively oppose Him; they would all be defeated to the point of prostrating themselves before God. (The NKJV footnote says the Hebrew word "Rahab" is here translated "proud." See Hailey for a study of the significance of the word.)

So God will punish men as He chooses, humbling even the most proud. This is true, though not always physically so during life on earth. But perhaps Job was describing that this is how he felt God had treated him.

So Job asked what He could say that would effectively give answer to God or reason with Him. He was convinced that He could never understand why God has treated him as He has. Nothing he could say or do would result in a satisfactory discussion with God. Again, he will have the chance at the end of the story, and sure enough he could not answer or reason with God.

9:15,16 – *Job thought that he could not reason with God.*

Job continued the point of verse 14 saying that, if he was righteous (as he believed he was though the friends denied it) he would still not be able to reason with God. He could not answer God. But he would still beg for mercy.

And if God spoke to talk to Job about the matter, Job would not be able to accept that God was really listening to him. He appears to be so convinced that God is ignoring and mistreating him that he could not bring himself to believe God was answering even if God tried.

These ideas are enlarged on in verses 17,18. Job was getting dangerously close to accusing God of mistreating him. He felt that he was being treated so badly that nothing would convince him that God was listening to Job's prayers. He had pleaded so long and been ignored (so he thought) that he had given up hope that God would really answer.

9:17,18 – *Job claimed that God was wounding him without cause and filling him with bitterness.*

Job thought that God was crushing him like a great tempest that overwhelmed him. He was repeatedly wounded, so continually that he could not even catch his breath. Job was filled with bitterness as a result.

A key phrase here is "without cause." Job blamed God for the suffering, yet he continued to affirm he did not deserve the treatment he received. This demonstrates that Job had accepted the friends' false concept that God is the one who it causing the suffering. He saw no other alternative. And since he correctly believed he had been righteous, he concluded that God had wounded him without cause. This is a dangerous thing to say of God and shows that Job has sunk to a point that he will need to repent.

9:19,20 – Job thought he would be punished no matter what he did.

Job granted that God had the power to overwhelm him. He did not question God's strength. But he definitely appears to be questioning God's justice. He asked who would give him a day in court. How would he be able to prove to God that he did not deserve the treatment he was receiving?

Even if he were righteous (as he believed himself to be), he would not be able to defend himself adequately. Despite being blameless, his words would make him appear to be perverse.

Because he suffered so and could see no reason for it, Job was convinced that nothing he could say would change the situation. He would never be convinced that God would listen. No matter how he tried, he felt like he would come out the loser. "Heads you win. Tails I lose." It appears that Job felt like he would be arguing with someone who would never admit He had mistreated Job. Job did not think he had done wrong, but he does not think God would ever be convinced of it so as to stop punishing him.

9:21-24 – Job claimed that God had destroyed both the innocent and the wicked.

Job again affirmed that he was blameless to the best of his knowledge, though he admitted he did not know himself. Yet he hated his life. This may be an admission that maybe he was guilty of something he was not aware of. But he was not aware of any guilt. But he knew he was displeased by his life as he faced it.

He then made some of his strongest statements against God to this point. He said God destroys the upright the same as the wicked. It is all the same to Him! Innocent people suffer, but wicked men prosper and appear to be in control. And the rulers, who ought to see these errors and bring justice, act as though they do not even see the injustice (their faces are covered).

Job has granted that God has great power, but he here denied that God uses His power to bless the righteous and harm the wicked, as the friends have stated. It seemed to Job that God uses His power against both the wicked and the innocent. If this is not the case, then Job admits he just does not understand what is happening.

God is the only One Job can think of who is responsible for these miscarriages of justice. If it isn't God, then who is it? This is a key question, but neither Job nor the friends seem to be aware of other possible alternatives. In a sense, Job is correct that both the good and the evil suffer in life. But he is mistaken regarding the source. Of course, the answer is that Satan is the one ultimately responsible for the evil and suffering in the world. But for some reason neither Job nor his friends think to blame the Devil.

Meanwhile, these are strong charges against God. He says that God even laughs when the innocent suffers the scourge. Obviously, this is Job's hardship motivating his thoughts. But still, this appears to be some of his statements for which he must later repent.

9:25,26 – Life passes quickly like a runner, a swift ship, or an eagle swooping on its prey.

Job repeated that life is short (compare notes and references on 7:6,7). He compared his days to a runner that swiftly flees away. Or they are like ships that sail swiftly by, or like an eagle swooping down on its prey. They are here and gone, almost before you know it.

Yet he added that his days see no good. Because he was suffering, he saw little or no value in the time he did have. He had repeated earlier that he wished to die. So he saw his life passing swiftly, but even so he saw no value in it.

9:27-31 – Job was convinced he would suffer no matter how innocent he may be.

Job said that it would do him no good to keep quiet about his concerns. If he tried to put off his sadness and put on a smile, he would still fear that he would have to suffer. God would not treat him as one who is innocent no matter what he did.

So he thought there was no reward no matter how hard he worked to be righteous. He would still stand condemned even if he was washed in snow water and his hands cleansed with soap. These were expressions for cleansing his life of any wrongdoing (compare Isaiah 1:18). Though his friends urged this course, he was convinced it would do no good. He would still be plunged into the pit. Everything around him would oppose and reject him to the point that even his own clothes could not stand to be near him.

Again, these were strong words of criticism of God's treatment of him. He was for all practical purposes accusing God of punishing him unjustly. He was suffering greatly, but his view was incorrect. He spoke without knowledge and in so doing made statements he should never have made.

9:32-35 – Job sought someone to mediate between God and himself.

Job knew God was not a man like himself, so he was convinced he would be unable to properly present his case before God, even if he were given a chance to face God as in a court hearing. One who thinks he has been wronged would seek a chance to prove his case before a fair judge. But Job was convinced that, as a mere man, he could never win a case against God, even though he was convinced he had a just complaint.

So he sought someone to stand between himself and God as a mediator, laying his hands on both of them. This expressed the concept of a mediator: one who can relate to both parties in a dispute. So Job thought such a mediator could state his case in a way that God would understand and give him justice.

Job thought that, if he had such a mediator, God might withdraw his rod of punishment, so that Job no longer would stand in dread and terror of God. With the help of such a mediator, he would be able to speak to God with confidence that God would hear and understand him (instead of fear of rejection). But unfortunately, he had no such one to help in his case.

Perhaps with the suggestion of a mediator, Job was at least suggesting hope that his complaints against God could be resolved. This may soften his criticisms offered earlier: maybe there would be a solution if someone else more on God's level could explain the case. Nevertheless, he knew of no such mediator.

In a sense, this is what we need with God when we are in sin: a mediator. And Jesus, of course, is that mediator, exactly as Job here described. What a blessing to have one who has experienced our needs and can relate to both God and us (1 Timothy 2:5; Hebrews 4:14-16; 7:25).

But again, Job's basic mistake was that he has accepted at least part of the error of his friends. He was convinced that God was the one causing his problems, and that such problems should be given only to those who are guilty of sin. This fundamental error characterized both Job and his friends. Neither could understand the truth till they got past these basic misconceptions.

Job 10

Job's Response to Bildad (cont.)

10:1-3 – Job asked God to explain why He was treating Job this way while appearing to favor wicked men.

Job then repeated how he hated his life, as he has stated earlier (see chapter 3). He insisted that he would not keep silent but would express his bitterness and complaint.

If he could speak to God, his complaint would include a request for God to show him why He contended with him. He would call on God to not condemn him. Job was sure he had done nothing worthy of punishment by God, and in this he was correct. So why was God acting like an opponent who contended with him and condemned him in a lawsuit?

He would ask if God thought it was good to oppress Job and despise the work of His hands. God had created Job, as He has all of us. One would think He would care for that which He made, especially when Job had done nothing against his Maker. Yet God acted (to Job's thinking) as if he was angry with his creature (compare verse 8).

In doing this, it appeared to Job that God was smiling on the counsel of the wicked. Perhaps this means that God treated those who were wicked better than He treated Job. He blessed those who rebelled against Him better than those who served Him.

10:4-7 – Job would ask God if he was like a man. God knew Job was innocent, yet he could not escape suffering.

Job asked if God was like a human. Did he have human eyes to see things the way people see them. He asked if God lived His days like a mortal man, even a mighty man.

If God was like a man and saw things like a man, this would explain why he would search for sin in Job's life, even when Job and God both knew Job had done nothing worthy of being counted wicked. Yet God is so mighty that no one could deliver Job from Him, if He determined to punish Job.

Job knew, of course, that God is not a human and does not see like men see. Yet it seemed to Job that God was acting like a man, perhaps like Job's friends. He found God's conduct to be incompatible with his concept of God. God should know when a man was a good man like Job and should treat him with kindness and reward him. But instead it appeared that he was mistreating Job. This is the kind of treatment one might expect from an imperfect human, but not from God. So Job expressed his confusion about how God appeared to be treating him.

10:8-11 – Job acknowledged God as his Maker, but asked why God would destroy him.

Job had stated that he was the work of God's hands (verse 3). Here he directly acknowledged that God had made and fashioned him. He was a unit – a complete entity or body – complex and intricate. Yet having made Job, God appeared to be determined to destroy him (compare verses 2,3). He had made Job of clay (perhaps like a potter molding clay or perhaps like God made Adam – Genesis 2:7) but was about to turn him back again to dust (Genesis 3:19).

Job compared God's creation of him to making cheese from milk. The milk is poured out into a mold and then curdled to make cheese. This was how Job expressed his making. He was clothed with skin and flesh, and tied together in bone and sinew. God did all this for Job, so why should He turn around and destroy him?

This made no sense to Job, but again the root problem was that he assumed God was the one responsible for his suffering. He failed to reckon Satan as the source of his problems.

10:12,13 – Job acknowledged that God had blessed him in the past.

Having made Job (as in the previous verses), God had then blessed him with life and favor. God had preserved Job's spirit by His care. This acknowledged God's providential blessings and provision. Job said he knew these blessings were from God, and he had hidden these things in his heart so that he would remember them. (Or perhaps this statement refers to other things in context that Job was convinced had come from God.)

Again, the point was that he did not understand why God had then turned against him. After doing all those great things for him, why reject and treat him as an enemy?

10:14-17 – Whether he was wicked or righteous, Job concluded that he must suffer.

Job seemed convinced that God would treat him as a sinner regardless of how he acted. If he really was guilty of sin, then God would put a mark upon him (identifying him as a sinner, marked for punishment) and would not count him as innocent. So if he was wicked, woe be to him.

But if he was righteous, he was still disgraced. He was in such misery that he could not even lift up his head. But if something should happen that his head was exalted, God would hunt him like a lion after his life till he brought him down again. Job was convinced God would act like an awesome enemy, no matter how Job acted, good or bad.

So God would testify against Job and direct ever greater indignation against him, no matter how he acted. War and uncertainty faced Job no matter how he turned.

This was how Job summarized his suffering despite the fact God had created him. It seemed as though nothing he could do would please God or relieve his suffering. And of course, again, the point shows his confusion and misunderstanding of the causes of his suffering.

Note that Job was disagreeing with his friends' views. They argued that only evil people suffered and good people were blessed. Job disagreed, claiming both the good and the evil suffered. Yet the result was an embarrassingly strong misstatement of God's treatment of him. Job's view effectively accused God of terrible injustice in treating good and bad the same.

10:18,19 – Again Job wondered why he had been born.

As in chapter 3, Job bemoaned his existence and wondered why God had ever caused him to be born. If he had perished before birth, no one would ever have seen him. It would have been all the same as if he had never existed, but would have gone straight from the womb to the tomb. See notes on 3:3-13. Job believed it would have been better never to have been born than to live and suffer as he was.

10:20-22 – Finally, Job asked God to at least let him alone so he could have some peace before he died.

Job said he would have preferred to have never been born than to suffer as he was (verses 18,19). But as it was, he had been born. Now he would be here for only a short time. So, if God had chosen to let him be born, he wondered why God didn't at least let him alone so he could have a little comfort. If God could not choose to bless him, then at least He might ignore Job instead of causing him to suffer so.

He would go to the place from which he would not return: death, which he described a land of darkness and shadow, dark as darkness itself. He seemed to view the shadow of death as darkness with no light at all: even what light there was would be darkness. And when it came, he would not return from it. This expressed a lack of understanding of death and resurrection, but Job knew it was coming and coming soon. So why would God not let him alone to have some peace till the end came?

Interestingly and importantly, for all his complaints, one thing Job does not do is to renounce God, as his wife had urged him to do. He may have questioned God and made statements that effectively accused Him of mistreatment and injustice. He in effect said there was no moral government in the universe. Yet he never denied God's existence or chose to turn his back on God.

Job 11

Chapter 11 - Zophar's First Speech

11:1-3 – Zophar began his speech saying that Job's boasting must be answered.

At this point, Bildad and Eliphaz have had their say, and Job has responded. So next came Zophar. He claimed he must answer because Job spoke a multitude of words, empty, mocking talk. Zophar insisted that Job's words demanded a response.

The implication is that Job must not be allowed to appear to "win" the debate simply by the fact he had so much to say. The person who talks the longest and loudest is not necessarily correct (Ecclesiastes 5:3; Proverbs 10:19). This, of course, is true. But Zophar's problem was, not just that Job spoke long, but that none of Job's friends had any real evidence for their view!

11:4-6 – Zophar argued that Job was so wicked he deserved more suffering than God had given Him.

Zophar pointed out that Job had claimed he was innocent ("clean") before God, and that he had taught the truth. This is basically correct, although it may have been an overstatement. What Job had really claimed was that he had done nothing to deserve the kind of suffering he was undergoing. In this he was correct.

However, Zophar proceeded to wish that God would speak out so Job and all of them could hear His words. He claimed that God would reveal true wisdom before Job, and give Job twice the wisdom he had. This was doubtless also true, and God later does speak and reveals true wisdom to all of them. But He does not say what Zophar expected Him to say!

Zophar then claimed that, if God would speak to them, Job would learn that he was so wicked that he actually deserved much more punishment than he had received! How is that for giving comfort to a man in the depths of grief over incredible hardship! The friends may have come with good intent to help Job, but instead their false views have led them into downright ridicule and false accusation on top of all that Job had suffered already.

Further, Zophar has chosen to speak for God, when he has no real knowledge of God's will in this matter. He admitted that God had not spoken, then he proceeded to reveal what God would say if He did speak! We need to take care when we choose to speak for God, knowing that we are attributing things to Him that we admit He never said.

In fact, we know what God has said regarding Job and it is the total opposite of what Zophar claimed. God had repeatedly spoken, before Job's trials began, and had told Satan that Job was blameless and upright (1:1,8; 2:3). This reveals the total bankruptcy of the views defended by Job's friends and the danger of assuming what God would say when we have no proof.

So the friends have offered various "proof" of their view. They offered dreams, human tradition, and here they offered Divine instruction that they admit they cannot prove God ever said. These are the same kinds of "evidence" we often receive when reasoning with people today. And it is as invalid now as it was then.

11:7-9 – Zophar claimed God's wisdom is so great that no one can know it.

Like all the speakers so far have done, Zophar then proceeded to extol the greatness of God. Of course, much of what he says is absolutely true, though it provides not one iota of evidence for Zophar's case!

He asked if we (including Job) can search out the depth of God or find His limits? He claimed these are higher than heaven and deeper than Sheol (the abode of the dead), so who can know them or do anything to compare to them? They measure longer than the earth and broader than the sea. All this is absolutely true, and is taught elsewhere in Scripture. (See Job 36:26; Ecclesiastes 3:11; Romans 11:33,34.)

But the implication is that God knows things about Job that Job did not know (verse 11), and that if God would speak (as in verses 5,6), He would reveal Job's real depth of iniquity. Zophar's statements about God were correct, but his conclusion about Job was simply assumed without proof. If God's wisdom is so great, then Zophar could not claim to understand it any better than Job did.

11:10-12 – Zophar claimed God knows the sins of men and judges them.

Having described God's unlimited knowledge and power, Zophar then claimed that God is able to observe the sins of men and punish (judge) them. He sees men's wickedness and deceit and takes it into consideration. When He does so, who can withstand Him?

This, once again, is quite true. But again the implication was that God had seen wickedness in Job and was judging him for it. So why does Job object or try to withstand it? The point was that Job may not have seen his guilt, but God did see it. That is the only explanation the friends can envision for why Job was suffering. And therefore Job should simply accept that the fact he was suffering proved he had sinned, so he should just admit his guilt and stop denying it.

Zophar then adds a proverb that is apparently of difficult translation. As translated here, the point is that a foolish brainless (empty-headed) man will be wise when a donkey gives birth to a man. Of course, the point is that this has never happened and never can happen. So likewise men with no sense cannot be expected to speak with sense; it is impossible. Apparently, this is his explanation for why Job will not accept the "logic" of the friends' view: he is so empty-headed that he will never be wise.

But Zophar's statement has some humorous implications for evolution. The force of the comparison is that everyone knows animals reproduce after their kind, so a donkey cannot give birth to a man. But apparently evolutionists do not know even this rudimentary fact of life. Evolution says, in effect, that given enough time, a donkey can give birth to a man! Of course, it must go through a number of steps on the way. But the resulting "logic" is as empty-headed as Zophar here describes.

11:13-15 – *Zophar urged Job to turn away from iniquity.*

As other friends had done, Zophar recommended that the solution to Job's problems was to repent. This followed from their conclusion that he was suffering because he had committed sin. So if he would repent, the cause of the suffering would be removed.

He said Job should prepare his heart or examine it and cleanse it of false motives. Then he should appeal to God (stretch out his hands to Him). He said Job should put far from him iniquity and not let wickedness dwell in his tents. He should turn to God with a face without spot. If he did these things, he could be steadfast and have no fear. In other words, the fears he had regarding his suffering would be removed.

Again, the clear implication is that the reason Job was suffering from fear and uncertainty was that He had not removed iniquity from his life and had not come to God without spot. So, if he would change his life and come to God with purity, etc., he could solve his problems.

11:16-20 – *Zophar said that turning from sin would solve Job's problems.*

Zophar continued to say that, if Job would turn from sin as in verses 13-15, his misery and suffering would be behind him and forgotten like water that has passed away. We would say it would be "water under the bridge." It would be over and gone, so Job could forget it.

Instead of suffering, his life would be brighter than noonday. Where his life had been dark with hardship and grief (compare 10:21), it would become as light as the morning. He would be secure and have hope for the future. "Dig around you" is translated "search" around you (ASV). Instead of being, perhaps like one who digs diligently searching for treasure and not finding it, Job could find the rest and safety that he sought.

He would lie down to sleep or rest with no fears from anyone. Instead of people looking down on him and making fun of him, as Job had implied people do, many people would come to seek his favor.

So Zophar concluded that those who are wicked are the ones who fail. Their eyes fail, meaning perhaps due to sickness and frailty, or perhaps meaning their eyes fail to see the good things that Zophar said men could see if they turn to God. They do not succeed in the blessings of life and will not escape from troubles. Their only hope for the future is in death.

This is the state that Zophar implied awaited Job. Job was suffering, so he must a sinner, in the view of the friends. If he would repent he could be spared and receive great blessings again. But if he refused, then he would continue to suffer the hardships that wicked people suffer. This is the view of the friends repeated over and over throughout the book.

Job 12

Chapter 12-14 – Job's Response to Zophar

12:1-3 – Job affirmed that he was as wise as the friends.

By this point in the discussion, all three friends had made their views known and Job could see the pattern. All had agreed that his suffering was the result of his sin, and all were determined to charge him with sin despite the fact that they had no proof other than his suffering. This, naturally, made him quite upset.

He responded somewhat sarcastically, saying that they must be the only wise people in the world so, when they died, that would be the end of wisdom! Of course, they had not claimed such a thing, but Job's point is that he was wise too. He claimed he understood as much as they did and was not inferior to them in knowledge and wisdom.

He asked who did not know such things as they had stated (compare verse 9). We would say, "You think I haven't thought of that?" He implied that they things they had stated were generally believed. But the problem appeared to be their conclusions from the information they offered. Or Job agreed with their observations in general, but denied that they fit his situation. In any case, they had offered no new or unknown ideas. They had not helped him, because he knew their accusations against him were not valid. So whatever, the real explanation was, they had not found it.

12:4,5 – Job said that it was easy for those who had no problems to mock those who were suffering.

He had called on God and God had answered. He had been just and blameless. This appears to refer to his past life. He had not been a sinner such as they had stated. But despite his good conduct and his relationship with God, his friends were mocking and ridiculing him. He did not deserve such treatment at their hands, just as he had not deserved to suffer as he was suffering.

Verse 5 involves translation difficulties. The ASV translates it such that those who are at ease (who are not suffering) despise or hold in contempt one who faces misfortune ("disaster" – NKJV footnote). They readily show contempt for one whose foot slips, as Job's had done.

But what is the significance as the NKJV translates the verse? One who is at ease despises a lamp (rather than misfortune as in the ASV), but it is ready for those whose feet slip. People who think they are in the light see no need for a lamp; they think the lamp is needed only by those who have trouble seeing their path. So the friends gave their advice freely to Job, thinking they did not need it – they were doing fine, so they must not be in sin. But Job (they thought) needed their advice to repent, since he was suffering. Perhaps this is the point.

The translations are significantly different, but the point ends up the same: people who have no problems are quick to criticize and find fault with those who do.

12:6 – Job affirmed that sinners often do prosper.

The friends argued that people suffer because of sin: Job was suffering, so it must be the result of his sins. Job knew that sometimes people suffer for sin. But he also knew that evil people sometimes prosper.

Thieves, for example, may get away with their crimes for some time and prosper as a result. Even though their conduct was an affront or provocation to God, yet they remained secure without apparent consequence for their evil.

The last phrase of the verse involves another translation issue. The NKJV appears to mean that God provides blessings for them too, despite their sins. This agrees with verses such as Matthew 5:45 – God does bless people in this life, whether good or bad. Final rewards are not determined according to physical prosperity in this life. Other translations imply that the wicked trusts in what he has provided by his hands as though it was his god who did it, or they trust in the work of their hands as in a god.

In any case, the point is that evil people do not always suffer, at least not right away and not in this life. Despite their evils against God, they seem to prosper and escape consequences.

12:7,8 – Job claimed that forces of nature testified that his view was correct.

Job then appeals to evidence from nature: animals, birds, fish, and the earth itself can testify that God is in charge in the affairs of the universe. The beasts and birds can tell this; the fish of the sea can explain it. The earth itself can teach it.

They teach many lessons we can learn from observing them. The most obvious lesson is that there must be a God who made them, so God must be in charge (verses 9,10). It must be that what occurs on earth is the result of God's will.

12:9,10 – God is in charge; everything on earth is under His control.

This is the first point Job says we learn from nature: God is in charge. He created all, so all must serve under His control. His hand gives life to all, and sustains the breath of all, including the people.

Perhaps the specific lesson Job here refers to is that suffering is not always the consequence of evil and prosperity is not always the result of righteousness. Animals suffer and the earth faces catastrophe, even when they seem to have done no wrong. Or they sometimes prosper when they appear to have done nothing better. Suffering or prosperity is not always the result of good or evil conduct. The Lord is in charge, but He brings good and evil on both good people and evil people.

This may be Job's point. In any case, he is claiming that God is in charge and this conclusion can be determined by observing nature.

12:11,12 – Men gain wisdom as they age, but each must test for himself.

Job states the general truth that people generally gain wisdom as they mature; understanding increases with length of days. Of course, this is not true for everyone, but it is generally true.

Nevertheless, each person must decide for himself what is right or true based on his own conclusions. He must test the words with his own ear, like he tastes food with his own mouth ("Here, try some."). He cannot simply take other people's word for what is wise, just like he cannot take other people's word for what a food tastes like. He must examine for himself and reach his own conclusions.

12:13-15 – Ultimate wisdom and power are found in God.

Compared to the wisdom man may develop from age or experience, God has true wisdom and true power. Real understanding and wise guidance come from Him. This means, of course, that regardless of other sources of knowledge that men may appeal to, nothing they say or do should be accepted when it differs from God's will. The three friends have cited all kinds of human evidence, but they have given no real proof that their teachings are from God.

No one can defeat God's work. Man cannot build what God determines to tear down. Man cannot escape if God determines to imprison him. If He withholds water, the earth must dry up. If He sends water, the earth must be overwhelmed.

Job does not make specific application of his points, so the applications are not certain. He could mean that he believes God has imprisoned him in suffering and torn down what he attempted to build up, etc. So there is nothing he can do to improve his condition so long as God determines to keep him suffering.

In any case, it appears that he is saying that neither he nor his friends may understand what God is doing (which was surely true) and none of them can withstand Him. They will understand only when they know what He says about it, not what their human wisdom indicates.

12:16-19 – *God's overruling strength and wisdom give Him strength over all leaders.*

Job affirmed again that God has true strength and prudence. All men are foolish and powerless compared to Him, and all are ultimately under his control.

He controls both the one who has been deceived and the one who deceives him. One may suffer at the hand of the other, but neither can overrule God. This could imply again that people who do evil (deceive) will not ultimately escape, but it also means the innocent people (the deceived) may suffer in this life. But God is ultimately in charge.

Likewise, men who exercise earthly power are under God's control. He plunders counselors (men known for wise advice) and makes fools of judges who ought to be wise. His wisdom is far greater than theirs (1 Corinthians 1:18-25; Proverbs 14:12).

Kings may think they can overpower others, but God loosens the bonds they place on others and makes them His prisoners as though binding them with a belt. Likewise, He overthrows those whom men consider to be strong and plunders princes who are viewed by men to be strong and rich. God's power is greater, so men cannot defeat His purposes.

These appear to be Job's observations. He makes no applications, but appears to be saying that God does these things whether men are good or bad. Suffering is not limited to the evil. And perhaps the point is that his friends, wise as they think they are, may not know as much as they think they know. In any case, he and his friends must obtain their explanation from God. Men may simply not understand why things have happened as they have.

12:20-23 – *God overrides the wisdom of wise men and overpowers the strength of strong men.*

Job has been showing that man's wisdom and power is insignificant compared to that of God. He continues here by saying the men in whom people put their trust and those who are respected as leaders (elders) lose their ability when He so chooses. Those whose words are trusted cannot speak, and those whose wisdom is trusted have no discernment. Men have abilities for which they are renown, but it means nothing to God.

Princes have fame and honor, but God views them with contempt. Men of war are known for might and strength, but God disarms them. Of course, this does not mean God hates or punishes all men. It simply means that the advantages men have, for which they are respected by other men, do not give them any special favors before God. If He chooses to defeat or overpower them, no man has the ability to stop Him. No one is great or wise compared to Him.

Things that are deep or dark – hard to understand or learn – God uncovers them. Men may have difficulty learning secrets or mysteries, but God knows them all and nothing is hidden from His wisdom. This may especially refer to plots by which men seek to cover their evils. Even the shadow of death comes to light before Him. We fear death and fail to understand many things about it, but God understands it perfectly.

Likewise, He has the power to control nations. He can bring them to greatness or He can destroy them. He can enlarge them (either in size or in power and influence) and guide them to blessings and well-being. His power over men is not restricted to individuals or even families, but it includes whole nations. He can control their prosperity or their decline.

Again, Job makes no application of all these points. He will show in chapter 13 that he has observed these things as well as his friends have. Perhaps he is just showing that he is as wise and informed as they are. But it may be that, in doing so, he shows that the human sources of wisdom on which they depend are not as wise or authoritative as they thought. Ultimately only God can answer the questions facing them.

12:24,25 – Compared to God, the wisest men wander in darkness.

As in the previous verses, Job said that God will remove the understanding of even the wisest, most respected leaders of men. The result will be that, instead of appearing as men of wisdom, they will wander like men lost in a wilderness and grope like men in the dark with no light. He will make them stagger helplessly like one who is drunken.

Again, the point is that God's wisdom is so great that the wisest, most respected men are foolish compared to Him. This may explain why Job and his friends are baffled by the suffering Job faced. His friends thought they knew the answer. Job implies their wisdom is folly, whereas he admits he is baffled. He knows their answer is incorrect, but He cannot determine the real explanation.

His speech continues in the next two chapters.

Job 13

Job's Response to Zophar (continued)

13:1,2 – *Job said he was aware of all that his friends argued, but he was not inferior to them.*

Job continued his response to Zophar by affirming that he has heard and understood all the things the friends know. Presumably, this refers especially to the power and wisdom of God to overrule the plans and wisdom of men, as in the last part of chapter 12.

Job claimed that he has observed these things and knows as much as the friends do about life. He denied that he was inferior to them (compare 12:3). This implies that they have left him the impression that they think they are right and he is wrong because they know more about life than he does.

This effect commonly follows from arguing from human wisdom and human observation, as the friends have done. Had they presented proof that God had spoken, the message would have the weight of Divine wisdom. But they had spoken about things they observed and things wise men observed. So naturally, Job would claim that his wisdom and observations were as good as theirs were.

We should learn this lesson today. If we try to convince people in religion on the basis of human wisdom, experience, and observation, they have every right to respond with their own wisdom, experience, and observations. Even if we are teaching truth, they may reject it because the impression is left that we think we are just smarter than they are. But when we cite God's word as evidence, then our words have the weight of Divine evidence behind them. People may still reject, but when they do they are rejecting God, not us.

Never leave the impression that we are right because we are so smart. Always appeal to Divine wisdom and give evidence from God's word to confirm it.

13:3-5 – Job wanted to speak with God instead of listening to the friends' lies. He said the friends were worthless physicians who should just hush.

Job claimed to be willing to speak to God and reason with Him. As in the notes on verses 1,2, he was tired of human wisdom. He wanted to know what God had to say. That is exactly the approach men should take in religion.

He stingingly rejected the friends' arguments, however, as lies they had forged. They were not speaking Divine wisdom – that he would listen to. They were speaking ideas they had forged themselves, and they were not true. This was especially true regarding their accusations that Job had sinned. All three of the friends had spoken and made that same accusation. Job forcefully denied the accusation and said it was a lie they had manufactured in their own minds. They had surely not given proof of any sin he had committed.

He further accused them of being worthless physicians. This is a powerful and almost humorous comparison. A physician's job is to offer a cure for one who has a problem. To do so, he must diagnose the problem. He must determine what caused the problem, and then find a solution to remove the cause. The friends had an entirely wrong diagnosis. They said Job was suffering because he had sinned, so they prescribed repentance as the cure. But Job argued (correctly) that he had not sinned, so as physicians they were worthless. They had no concept of the problem or the cure. Instead of making things better, they were making them worse. They added to his suffering instead of helping relieve it.

So Job concluded that, if they wanted to show true wisdom, they would just hush: be silent! That would show far greater wisdom than their speeches had. In effect, he was saying that the most help they had been to him had been when they first arrived and sat for seven days speaking nothing (2:13). As soon as they started speaking, they caused problems. So the best thing they could do at this point was to hush!

13:6-8 – Job accused them of speaking deceit as if it was from God.

Job called on them to now listen to his reasoning, the things his lips would plead. He then asked questions designed to show what he believed they had done.

Would they speak wickedness on behalf of God, speaking deceitfully for Him? They claimed their conclusions accurately described how God viewed Job and the reasons God was causing Job to suffer. But what they spoke was wicked and deceitful, since it falsely accused Job of sin. So they spoke wickedness and deceit, claiming it was God's will. Many religious teachers today do the same by teaching various false doctrines as though they are truth from God. This is a great danger that we must carefully avoid.

He then asked if they would show partiality and contend for God. They spoke as if they were arguing the case as God would want them to argue it, but they argued incorrectly. They had presumed to argue as God would argue, when they did not really know His will.

I am unclear in what sense this constituted partiality. Perhaps the point is that they argued he had sinned simply because he was suffering, yet other people did not suffer just because they sinned. So the friends made their argument selectively, when it appeared to work. Perhaps his point is that they were not consistent in applying their arguments. See verse 10.

13:9-11 – God would search out the friends and judge them to be wrong.

Job proceeded to remind the friends that God would judge them for their words. He would search what they had said to determine whether or not they spoke the truth. He claimed God would rebuke them for their errors. This is exactly what happened in the end (42:7ff).

He asked if they could mock God like one mocks a man. The idea of mocking God sometimes means to act as though we think we can get away with evil. See Galatians 6:7. God searches men's lives to judge us accordingly. To think you can speak or practice evil and get away with it is to mock God: to ridicule or make fun of His wisdom or power to punish for sin. You may be able to do this to men, but not to God.

Job then spoke again of the friends' secretly showing partiality. As in verse 8, this could mean Job thought they were applying their teaching inconsistently or unfairly. Perhaps the idea could include that they acted as though God would overlook their sin, when he clearly had not (in their mind) overlooked Job's sins. This too would be showing partiality in their view of God's treatment of them.

God is so excellent – so righteous and holy and just – that men should fear before Him. The dread of God's goodness should have caused the friends to fear to do or speak wrong, especially when they claimed to teach His will. We must be sure we are right, for He will search us out. Fear of His righteous judgments should have taught the friends to be more careful to speak truth.

We too need to take care when we speak. God will search out our words and judge us for our speech (Matthew 12:34-37). Will He rebuke us then? One way we can err in speech is to accuse people of sin, like Job's friends did, when we lack the real proof that they are guilty.

13:12,13 – Job claimed that the friends' proofs were worthless. He would speak and accept the consequences.

Job had vigorously disputed the claims of the friends that he was a sinner just because he was suffering. He had called their accusations lies (verse 4). He here argued that their defenses and proverbs were made of clay and ashes – they had no strength or value. Ashes are waste left over after that which has value has been used up. Clay is dirt, having little strength or value. So Job discounted the worth of the friends' proofs.

He then called on them to listen to what he had to say (in contrast to their arguments), then he would take whatever consequences came as a result.

13:14-16 – Despite his suffering, Job yet trusted God to save him.

Commentators view verse 14 as difficult to understand. Job said he was taking his flesh in his teeth and putting his life in his hands, and he asked why he should do so. Perhaps parallelism implies the first part of the verse means the same as the last part. Taking your life in your hand, as a common modern expression, means that a person has chosen to take a course of action, even though he knows it is a very serious matter (life or death). Job had just said he would speak, then accept whatever consequences followed (verse 13). Perhaps taking your flesh in your teeth was a proverb with similar meaning: he was determined to speak or act, even if it meant in the end that he had devoured himself.

Job concluded that he was determined to maintain his faith in God, even if God chose to kill him. Though he was deeply troubled by the problems he thought God had brought on him, he still believed in God. And furthermore, he still wanted to present his case to God, whether to convince God Job was righteous or to learn God's reasons for allowing him to suffer.

In the end, he believed God would yet save him. He knew that God would not justify or accept one who was a hypocrite; perhaps the meaning includes that an evil man would not even be allowed into God's presence to present his case. Yet Job was maintaining his integrity before God. If he was attempting to lie or deceive, God would know it and would not accept him. Yet he was convinced in the end that God would recognize him to be upright. He did not understand why he was suffering, yet he still trust God to render a just verdict in the end if Job could only present his case before God.

13:17-19 – Job had prepared his case to present and could not hold back.

Job called upon the friends (and perhaps God?) to listen carefully to what he spoke and declared. He had prepared his case – his reasons or evidence – to present to God (verse 15). He was convinced his evidence was persuasive and would be vindicated before God if he could only present the evidence. He could not hold back from speaking out, or it would kill him to keep quiet (obvious exaggeration). (Note that the translation of 19b is also uncertain.) He was convinced no one could successfully disprove his evidence.

13:20-22 – Job called on God to discuss the case with him.

Job said he had two requests to make of God. Then he would no longer hide or refuse to speak about this matter to God. Of the various things he then mentions, I am not sure which "two" he refers to, since he actually makes several requests (though the number "two" could be symbolic, simply meaning that he had more the one point to make to the Father).

He asked God to withdraw His hand from Job and not let fear of God keep Job from speaking. Doubtless it would be very hard to speak to God of such matters, even though Job has repeatedly sought opportunity to do so. So Job hoped this dread would not prevent him from speaking clearly. "Withdraw your hand" might be a request for God to allow Job's suffering to cease while they reason about the case. If so, then Job could speak without as great a dread of God.

So he urged God to speak to him and give Job a chance to respond, or else let Job speak to God and God can respond to Job.

13:23-25 – Job sought to know what his sins were and why God treated him as an enemy.

Job asked for evidence to convince him how many sins he had committed and what those sins were. This could be addressed to the friends, since they had accused him of sins. But it appears (based on context) to be addressed to God, in which case the result would be far more convincing than if the friends just made more accusations.

He wanted God to explain why He had hidden His face from Job and regarded Job as an enemy. This asks, in effect, why was God punishing Job. Job felt that his suffering meant God viewed Job as an enemy who did not deserve to be in God's presence but should be attacked. Job asked God to explain why He treated Job so. This was Job's main issue. He could think of no reason why God would cause Him to suffer, yet he could think of no other reason why he was suffering.

In Job's view, by causing Job to suffer so, God was attacking (frightening) a dead leaf that was driven back and forth in the wind. It was like persecuting dry stubble. Stubble is the worthless material left over after a field has been harvested. A dead, fallen leaf is likewise of little value to anyone. How foolish for a man to spend his time attacking something so worthless and harmless. Job viewed that he was likewise unimportant to God, especially since he had been humbled so by his suffering. So why did God bother to continue to attack him? Why not just let him go, now that he was reduced to something of no value?

13:26-28 – Job wondered if God were punishing him for things done in the distant past.

Job claimed God was writing bitter things against him – i.e., God must have some strong accusation against Job to treat him so, and Job wanted to know what it was. He thought maybe God was punishing him for sins committed in his youth. He could think of nothing he had recently done against God, so could it be something done in the distant past that he either did not remember or had not repented of? He sought God to explain what the grounds were for the treatment Job received.

He viewed God as punishing him like men were sometimes punished by having their feet put in stocks. Then God stood guard over him, watching closely all that Job did, putting a limit on where Job's feet could take him. He was like a prisoner restricted and punished, unable to go where he wants, yet for no reason he could think of.

He felt like a moth-eaten garment or some other rotten, decayed object of no value to anyone (compare verse 25). This is how he felt after his life was consumed by such tragedies, and yet God continued to punish him. His questions sought to know what he had done to deserve such treatment, and why God did not now let up on the suffering since Job had been already ruined to the point of having a meaningless life anyway.

Job 14

Conclusion of Job's Response to Zophar

Job concluded the first round of speeches by expressing further lamentation about his condition.

14:1-3 – Man lives a short, troubled life. He fades away or flees like a flower or a shadow.

Job affirmed that people are born to trouble. Life is short and filled with hardship. This is true – though Job does not directly say so – for the righteous as well as the wicked. It is the general experience of mankind. Ever since the sin of Adam and Eve, people good and bad have suffered in this life. This is not just true for Job. It is true for all people, including his friends.

Man flourishes for a short time, like a flower that grows and blooms. It serves a purpose and gives some blessing to others, but then it dies and fades away. So a man's life is like a shadow that appears and then flees away. He is soon gone, leaving little lasting impact. For other Scriptures on the brevity of life, see notes on 7:6.

Job then wonders why God would look at such a one as himself and bring him into judgment (note the capitalized pronouns, indicating the translators believe Job is here addressing God). This may indicate that Job's life is so short and sad that he did not view himself important enough for God to bother with judging. Or perhaps he is just wondering, once again, why God chose to bring such suffering on him.

14:4-6 – Job asked God to give him a chance to rest from his calamities.

Verse 4 is difficult to understand and see its connection to the context. Job asks who can bring something clean out of something unclean, and says no one can do so. Could he mean that all people suffer, so how can someone live life without suffering? Or does it mean that all people sin eventually, just like the people they came from? If so, this could be taken to mean Calvinistic depravity, but that would not necessarily be so. It would not require inherited guilt, but only that all people are born into a world of sinners, and they themselves eventually sin. Even so, I don't see the connection to the context. An explanation that fits the context is that all people die, because they come from people who die. That would fit the verses before and after.

Job then says that man's days are determined, God sets the number of his months so that he cannot exceed the limits God has set. We would say, "His days are numbered." This does not mean God determines or even knows ahead of time exactly how long each person will live. But generally speaking, we know that man's lifetime has a maximum limit – not an absolute limit, but men live only so long and then they die. This is how God has set up the world.

So Job will only be here so long, so he asks God to "give him a break." Just let Job rest (from his suffering) awhile. The end will come soon, so why not let him have a little peace? Death will come like a hired man's day comes to an end. Then his time of suffering here will end.

14:7-10 – Even a dead tree may sprout again from the stump, but when man dies, what then?

Job uses a tree as an illustration. When a tree is cut down, there is still hope that it may grow again. It may send out shoots from the stump. And even if the stump appears dead, so long as the root is alive, when water and other conditions are right, it may send forth new branches. These may grow into a tree again.

But Job contrasts this to a man. When a man dies, breathes his last, and is buried, what then? What hope is there for him? Job wonders about such questions, but appears not to know the answer. The New Testament teaches much more clearly the concept of resurrection from the dead, because we see it demonstrated in our Master. But at this early time, such revelation apparently had not been clearly given. Job does not deny the concept of life after death, but he seems to have no clear knowledge of it (compare 10:21,22). See more notes on v14 below.

14:11-13 – Job compared death to a dried up river or sea.

A river that dries up has no use or purpose of any kind. Likewise, water evaporates from a sea and appears to be gone forever. So when a man dies, he lies down and rises no more. At least that is the observation of mankind. Such people will not be aroused from sleep (death) till the end of the heavens. (Then comes the resurrection, but Job does not mention that.)

So Job sought to go to the grave in order to rest from his suffering, which he believed was caused by God's wrath. But he yet hoped that God would at some appointed time in the future remember him. This seems to imply hope in life after death – perhaps a future opportunity to stand before God to understand why things happened as they did. But then note how he continues in verse 14.

14:14,15 – Job asked if there is life after death.

Job asked whether or not a man will live again after he dies. As noted on verse 13, Job does not appear to have a clear understanding of life after death. Yet this verse may imply that he has hope. He says he will continue to wait, even though his work here is a time of hard service, till the time of his change comes. Does this change refer to the change from this life to the next? God will call, and Job will answer the call; God will be favorably interested in the one who had been made by His hands.

This sounds like Job hopes that, after this life he will sometime have an opportunity for a favorable reward from God.

14:16,17 – Job hoped God would cover his sins.

God numbers Job's steps. This probably means that God records everything man does. He keeps a record of each action. As translated in the NKJV, Job asks that God not keep a record of his sins. However, other translations translate this as a rhetorical question, implying that God does watch or see and record man's sins.

Job says his transgression is sealed in a bag and God covers his iniquity. The first clause appears to mean that God has recorded and preserved his sins so the record will permanently remain. If so, the covering of the iniquity in the last clause could mean, not hiding it so it cannot be seen, but putting it in a protective coating so it is preserved for future reference. Another possibility is that it is sealed from Job, so that he does not know what his sin is.

So, it is unclear whether Job is expressing hope that God will hide his sins so they are not held against him, or whether he states a sense of hopelessness that God will preserve his errors and continue to hold them against him. The following verses seem to imply the hopelessness of the second alternative.

14:18,19 – As a mountain gradually wears away, so God destroys man's hope.

Mountains gradually erode and wear away. The rocks crumble and fall, being moved out of their place. The rain gradually wears away even seemingly solid stone. Floodwaters wash away soil.

In the same way, Job claimed that God destroys man's hope. At first he had hope of deliverance from his suffering and heartache (and perhaps hope of life after death – verse 14). But as time passed, he gradually lost hope, like the soil was washed away. His hope faded the longer he continued to suffer.

14:20-22 – Man dies never to return or have any reward on earth. He does not know what happens to his children after he dies.

Job continues speaking of man after death. God prevails against men so that they eventually die, as God willed. His countenance changes (as he grows old or after he dies) and eventually he is sent away (from life).

Having died, his involvement of affairs on earth has ended (Ecclesiastes 9:6). He does not now what happens to his descendants after him. They may come to the favorable result of honor or may come to defeat and lowliness. But either way, the father does not know because he has gone.

Nevertheless, death will come, with all the pain and grief attached to it. The body endures pain as it comes to death. The soul grieves as it suffers and knowing it will suffer. Throughout it all is the knowledge that this is the way life will end.

So Job ends a tragic expression of his view of life. Suffering has deeply affected his view of God. He needed some sign of hope from God, but could find none.

Job 15

Chapter 15-21 – Second Round of Speeches

Chapter 15 - Eliphaz' Second Speech

At this point all three of Job's friends had expressed their views and Job had responded. So the discussion then went around in the same order the second time as each of the friends stated his response to the discussion and Job responded.

15:1-3 – Eliphaz claimed Job was like the wind blowing.

The second round of speeches began as Eliphaz took up a response to Job's statements. In this round, the friends and Job each defended their same views as before, but each stated his case more strongly as he became more determined to stand his ground.

Eliphaz criticized Job's statements as empty knowledge, like the wind blowing (he was a "windbag"). He asked if that is the kind of speech one would expect from a wise man. He accused Job of using unprofitable talk that could do no good to prove his case.

Such statements are typical when one person disagrees with another person's view, but the other person refuses to accept the arguments that have been made. In short, this kind of talk is common in debate. If men cannot agree, they naturally view the other as making useless speeches that prove nothing.

15:4-6 – Eliphaz claimed that Job's speeches were based on sin and condemned him.

Eliphaz claimed to have an explanation for why Job argued as he does. He claimed that Job was guilty of sin (based on the assumption that all suffering is the result of sin), and his speech resulted from his sin. In other words, his sin taught his mouth to speak evil and his tongue to be crafty. The implication was that Job spoke to defend himself, because he refused to admit his error, not because he was really innocent.

So Eliphaz claimed that Job cast off fear – he was not afraid to defend himself (though by implication he should have been afraid), because he was determined to deny his guilt. He claimed this hindered or restrained prayer before God. This seems to mean that Job's failure to admit his error prevented him from truly repenting and being forgiven so he could worship God properly.

He then argued that Job's own words testified against Job and condemned him. Eliphaz thought he did not have to condemn Job, because Job stood condemned by his own speeches. Of course, Eliphaz did not demonstrate or prove in what way Job's speeches had condemned him. As usual, he just made the claim and expected it to stick even without proof.

It is sadly true that people often do speak to justify themselves, even when they are guilty. They don't want to admit error, so their speech is the result of their sin. We encounter it often, and if we are not careful we are guilty.

However, Eliphaz' statement overlooks the fact that a truly innocent man will also claim to be innocent! The fact a man claims to be innocent does not automatically prove him to be guilty! There are two classes of people who claim to be innocent: (1) those who are guilty but refuse to admit their guilt, and (2) those who are really innocent! The only way to distinguish which is true in a particular case is to present convincing proof of a man's guilt. If the proof does not exist, then it is not proper to assume the man to be guilty.

So Eliphaz' statement simply repeated the fundamental error of the friends: they were convinced Job was guilty simply because he was suffering so terribly. This assumption was foundational to everything they said. If Job then claimed to be innocent, he must be speaking deceitfully, because of course he was guilty. How did they know? Could they produce evidence or testimony of sins he committed? No. The fact he was suffering was proof enough to them!

15:7-10 – Eliphaz then attacked the source of Job's knowledge and claimed that aged wise men were on the friends' side.

He asked if Job was the first man born, made before the hills. This point prepared the way for the claim in verse 10 that aged men agreed with the friends. So how could Job disagree with them: Was he older than the old men who supposedly agreed with the friends? If not then, by implication, he could not disagree with the conclusion: he did not have enough seniority!

Eliphaz then asked if Job had somehow received some special revelation from God that gave him the wisdom to know the things he taught – wisdom that he alone possessed but was hidden from all others. Of course, Job had already stated that he wished to discuss the matter with God.

So Eliphaz asked how Job knew he was right and the friends were wrong. What source of information did Job have that the friends did not have?

Then Eliphaz made the bold claim that he and the other friends had to be right, because the view they defended was held by the wise, aged men among them. Why, men even older than Job's father agreed with them! This was the argument Bildad had made in 8:8-10 (compare 12:12; 32:6,7).

But again, the friends appealed to human authority and wisdom, as they had done throughout. They had no evidence from God. And like all human authorities, the ones they cited could be wrong. No men are infallible, no matter how old they are.

So as is often the case, those who were wrong (the friends) accused others of being wrong. They said Job refused to admit his error, when they were the ones refusing to admit their error.

15:11-13 – Eliphaz claimed that Job did not appreciate God's word, else he would not turn against God as he had.

He asked a question that implied Job did not appreciate the blessings God gave him. God had consoled or comforted Job and had spoken gently to him. Perhaps he was referring especially to the things the friends were trying to teach him – they thought they were giving him gentle consolation from God, but he was rejecting it.

He claimed that Job's heart moved him away from God's revelation and caused him to wink at or overlook what God had done for him (other translations say his eyes flashed at it, implying he rejected it in anger). He claimed that Job spoke as he did because his spirit had turned away from God.

15:14-16 – Eliphaz claimed that no one is pure in God's eyes.

Eliphaz here appears to be attempting to disprove Job's claims that he was upright by arguing that no one is upright before God. He said that no man, born of woman, could be upright or righteous before God. He claimed that God does not trust anyone, not even his saints (holy ones – angels?) and the heavens themselves are not pure before him. So how could man be pure before God, since man is abominable and filthy, drinking iniquity like water? This last verse appears to be a direct accusation of Job.

This argument is patently foolish. In the first place, what proof did Eliphaz have that even the heavens are not pure before God? And if his statements were true, then they would condemn Eliphaz and his friends, as well as Job. So why aren't they suffering like Job?

But the biggest problem is that it simply is not true that everyone is as wicked as Eliphaz makes out. We know from chapter 1,2 that Job was upright, even as he claimed to be. This may have been the result of both right living and forgiveness received for his wrongs. But in any case, some people were upright and worthy of God's favor, for Job was one of them. It is interesting to observe how some people still today, in attempting to prove unscriptural doctrines, make men out even worse than they are. It is true that all men sin, but some do repent and have a right relationship with God.

15:17-19 – Eliphaz attempted to declare the condition of evil men based on what wise men told him.

These verses are preparatory, leading up to the description Eliphaz gave of the wicked in verses 20ff. He said that he is about to declare things he has seen and has been told by wise men. The land was given to them with no foreigner in their midst (perhaps meaning no one had come to contaminate the truth they had discovered), and they did not hide what they had received. Again, the friends appeal to the wisdom of men, especially those who are older.

15:20-22 – Eliphaz claimed that a wicked man suffers pain all his life.

He said the wicked writhes in pain every day, but no one knows how long his suffering will continue. (I am unsure whom the oppressor refers to, but it seems to be the cause of the suffering.) His ears hear dreadful sounds, apparently bad news because he is bad. Even when he prospers, suffering is about to come, for the destroyer comes upon him despite the prosperity. Nothing he can do will prevent the consequence. He has no confidence that his suffering will end and he will return from darkness (see verse 23), because a sword (death) awaits him as a result of his suffering.

All this appears to be an exaggeration. Job was surely suffering in these ways, but his was an extreme case. Not all sinners so suffered. Yet Eliphaz seems to take for granted that every evil person will suffer like this.

15:23,24 – He said the wicked face trouble and hunger.

The wicked man cannot even find food to eat. He wanders around seeking food but cannot find it. He knows a day of darkness (suffering, maybe even death) awaits him. He fears that trouble and anguish will come upon him, and sure enough they do. They attack and overpower him like being attacked by a powerful king prepared for battle.

This in many ways described Job's case. But remember that Eliphaz was describing the suffering that comes on a wicked man (verses 20,25). He went to great extremes to argue that suffering comes from being evil.

15:25,26 – Man suffers because he has rebelled against God.

Eliphaz argued that the suffering he has described comes upon man as a consequence of sin. The man has stretched his hand out as an act of defiance against God. We might express it that he is shaking his fist in God's face. He is stubbornly pursuing a course of antagonism against God, as though he is an enemy armed for battle against God.

Again, this was how Eliphaz viewed men who suffered as Job was. It was the consequence of blatant rebellion and stubborn antagonism against God. While many people act this way, and they sometimes suffer in this life for it, not all rebels against God suffer this way. And not all who suffer are guilty of such rebellion. This simply was not Job's case, and the whole description is an incredible slander against him. To speak so to a righteous man who is suffering as Job suffered is just unconscionable.

15:27-30 – The wicked man may grow fat but it will not continue; he cannot avoid suffering.

Just as the wicked man may seem to prosper temporarily, so Eliphaz said he may increase fatness in his face and waist. But he will dwell in desolate cities that no one else wants to inhabit, destined to become ruins. He will not be rich or continue in wealth. His possessions will not spread over the earth.

He will not be able to escape from the darkness of this suffering and agony (compare verses 22,23). He will be like a tree whose branches dry out due to flames: this could refer to his offspring being destroyed. The breath of God's mouth will ultimately destroy him.

15:31-33 – The wicked should not think anything can help him escape, but he will suffer before his time.

Eliphaz continued to enlarge his description saying that the wicked man should not trust in anything that might deliver him from this suffering. Anything that he would trust to do so would be futile and he would just be deceiving himself. His reward will be futility or emptiness, and it will come before his time.

His branch will not be green and he will drop unripe fruit like a grapevine and blossoms like an olive tree. All these expressions appear to refer to his offspring. Not only will he suffer himself, but he will have no children or his children will die prematurely. They too will not prosper.

Of course, all this happened to Job. But Eliphaz improperly assumed it was because of sin.

15:34,35 – So Eliphaz summarized the troubles of hypocrites.

Eliphaz concluded his description saying hypocrites will be barren of company and fire consumes the tents of those who commit bribery. The barren company may refer to family or friends, but the point appears to be that the hypocrite will lose his offspring and/or friends. Those who obtain possessions (tents) by bribery will lose them to tragedy (fire).

Such men, by their wickedness, are like a woman who conceives and gives birth, but what they conceive is trouble and what they bear is futility. From their womb is born deceit.

What a tragic description of evil. Some people do suffer such consequences in this life for their sins. And those who do not repent will receive even worse after this life. But the sad part was that none of this fit Job's case. Not everyone who suffers is guilty of sin. And such a description constituted an unbelievable accusation against an upright man.

Job 16

Chapter 16,17 – Job's Response to Eliphaz

16:1-3 – Job accused the friends of being miserable comforters.

Job responded to Eliphaz's speech by saying he had already heard many claims and arguments as Eliphaz had offered. In fact, he had heard it now many times from the friends!

He accused them of being miserable comforters. They had supposedly come to comfort him (2:11). But if this was their idea of comforting, they were doing a miserable job of it! Instead of helping him know how to overcome his problems or at least sympathizing with him, each of them had repeatedly accused him of sin. What comfort is that to a man who suffers and has really done no wrong?

He views their words as like a wind that keeps on without end. They just kept saying the same false accusations over and over. He asked what had provoked them to treat him in this way.

16:4,5 – Job claimed he would encourage them if they were in his place.

Job suggests that, if he were in their place and the shoe was on the other foot, he could criticize and condemn them too. He could heap up accusations and shake his head at them as though they had done shameful things. But he would not do so, he said, but would speak to give them strength and relieve their grief.

Job's point, of course, was that they ought to be treating them as he says he would treat them. They should have been encouraging and comforting him

16:6-8 – Job renewed his complaint that God had worn him out with opposition.

Whether Job spoke or remained silent, neither way would help his condition. He had tried keeping silent and he had tried speaking to the friends, but he still had his problems without relief. Nothing seemed to ease the hardship.

He said that God had worn him out with his suffering. He was desolate of true company. Other associates had deserted him, and his friends were no companionship as long as they continued to treat him as guilty.

He felt shriveled as though his life and spirit had dried up in a desert. He was lean, as from hunger, but in this case it was the result of suffering. But people (like the friends) acted as though his very leanness and weakness themselves testified against him to his face. No matter what he did, he could neither find relief nor obtain sympathy. People used his suffering, not as a reason to give him comfort, but as "proof" that he was evil.

16:9-11 – Job was convinced both God and man treated him as an enemy.

Job felt as though God Himself had determined to act as an enemy toward him. He tore Job in anger and hated him, gnashing at him with His teeth. He acted as an adversary gazing sharply at Job (perhaps to seek for faults or at least to express anger). All these were acts of antagonism and hatred.

Other people also stared at Job with their mouths open, striking him on the cheek. They assembled together to attack him. But God, instead of defending or protecting him, turned Job over to ungodly enemies so they could torment him.

16:12-14 – Job felt like a target for God's armies.

Job claimed that he had been at ease without problems (before the suffering began). But God shattered that ease and peace. He took Job by the neck and shook him, like a wild animal might take a small prey by the neck and shake it in violence.

Job felt as though God had determined to let his armies use Job for target practice! His archers surrounded Job and shot at him. His heart was pierced by their arrows without pity; his gall – the contents of his internal organs – was spilled on the ground by the attacks. Like an enemy warrior, God ran at Job to attack him, breaking his body open with wound after wound. (Compare 6:4; 10:17).

Again, this is how Job viewed his condition. But we know from the introduction of the book that it was not true. God did allow the suffering, but He did not contribute to it. Again, Job is mistaken in a way somewhat like his friends in that he blames God for the suffering.

16:15-17 – Job maintained his claim that he was suffering even though he was pure.

Job again described his sorrow so great that sackcloth was sewed on his body. Sackcloth was coarse, uncomfortable cloth, worn next to the skin only to express great sorrow. But Job did not just wrap himself in it temporarily, but sewed it in place. It was like a permanent garment that he wore all the time as though he would never be free of it. He did not just sit in dust, but laid his head in it. (Other translations, instead of "head," use "horn" – a symbol of pride or honor.)

Job wept so much that his face was flushed by crying. His eyelids looked like those of a dying man. And all this despite the fact that Job continued to maintain that he had done no violence. He was pure in his prayer and worship of God. Had he believed himself to be guilty, he could at least feel that he was suffering deservedly. But to know that he was innocent just made it worse, because he could not understand why all this was happening.

16:18-20 – Job hoped that his case might stand open as a testimony to his uprightness.

Job called upon the earth to not cover his blood. When blood was covered, there was no longer any evidence that it had been shed. The proof was hidden. But Job wanted the evidence of his suffering to continue. He wanted his cries to continue to be heard. (Compare the case of Job to Genesis 4:10; Ezekiel 24:7,8)

He hoped that even in heaven his witness would be heard and his evidence brought before God. His friends were no comfort. They did not consider the evidence of his innocence but just continued to scorn him as evil. So he poured out tears to God, hoping that someday God would examine his case and recognize his innocence.

16:21,22 – Job felt like one about to die, so he hoped yet for God to hear his case.

He sought for an opportunity to present his case to God as one could plead his case to or on behalf of a neighbor. In the same way, he hoped that he would be able to plead on his behalf before God. He knew he had only a few more years before he died, going the way of no return. He hoped for a chance to make his case known before he died; but if not, he hoped his case would remain open before God so that someday he would be vindicated as not guilty as charged by the friends. (These verses are difficult in translation and explanation.)

Job 17

Job's Response to Eliphaz (cont.)

17:1,2 – Job's spirit was broken because he saw death ahead of him and mockers around him.

These verses appear to be just a continuation of chapter 16. Job was so discouraged he thought his life was ready to end. His spirit (or breath, depending on translation) was broken and his days extinguished, so that the grave faced him. He had nothing to look forward to, that he could see, except death and the grave. He saw no hope for justice or relief in this life.

While he saw no hope ahead of him, he also saw nothing but discouragement around him. The friends surrounded him with mockery. He could see clearly the way they provoked him with their false accusations and false doctrine regarding the cause of his suffering.

No matter where he looked, he saw only hopelessness, discouragement, and opposition despite the fact he was convinced he was innocent.

17:3-5 – Job sought a pledge and urged God not to exalt his friends since they lacked understanding.

Job called upon someone, presumably God (see the capitalization in the NKJV), to make a pledge and shake hands (other translations say to strike hands) with him on it. Striking hands was an expression for sealing an agreement, as we do by shaking hands (compare Proverbs 6:1,2; 17:18; 22:26). He wanted a promise or guarantee on some point.

Some think this pledge would be that Job would eventually be justified and shown to be innocent. The connection to verse 4 indicates to me that the pledge involved not exalting Job's friends. They had mocked Job by falsely accusing him (verse 2). Because of their closed minds, God had hidden understanding from them (verse 4; compare Matthew 13:13-15). So they did not deserve to be exalted.

Since they were accusing Job of sin, exalting them would make it appear they were right and Job was a sinner as they accused him of. But if God would refuse to exalt them, then Job would appear exonerated. So the end result of whatever view one takes appears to be that Job is seeking for God to agree that, eventually, Job would be exonerated and the friends would be proved wrong. This, of course, is what does happen in the end.

Job continued that, if one speaks flattery to his friends, his children's eyes would fail. The ASV translates this as denouncing one's friends, rather than flattering them. This meaning would surely apply to the case of Job's friends who had denounced their friend in falsely accusing him. They had in some ways also flattered him by pretending to be his friends and to care about him, when their speeches really instead accused him.

The idea that their children's eyes will fail may just be Job's expression for the fact they would not see or receive good but would suffer for their father's evil. Children are not guilty of sin and are not punished in eternity for their parents' sins (Ezek. 18:20), but they often do suffer consequences in their life. This would be the case of the children of the friends, if they did not change.

17:6,7 – Job viewed himself as one whom people spit upon and whose eyes have become dim because of sorrow.

Job believed he had become a byword in the eyes of people – an object of mockery and ridicule – so that men spit in his face. Men may not have literally spit upon him, but he felt as though they had by the accusations his friends made against him. He viewed this as something God had done, though we know it was Satan who was responsible.

His sight had become dim because he had grieved so much that his vision was affected (perhaps as by crying). The members of his body had become like shadows, perhaps referring to how his body had wasted away.

17:8-10 – Those who appreciated uprightness would be astonished at Job's treatment, yet a truly righteous man would maintain his ground.

The treatment Job had received, especially at the hands of the friends, would cause upright people to be astonished. Truly innocent people would be stirred up against such hypocrisy. Job did not understand why he was suffering; yet he was convinced that people who really understood justice, unlike his friends, would be appalled at their accusations against him.

Yet despite such mistreatment, a truly righteous man would not give way or admit that their accusations were valid. He would continue to maintain his cause, defend his innocence, and become stronger and stronger as a result of the debate. This is how Job expressed what he believed his responsibility to be in the light of the friends' accusations.

Nevertheless, having denounced his friends and affirmed that they did not understand the truth and that truly upright people would recognize their error, he invited them to come at him again. This seems to be ridicule, not that he really wanted them to come back again, for he accused them of not having even one truly wise man among them. There was no true wisdom in their viewpoint, nor did he expect them to have learned anything from the debate. His statement is similar to our expression, "bring it on." He expected more of the same from them, and he expected that he would need to continue to oppose them.

17:11,12 – Job complained again that his goals in life had been broken, but others claimed that the light was about to dawn.

Job drew his speech to a close by again observing how greatly he was suffering. He viewed that his days were past and his purposes broken off. Perhaps this means that he viewed that any meaning in his life was behind him. He no longer had hope that he would achieve with his life the goals he had set out to achieve. His hopeful thoughts for his life had been defeated.

But other people changed night to day by saying that light is near when times are dark. This is difficult, especially since the context does not make clear who the "they" are that Job referred to. Does this refer to people in general, or to his friends? Perhaps he referred to the concept some people express that night is often darkest just before day begins to dawn. This would indicate that he should have hope even in his darkest hour. Or perhaps he refers to the claims of the friends that, if he would repent, his darkness would be turned to day. In any case, Job does not appear to accept the idea but just attributes it to others.

17:13-16 – Job poetically claimed that only death and hopelessness awaited him.

Perhaps in contrast to others (verse 12), Job saw only death and darkness ahead of him. He waited for the grave and darkness as his house and his resting place. He viewed corruption and worms as his family: father and mother, sister, etc. They were the only close companions his could see awaiting his future.

So he concluded by asking what hope existed for him. Who could see any real hope? Obviously he could not. Sheol is the place of the dead, perhaps here the grave. So he asked if they would go to the grave and rest in the dust with him. To whom does his refer? Perhaps to the hope of verse 15 and the purposes of verse 11. They would die, just as he would die. He saw no hope for the future, but all would end in the grave.

What a sad, forlorn picture, but what can be expected to come from one who suffered so as Job had?

Job 18

Chapter 18 - Bildad's Second Speech

The cycle of speeches continues as Bildad speaks for the second time.

18:1-4 – Bildad claimed that Job lacked understanding and treated the friends like stupid beasts.

Bildad the Shuhite continued the pattern established by the friends in which they accused Job of sin because he was suffering. He began, as often the speakers did, by rebuking Job for rejecting the arguments of the friends. He implied that Job's statements had no value and were without understanding (verse 2).

He asked how long it would be till Job stopped making his arguments (some translations ask how long will you hunt for words). He urged Job to improve his understanding, then the friends could speak to him. He said that Job's responses treated the friends as though they were stupid (some translations say "unclean") beasts.

He accused Job of tearing himself in anger – Job's reaction to his problems and to the friends' teaching was only hurting Job himself further. He asked if the earth would be forsaken or rocks removed from their place for Job's sake. This seems to imply that, in order for Job's statements to be true, the whole course of affairs on earth would have to be upset. He is implying that Job's view contradicts the fundamental moral order of the universe.

Of course, all such statements prove nothing. Anyone can say such things when others reject their statements. But Bildad surely shows that the friends have not been convinced by Job's arguments.

18:5-7 – Bildad claimed that the light of the wicked goes out and he is defeated by his own schemes.

Repeating the view that wicked people do suffer in this life, Bildad argued that their light goes out and their flame does not shine. So his lamp is put out and his tent is dark. He becomes weak because of sin so that he cannot even walk properly. He suffers consequences (he is cast down) because of his own counsel. That is, his improper decisions to practice evil are what lead to his downfall.

Light can represent understanding, life, or pleasant prosperity. Bildad's reference could refer to any or all of these. The point is that sin leads men to suffer so that they do not receive the blessings of life. He lacks the strength to actively pursue life and achieve worthwhile work. All this is the hardship that comes as consequence of his lack of understanding that leads him to do evil. He will be defeated because he does not have the wisdom to do right.

Again, Bildad here begins a lengthy description of how people suffer for their sins.

18:8-10 – *The wicked man falls into a trap.*

These verses use repeatedly the illustration of a trap or snare. The wicked person is caught in a net by his feet or heel. He walks into a snare that takes hold of him. A noose or trap is hidden in the ground by the road.

All these express the idea that his evil causes him to suffer consequences like a bird or animal that is caught in a trap, net, or snare. His unrighteousness leads to consequences that defeat him.

Again, this is true if one considers the long run, especially the eternal consequences of sin. And sometimes people suffer for evil in this life. But the point is that people do not always suffer in this life for their sins. And it simply is not true, as the friends were arguing, that only the wicked suffer so that must be the explanation why Job was suffering.

18:11-13 – *The wicked suffers fears, weakness, and disease.*

Bildad continued to describe the consequences he believed come on the wicked man by saying he is surrounded on every side by terrors that frighten him. These terrors drive him to his feet. Other translations say they chase him at his heels. The point seems to be an illustration of one who flees from terror.

Instead of being strong, he loses strength like one who is starving. He is accompanied by destruction traveling at his side. He is diseased as one who has patches of skin being devoured (such as in leprosy or a skin cancer). Other translations refer this to disease that wastes away the body. In short his limbs are devoured by the firstborn of death – i.e., death of the most severe or outstanding kind.

All this appears to allude to Job's troubles. He had expressed great trouble as a result of fears. He was obviously wasting away with disease of the skin (boils), and he had repeatedly stated that death awaited him. Bildad appears to cruelly and mercilessly be citing all these as evidence of guilt of sin.

18:14-16 – *The wicked is driven from his home, and he is cut off root and branch.*

The wicked further, Bildad claimed, would lose the shelter of his tent. Apparently Job and his family lived in tents. Wickedness would cause one to lose his happy home. He would be uprooted from his tent and paraded before the king of terrors. This probably refers again to death, the greatest terror of all.

Instead of the wicked man dwelling safely in his tent, other people whom he does not know will dwell there. Or brimstone (burning sulfur) will be scattered on his dwelling, such as happened to Sodom and Gomorrah. The dwelling could refer to all his land and possessions, including the fields and shelters where he kept his flocks, etc. In short, he would lose all that he owned. His roots would die below the ground and his branches would wither above the ground. Like a dying tree, he would be destroyed.

The figures of speech continued seemingly without end. But the point of them all was that people suffer because they are wicked. Job was suffering, therefore Job must be wicked.

18:17,18 – The wicked is not remembered among those who are honored with respect.

When the wicked man dies (as has been described), people forget him as soon as they can. They have no reason to remember him favorably, as is done with respected or renown people. When people die who have been beloved for their good works, people make memorials to honor them and respect their memory. But no such would be done for the wicked. This is especially the case when one has no children to respect his memory (see verse 19).

Instead, the wicked would be as though he was chased out of this life like one is driven from light to darkness. People who are pursued by an enemy may flee to places of darkness to hide. But the wicked would be chased entirely out of the world into the darkness of death.

18:19-21 – The wicked has no offspring. He leaves behind him only astonishment that such a man lived.

When the wicked man dies, he leaves no posterity to inherit his property. He has no children to live in his dwelling. This was a terrible tragedy, especially to people in those days. Again Bildad's statements would apply with bold cruelty to the death of Job's children. Instead of mourning with Job and comforting him for the loss of his children, Bildad openly implied that they died because Job was so wicked!

People from the west to the east – in other words all around who hear about such a man – will be astonished and frightened at his life. He will not be remembered with respect (verse 17). Instead, people will be amazed at the terrible consequences he has suffered for his evil.

Bildad concluded that what he had described is the dwelling or place of the wicked man who does not know God. This would be the outcome of his refusal to serve and have proper fellowship with God.

Again, in a spiritual sense and in eternal consequences, all this is true. But the arguments of the friends have meaning and application to

Job only if they apply in this life. That is where they miss the point for it simply is not always true that the wicked suffer so horribly in this life. And as in Job's case, it is often the good and righteous who do suffer.

Job 19

Chapter 19 - Job's Response to Bildad

19:1-3 – Job claimed that the friends had wrongfully reproached him ten times.

Job responded to Bildad, as he had to the other arguments of the friends. He began his response, as he had several times before, by rebuking the friends for their error in wrongfully accusing him of sin.

He said that their words tormented him and broke him in pieces. This is interesting in light of the children's taunt that "sticks and stones may break my bones, but words will never hurt me." This is indeed childish, and all who know the truth are aware that words can cut deeply. Job had truly done nothing worthy of suffering, yet he suffered greatly. The friends ought to have comforted and encouraged him, but instead they persisted in accusing him of sin, simply because he was suffering.

He said they had reproached him ten times. And although he had repeatedly shown them their error and denied their accusations, and although they could offer no proof for their accusations except that Job was suffering, yet they were not ashamed. Job plainly said that they had wronged him.

The reference to ten times does not mean that Job could itemize ten specific instances. It is symbolic of a large number of times – poetic exaggeration (compare Genesis 31:7; Numbers 14:22; etc.). The friends had repeatedly and frequently wronged him, yet they refused to admit they were wrong.

19:4-6 – Job claimed that God too had wronged him by causing such suffering.

Job said that, if he had done wrong, his wrong was to himself alone. There was no evidence of it, so how could they know? He had done nothing wrong to others, so there was no proof of the friend's claims against him. In fact, of course, he had repeatedly stated that he did no wrong. But if he had, they could not know it.

Verses 5,6 appear to mean that he did not need them to cause trouble for him – exalting themselves against him and pleading that he was (or should be) disgraced. He already had enough problems dealing with the wrongs he believed had been done to him by God. God had surrounded him with troubles like an animal caught in a net.

19:7-9 – *Job claimed that he had called for help but God had withheld justice, capturing Job and removing his glory.*

Job then returned to his lament, describing his agony and especially how he viewed himself as having suffered at the hand of God. He cried out that he was being wronged, seeking someone to correct the unjust suffering he endured, but there was no one to hear or respond. No matter how hard or long he cried out, justice was not done, so he continued to suffer.

He felt trapped like one who was fenced in and cannot escape. Every path that he pursued to escape simply led to further darkness. We would say, there was "no light at the end of the tunnel." No matter where he turned, he saw no way out.

Job appears in all this to still be blaming God. He claimed that He (God) had stripped Job of glory, removing the crown from his head. Job may have been a ruler of sorts before all this trouble began. He surely was honored and respected among his people (see 1:3). Or perhaps he viewed his family and possessions as a crown of honor. But as a consequence of the evils that had befallen him, he had lost these sources of honor so that people no longer looked at him with respect.

19:10-12 – *Job felt as though God had uprooted him like a tree or sent armies to attack him.*

Job continued his complaint describing how he felt about what was happening to him. He felt that he had been broken down like a house whose walls are crumbling till he is destroyed. Or he was like a tree in a tornado that everything in his surroundings is torn apart till even he himself is like a tree pulled up by the roots.

He considered himself to be the object of God's wrath, as though God viewed him as an enemy and sent His army of troops to attack him. The troops gathered for battle, made a path to Job's tent, and surrounded Job like an enemy army encamped around his tent.

In all this, Job continued to blame God. Perhaps his expressions are not so much rebellion against God as just grief and confusion. He can see no explanation for what has happened other than that God caused it, but he could see no reason for God to so treat him. In any case, he was mistaken in charging God with the problems, and eventually God did speak to him and correct him.

19:13,14 – *Job viewed himself as alienated from relatives and friends.*

Next Job turned to describe how his suffering had affected his relationship with loved ones. His brothers had removed themselves from him and relatives failed him. Acquaintances were estranged from him, and close friends had forgotten him.

Job did not explain why or how this had happened. Perhaps these people, like the three friends speaking to him, had concluded that he was to blame for his problems. Or perhaps they were so overwhelmed by his problems that they did not know how to help. In any case, they had turned from him, even as his wife had (2:9) and as his three friends had. They not only offered him no comfort, but they broke off their relationship with him.

All this added the burden of broken relationships to the loss of his possessions, his children, and his health.

19:15,16 – Job's servants had ceased to help him.

Prior to his misfortunes, Job had a number of servants (compare 1:14,16,17,18). He had maidservants and other servants. In addition, there were those who had dwelt in his house, perhaps referring to guests to whom he had shown great hospitality. But now they were treating him as a stranger or an alien. They acted as if they did not know him. They refused to serve him or obey his instructions. Even if he pleaded with them for help, they did not even answer.

Again, the reasons are not explained. As with the friends and relatives in verses 13,14, they may have felt that he was guilty of sin and unworthy of their help. Or they may simply have not known what to do to help. In any case, they had long benefited from his provision of them, but now when he needed their help they refused to give it.

19:17-19 – Even Job's family members found him repulsive.

Job's wife apparently continued with him, after their confrontation in 2:9,10. But she found him offensive. Job mentioned his breath. Perhaps his disease caused a stench that she could not bear. Or perhaps this is just an expression for the repulsion she felt toward him.

The same was true of the children of his own body. This is strange, since chapter 1 indicated that his sons and daughters had been killed. The ASV says "children of my own mother." If that is a correct translation, then Job refers here to his brothers in the flesh (where perhaps verse 13 referred to more distant relatives, maybe even other tribesmen as his "brothers").

If the NKJV is correct, then somehow Job must have had children other than those in chapter 1 (maybe those had been specifically mentioned because they were grown children who later died). The KJV says he entreated for the sake of the children of his body, perhaps meaning he entreated his wife to care for him on the grounds that they were married and had children together. Regardless of the proper translation, the point is that Job's closest family members turned from him in his time of greatest need.

Other children despised him. Children tend to object to anyone deformed or seriously ill. Surely they would be repulsed by one such as Job. But these went so far as to despise him and speak against him, perhaps making fun of him.

He concluded that all his close friends and those whom he loved had turned against him. Job's great problems were made increasingly unbearable because other people refused to bear his burden with him (Galatians 6:2). Instead of helping him, they either ignored him or worse yet rejected him as unworthy of their concern and help.

19:20-22 – *Job's flesh and bones barely hung together; he pleaded with the friends for mercy.*

Job's suffering, especially his boils, had left his skin and flesh as though it hung from his bones. He said he had escaped or perhaps survived by the skin of his teeth. This is the origin of this expression for just barely surviving, since there is surely not much skin on one's teeth. (Apparently the translation here is difficult or uncertain.)

Having suffered so greatly and been repulsed by his family and friends, Job turned to these three friends who had come to speak to him. In his great grief and suffering, he called on them to have pity on him. They could see how he was suffering, and they all (mistakenly) viewed it as the hand of God upon Job. He asked why they couldn't be satisfied with the suffering he endured in his flesh. Why did they have to add their own persecution to his suffering? Why could they not sympathize with him? That is what true friends ought to do in such cases.

19:23,24 – *Job wanted his words written in a book or on a rock.*

Job was so convinced that he was justified and that his view was correct that he was willing to have it written down. It could be inscribed in a book or even "written in stone" or with an iron pen and lead, so that it could be read by future generations forever. He was not afraid for others to hear his words. He was sure he was right to the point that he would let even future generations judge the correctness of his case. Of course, unknown to him at the time, this is exactly what did happen. So we now have his history written and can judge and learn from him.

19:25-27 – *Job expressed confidence that he would see God.*

These verses are apparently difficult to translate. But the general meaning appears to be that, despite his suffering and his statements against God's justice, Job had confidence that someday he would be able to stand before God. He continued to have confidence that His redeemer does live. God is alive, and we will all someday stand before God. "Redeemer" refers to God as the one to deliver us from our problems or sins. It is an expression often used in the Old Testament, such as in Isaiah, for the true God.

Job appeared to realize that this might not happen in this life, as he had called for it to happen. He might not be able to ask his questions of God and receive explanation from him during this life. But after his skin was destroyed – i.e., after he died – he was convinced he would see God for himself. He himself – not just other people – would see God with his own eyes. His heart yearned within him for this privilege.

It is not clear, as the book proceeds, exactly what Job believed about life after death. At times he appeared to have some concept of it, but not at other times. In any case, these verses seem to affirm that he was confident he would eventually have an opportunity to stand before God and be justified before Him, as he had often requested to do. If it could not be done in this life, then perhaps it would come afterward, but he was confident it will happen.

19:28,29 – Job warned the friends to fear judgment if they continued to persecute him.

Job concluded his speech by reminding his friends that judgment for wrongdoing applied to them too. They had claimed repeatedly that he was suffering for wrongdoing. He denied having done wrong, so he did not understand why he was suffering. But he did not deny that God judges men for sin. They seemed to think that the root of the problem lay in Job – it was all a matter of what he had done. But he reminded them that what they did mattered too. So, if they should determine to continue their persecution of him, falsely accusing him of wrong, they should remember that judgment awaits them too.

It is easy to think that we can point out the sins of others and forget that we will be judged for our wrongs. And one of those wrongs might be false accusation against those who are innocent. Their conduct toward Job had been cruel almost to the point of viciousness. They had reviled and accused one who needed encouragement and sympathy. He warned them to be afraid of the sword of punishment that may come upon themselves. He was not threatening them that he would punish them, but that they would give answer to the sword or wrath of God. We should take care lest we accuse and wound one who has done no wrong, so we ought to uplift and encourage him.

Job 20

Chapter 20 - Zophar's Second Speech

20:1-3 – Zophar said Job's rebuke insulted him, so he had to respond.

Zophar responded to Job claiming that he had heard Job's reproach against him and the other friends. This probably included Job's general comments about the wicked and the righteous. But it may have especially been provoked by Job's concluding remarks (chapter 19) that pointed out that the friends may be the ones who are doing wrong here – that Job is innocent but his friends have done wrong by falsely accusing him.

Zophar claimed that his anxious thoughts and his understanding compelled him to speak. He was upset by Job's views and believed he had a proper understanding that required him to respond. He proceeded to again claim that the wicked suffer in this life for their sins.

20:4,5 – Zophar claimed that any apparent prosperity of the wicked is short-lived.

Zophar appealed to history for his conclusions. He claimed that what he was arguing had been true since the foundation of the world. Note again that the friends never cited any true authority for their views, but only the same kind of human authorities often cited by people today who cannot prove their views on the basis of Divine revelation.

He could not completely deny Job's claims that wicked people do prosper, but he responded that such triumph would be short-lived. The joy of the hypocrite would last for just a moment.

Zophar refused to abandon the basic position the friends had defended: people suffer because they are wicked, and since Job was terribly suffering, he must be wicked. He acknowledged Job's argument that sometimes the wicked do prosper, but he argued that it would not last long. Soon they would again be suffering.

20:6-9 – No matter how exalted the wicked may be, he will perish and be seen no more.

Zophar continued specifically claiming that the wicked may be haughty and exalted in his own view. He may appear to prosper for a time. But no matter how exalted he may be or how high he might raise his head (even to the sky), still he would perish like garbage that is rejected.

After the wicked man fell, men would ask what happened to him? He would be like a dream that vanished and cannot be found, or like a vision of the night that appears and then disappears. No eye would continue to see him. His place would be as empty as if he had never existed.

Zophar was trying his best to convey the idea that, no matter how the wicked person may prosper, it would not last.

20:10-15 – The wicked man and his family would lose the pleasures and the fruits of evil.

Zophar continued to claim that the wicked would not prosper long. He claimed that their children would beg favors from poor people. The poor would be expected to beg from the wealthy, but the children of this man would suffer such need (because of his sins) that they would have to beg from poor people. His hands may enjoy his wealth for a while, but would soon have to give it up or restore it to the source from which it came (verse 18).

He may have the energy and enthusiasm of youth, but he will soon lose it and that youthful zest will simply follow him to die in the grave.

His evil conduct may seem pleasant and taste good to him at the time that he participates in it, so he may seek to continue to relish the taste. He tries to hold onto it, like a man who enjoys a good meal so he keeps the food in his mouth as long as he can before swallowing it. Nevertheless, when he finally swallows it, it will turn his stomach sour. It ends up poisoning him like cobra venom. When he swallows down what he thought he so enjoyed, it will so upset him that he will vomit it up again. God causes his belly to reject what he thought would be so pleasant.

Zophar here again granted that the evil man might enjoy should profit, gain, and pleasure in life. Yet he was convinced such a man would soon suffer hardship.

20:16-18 – The wicked would not enjoy the fruit of his efforts.

Whereas the wicked man sought great joy and pleasure from his work, afterward it would seem like sucking poison from a cobra. The consequences would be like a man found by a viper and slain (Zophar seems to mistakenly think that the viper's poison is in its tongue).

He would not continue to enjoy the blessings of life, especially the fruit of his evil conduct. He may anticipate the joy, like the beauty of a stream or like a river flowing full of honey and cream. Of course this is figurative. He may anticipate the enjoyment of his wealth, like a man who dreams of pleasures coming richly to him. But in the end, he would have to give up the blessings he enjoyed. Instead of swallowing them down to benefit from them (as in the previous verses), he would have to restore or give up to others that which he labored for. In the end he would not enjoy the proceeds of his business.

Again, this is clearly untrue in many cases. We all know evil people who enjoy the fruits of their evil throughout life. Some surely do suffer in this life for their evil, but many will wait till after this life for their rewards.

20:19-21 – The wicked man cannot enjoy the fruits of his labor, because he has mistreated others.

Zophar mentioned especially that wicked people will oppress or neglect (forsake) other people in their needs. Instead of helping those in need, he will violently take the house of the poor man who built it. The wicked man did not build the house, but he will seize it for himself as if it was his. This is the kind of conduct Zophar says will lead to suffering in this life. Presumably this is the kind of thing he was accusing Job of committing, though of course he had no proof because it was not true.

Such a man is disturbed in his thoughts. He can find no peace or quietness, either because of the guilt he feels or because he suffers in this life as a consequence of his sins. Or perhaps he is never satisfied because, no matter how much he has, his greed always leads him to want more. What he seeks to hold or save for his own purposes, he cannot hold on to. He will lose his prosperity to the point there will not even be food to eat. He cannot continue to enjoy well being.

20:22,23 – The wicked man will suffer misery instead of enjoyment.

The wicked man considers himself to be self-sufficient. He thinks he can care for himself and provide for himself all that he wants. This is typical of the greed and selfishness of the wicked. Yet Zophar says that, instead, the wicked will suffer distress and every misery will turn its hand against him.

When he is about to fill his stomach with the fruits of his evil (verse 18), God will come upon the wicked and rain His fury and wrath upon him, even as the wicked man is eating the fruits of his evil.

Zophar's theory is that the evil person may indeed experience some success in life as a result of his evil, but it will not last long. It will be cut off soon. Of course, it is true that the evil man will suffer in the long run, especially after this life. But it simply is not true that he always suffers in this life for his evil, or that such suffering comes quickly, or that this is the only reason some suffer.

20:24-26 – The wicked will suffer as from weapons of war or fire. He cannot escape.

Zophar continued his description of the consequences to come on the wicked. He claimed the wicked would flee as though attacked by an iron weapon. He would be like one who, fleeing from an enemy, is shot with an arrow from a bronze bow that strikes him and pierces completely through his body, piercing his innermost organs, such as the gall bladder. Gall is a symbol of bitterness. So he is faced with fears of bitter suffering, even the terror of suffering and death.

Whereas he hopes to enjoy the treasures he has accumulated by his evil deeds, instead his treasures would go into darkness. This might express that they are lost to him; they do him no more good than if he had no idea where they were.

He is like one who is consumed by fire. The fire is unfanned, probably meaning that it burns of itself, needing no external encouragement. It is the consequences of the evil of the wicked man himself. Even the people who live with him in his tent will suffer the consequences of his evil.

20:27-29 – The wicked man will be revealed before all and will lose his possessions.

Zophar's parting description of the wicked man was that all would know his evil. The heavens (presumably meaning God) will reveal his sin and even the earth (people) will rise against him. This is true in a sense after this life at the Judgment Day. But to claim that it is true in this life is simply nonsense. Many wicked people live for many years keeping their evil hidden so that it is unknown. And even when the evil is known, people often overlook it, simply don't care, or even admire them for it.

Finally, Zophar said that the wicked man would lose his prosperity. His increase or income will depart, and his goods will flow away in the face of wrath (again, presumably God's wrath). This appears to be a severe condemnation of Job, since this is exactly what happened to Job's wealth. This is the friends' explanation for why such things happen. But it was not the reason in Job's case, and there are many wicked people for which this does not happen at all in this life.

Zophar concluded that what he had described was the portion or heritage that God has assigned to the wicked man. And this would be true if one considers the final reward of evil men in the Judgment Day. But the friends' claim was that this is true in this life. In many cases, that is simply false. And in Job's case their statements constituted false accusation – the very thing Job had warned them about at the end of chapter 19.

Job 21

Chapter 21 - Job's Response to Zophar

21:1-3 – Job said he would speak, then the friends could continue mocking.

Job spoke in response to Zophar, as he had with each of the other speakers. He urged them to listen to his speech so they could find some consolation in it. However, he was convinced that, if they bore with him so he could speak, they would just continue to mock or find fault with him. He had come to the point of frustration with them, so he was convinced nothing he said would convince them, no matter how truthfully he might speak.

Some would try to convince us that men of God should never be sarcastic when dealing with those in error. But how do they explain Job's response here to his friends?

21:4-6 – Job asked them to consider his case and be astonished.

Verse 4 is difficult in translation and meaning. Job asked whether or not he was complaining against men. This was likely a rhetorical question, and likely he meant that he was not complaining to men, but was calling on God for a response. If he was speaking against men, he would have the right to be impatient, considering all that he suffered especially compared to how evil men prosper (verses 7ff). Perhaps the point was that, he knew he spoke against God, yet he was aware that he should exercise some restraint in such a case.

He said that just looking at him should cause them astonishment enough to put their hand over their mouth and quit criticizing him. He had suffered enough without their added revilements.

In verse 6 he said he trembled and was terrified when he remembered. This might refer to verse 7, where he began to describe the circumstances of the wicked in this world. He trembled and was terrified because he knew they deserved punishment, yet it did not appear that they received it as they ought to. He might also be terrified when he realized how wrong the friends were in their analysis of the case of wicked men. (Yet perhaps he meant to say that he was terrified when he remembered his past life and how he had so terribly suffered recently.)

21:7-9 – Job described the wicked as being safe in their lives and families without suffering at the hand of God.

Job directly challenged the theories of the friends by directly denying their view of what happened to wicked people. They (most recently Zophar) had argued that the wicked would inevitably suffer in this life and only the righteous would prosper. Job claimed the opposite is often true.

He first said that, instead of suffering bad health and dying young, the wicked often live long lives, come to old age, and even have great power and influence. If the friends' arguments were correct (compare 20:11), why would this happen?

Furthermore, wicked people prosper in their families. Their descendants are established before their eyes (the "offspring" may be the children of the "descendants," which would mean the grandchildren of the older wicked generation). That is, they have children who grow up and they also prosper. And the wicked man lives long enough to see the well-being of his children (and grandchildren). This would contrast to Job, whose children had already died. Why is this so if the friends are right that only wicked people suffer in this life, including loss of children (18:19)?

Furthermore, the houses of the wicked are safe from fear, for they do not suffer punishment (the rod) from God. Their houses would mean their households or families, which do not suffer from calamity. But if the friends were correct, only the righteous should dwell safely (5:17,24). Instead, the wicked face no fears and do not suffer at God's hand. This is a generalization, but is often true in this life. Here Job directly contradicts the theories of the friends.

21:10-12 – The wicked has good flocks, and his family has joy and celebration.

Job continued saying that the flocks of the wicked man also prosper. His bulls breed successfully and the cows bear their calves with no miscarriages. This meant great prosperity to those who made their living from their flocks. And, of course, this was the opposite of Job, who had lost his flocks and herds (chapter 1). If the friends were right, why did wicked people prosper?

Furthermore, the families and children of the wicked man enjoy happiness and contentment. They go forth like flock (in great numbers and safety), dancing in joy, singing and rejoicing to the sound of musical instruments.

Again, Job is flatly denying the arguments of the friends that wicked people and their families suffer for their sins.

21:13-15 – The wicked prosper through life and then die without suffering, despite their rebellion against God.

Job summarized the life of the wicked as days of wealth: prosperity and comfort in every material way. Then when their time comes to die, they die peacefully in a moment – without great suffering. Again, all this contrasted to Job, whose recent life had been filled with suffering and pain after the loss of all his wealth.

These blessings come to the wicked man despite his overt rebellion against God. Job described them, not just as careless and negligent, let alone sincerely mistaken. Rather, they were openly defiant against God. They tell God to go away and leave them alone. They don't want to know His ways. They are not just ignorant due to lack of opportunity to know; they refuse to listen to God's word.

They ask who God is, that He should tell them what to do or they should bow to His will. They claim to see no benefit could come to them from worshiping or praying to Him.

All this describes open, extreme rejection of God, His will, and all He stands for. Surely if the friends' theories were correct, such extreme evil should lead to swift punishment in this life. Yet Job had affirmed it was often not that way at all. The wicked prosper in all the ways he has described.

21:17,18 – Job denied that God brought sorrow on the wicked in this life.

Verse 16 is difficult. It appears to say that the wicked do not have their prosperity in their possession, but that appears to contradict what he had just said. Perhaps Job is here saying that this is the way it really is: "indeed." That is, they seemed to prosper by their own power, but despite what they thought, it was not their own hand that brought their prosperity. They were not in control as they thought. Their counsel or way of thinking was far from Job. He could not begin to share their rebellious attitude toward God, yet he suffered greatly where they prospered. This was a denial that he was guilty of evil as the friends had accused.

Job then bluntly asked how often it happened that the lamp of the wicked is put out and destruction comes upon them (compare 18:5,6). In other words, how often did it really happen that the wicked lose their lives and prosperity as the friends had argued? Did God really distribute the force of His anger against them? Of course, it sometimes does happen in this life, but not universally as the friends claimed. Job here cited the claims of the friends and flatly denied them, challenging the friends to prove how often these things really happen to the wicked.

Verse 18 says they are like straw before the wind, and like chaff that a storm carries away. The language of verse 17 appears to continue into verse 18, so Job is still asking how often this happens. Is the wicked man really carried away by the forces of life into oblivion and emptiness? If so, how often does it happen? Where is the proof that the friends' claims are true?

21:19-21 – Job discussed the claim that God punishes the children of the wicked, but says the wicked will not care after he dies.

In these verses someone is cited as saying that God brings the consequences of a man's wickedness on his children. But it is hard to know who is saying this. Since the context is surely a rebuttal of the friends' arguments, I assume Job here discusses an argument made by the friends (see 5:4; 20:10). If so, then the friends have argued that even the children of a wicked man suffer for his sins, and perhaps this is intended to explain the death of Job's children.

It is true that sometimes children suffer problems because their parents are evil, though God does not consider them to be guilty simply because their parents are guilty (Ezekiel 18:20). But again, this is not always true in this life.

Job's response seems to mean that, if God is going to punish someone for sin, he should punish the wicked man himself. He himself who sinned should be recompensed so he knows he is suffering and seeing destruction for his sins. Let him (the wicked man himself) drink the wrath of God.

Job argued that the wicked man would not much care if his children suffered for his sins. When his life ends (is cut in half), what difference would it make to him what happens afterward to his children? If God is going to punish him, He must bring the suffering on the wicked himself so he learns the lesson or at least suffers for his own wrong.

21:22-26 – Job claimed that men suffer or are blessed regardless of sin.

Job asked if anyone can teach knowledge to God. God is the Judge, even of the most exalted beings. What man could presume to give God instruction how to do His work? Of course, no one can, though Job himself seemed at times to want to do so.

Then Job said that sometimes a man dies at a time in life when he is in good health with full strength, at ease and secure. He is prospering well, as shown by the fact his pails are full of milk – his animals provide well for his needs. His bones are healthy and strong, even to the marrow. In short, all is well through his life. He suffered not at all for his sins.

But another man may die having lived a bitter life. He has enjoyed little or no pleasure. His life, like that of Job, is filled with grief.

Then both men die and their end is the same. Their bodies are buried and eaten by worms. So what is the advantage in this life of living righteously?

Job simply cannot see the friends' arguments that the wicked suffer more than the righteous in this life. So far as Job can see, there is little difference or at least no consistent difference in how people prosper in this life, regardless of whether or not they live wickedly.

21:27,28 – Job claimed that the friends' arguments did him wrong.

Job had reached the point of directly confronting the friends for the accusations they have made against him. He claimed that they had schemed together to do him wrong.

They claimed that his house (speaking of him as a prince) and his tent were gone. The dwelling place of the wicked could not be found (house may also refer to family, again referring to the death of his children). This apparently is his expression of their view of him. He lost his possessions because of wickedness. This is exactly what they had said, and he was right to confront their accusations against him.

21:29,30 – The wicked will be brought to doom and a day of wrath.

Job asked if the friends had traveled the road and knew the signs. This is a figure of speech. One who has traveled a road knows the signs and what to expect. He has experience that guides him when he travels the road again. So Job asked if the friends had experience that taught them about the problems of suffering and of the punishment of the wicked. The implication is that they are inexperienced and don't know the truth about the matter.

Verse 30 indicates that the wicked will be punished. They will come to a day of doom and day of wrath. But that does not mean they will suffer in this life. The doom or wrath will come after this life. It is not clear how well Job understood the concept of life after death or punishment after death. Here he seems to know that the wicked will be punished, but not necessarily in this life. And it does not follow that the righteous will not also suffer in life.

21:31-34 – Job concluded that the wicked would ultimately die as do others.

Job continued to describe the wicked man and how he often escapes retribution in this life. He asked who confronted the wicked man and rebuked him to his face. And who would repay him or cause him to suffer or be punished for his evil? In this life far too often there is no one who will do so.

As a result, he gets entirely away with his evil. That is Job's point. Conduct that is horrible enough to constitute crime against the law of the land may lead to punishment, but even that is often escaped. When people commit sins that are not against the law, they often suffer little or no consequences in this life at all.

Nevertheless, eventually the wicked will die, as does everyone else. But even then he will die in peace and even honor. A vigil is kept over his tomb as a memorial of his life. That is, he dies with honor and respect. Mourners grieve over him as much or more than when a righteous man dies. So even in his death he does not suffer among people for the sins he committed.

His death will appear peaceful. He will go to his grave as through the clods of earth are sweet to him. Not even death will seem to him to be objectionable. He will simply die, like countless people before him have and like many will follow him in doing. Nothing seems very sad or offensive about his life, even when it comes to an end. He dies without deep regret for his life. (Of course, he will have regrets after this life. But Job is discussing this from the view of the friends, making the point that the wicked man will not appear to suffer in life or in death as the friends claimed.)

Finally, Job rebuked the friends plainly saying that their words could never give him comfort, since they were false. They did not understand the true cause of his suffering, and worse yet they made false accusations against Job.

Job's conclusions regarding the wicked cannot be taken as universally true. The wicked often suffer far more in this life and death than he described. Nevertheless, his point is correct that wicked people often do not suffer in this life for their sins, and good people often do suffer. The friends' explanation for why Job was suffering simply cannot be correct.

Note that the friends have taken an absolute view that there is one reason for suffering: because the sufferer committed some sin. To prove their point, they can allow no exception. Job does not need to prove all his possible reasons why people suffer in order to prove the friends are wrong. All he needs to do is to find some other reason or reasons why people suffer, and the friends' view is disproved.

Job 22

Chapter 22-31 – The Third Round of Speeches

Chapter 22 - Eliphaz' Third Speech

22:1,2 – Eliphaz began his third and final speech by arguing that man cannot profit God.

At this point, each of the friends has had two chances to try to convict Job of sin, and Job has responded to each. This chapter begins the third and final round of speeches. As the speeches have continued, the friends have become increasingly forceful in openly accusing Job of sin and arguing that he must be suffering because of sin. This last round of speeches is the most forceful of all. But Eliphaz is the only one of the friends who makes a lengthy speech. Bildad's is quite short, and Zophar makes no speech at all.

Eliphaz began in verse 2 by asking if a man can be of profit to God. If he is wise, that may benefit him in some ways, but why does God need man's wisdom? This argues that Job's righteousness – if he really was righteous – would be of little value to God. Job could not be of profit to God nor produce gain for God by being righteous.

Hailey thinks the point is that God would have no reason to test Job, if Job was righteous as he claimed to be. What benefit would God get from bringing these problems on Job if Job was righteous? Of course, that is exactly what Job cannot understand, yet he knows he has committed nothing worthy of such suffering. But Eliphaz' point was that Job must not really be righteous. The only reason God would have for sending such suffering upon Job is that he is not righteous.

22:3,4 – Eliphaz argued that God is not punishing Job because Job fears Him.

Eliphaz continued the point of verse 2 by asking that, if Job was righteous or blameless (as he claimed to be), what pleasure would that give to God or what gain would that be to Him? Of course, the point is that it would be none, as in verse 2.

So in verse 4 he then asked whether God would correct Job or bring him into judgment, as He appeared to have done, if Job feared God as he claimed. Would God have brought such suffering on him in such a case? And again, the implication is that He would not. What good would God get out of causing such suffering if Job was upright? So, it must be that the suffering was caused by Job's evil, not by His righteousness (see verses 5ff).

The truth is, however, that God does benefit when men endure trials and demonstrate themselves to be righteous. He gains the assurance that His creature loves Him enough to serve with commitment, which is a major part of the reason why He created people anyway. This was surely the case with Abraham in Genesis 22. And in the current case, God would gain a proof case to demonstrate to Satan that some people will do right no matter how greatly they suffer (Job 1,2). But such benefit is not measurable in material profit.

22:5-7 – Eliphaz then began directly accusing Job, saying he had mistreated the hungry, the poor, and the thirsty.

Since Eliphaz argued that God would not bring such judgments on Job if he was righteous, it must be that Job is guilty of great wickedness and unending iniquity. This is a conclusion that follows from Eliphaz' conviction that all suffering is the consequence of sin. In this chapter he argued that view as plainly as anywhere else. Since he could think of no other explanation for suffering, he repeatedly accused Job of horrible evils.

He began by accusing Job of taking pledges from relatives and then for no reason taking away their possessions even to the point of leaving them with nothing to wear. In other words, Job had loaned money to people requiring that they put up collateral, then foreclosed and took everything they owned. He made Job out to be as a villainous landlord. Compare Exodus 22:26; Deuteronomy 24:6,17.

He then claimed Job had no care for the poor and needy. He had refused to give bread to the neediest of people and refused to give water to the weary.

Of course, all this was completely baseless and unfounded. Compare this to the complimentary things Eliphaz had said in 4:3,4. False accusation without proof is a terrible sin of itself. See Proverbs 17:15; Isaiah 5:20; 1 Peter 2:12; 3:16; 4:4; 1 Kings 18:17,18; Matthew 5:10-12; Luke 6:22,23,26; 3 John 9,10; Luke 3:14; John 7:24; 2

Timothy 3:3; 1 Corinthians 5:11; 6:9-11 (revilers); 1 Timothy 6:4; Titus 3:2; 1 Peter 2:1; Ephesians 4:31.

It is amazing that Eliphaz would say such things about one who was supposed to be his friend. Surely such vicious accusations require specific proof of Job's guilt. Yet we know that such proof did not exist, since we knew from the beginning that Job was upright. It just appears that, as we often see today, when a person has become wedded to a viewpoint but cannot establish it by evidence, he may well simply make every kind of imaginable personal attack hoping that someone will believe his points are valid.

22:8,9 – Eliphaz continued by accusing Job of neglecting widows and orphans.

He said the mighty and honorable man possessed the land and dwelt in it. Perhaps Eliphaz referred here to Job himself. If so, the point would be that Job (before tragedy struck) was a mighty, honorable man with great possessions in the land. Yet he showed no care for the poor or hungry, widows or orphans. Despite having great wealth, he was unwilling to share with others, but sent them away empty. For this reason God had humbled him by taking away his possessions. This view would fit the context. (Another possible view would be that Job would honor mighty and honorable men, showing care and concern for them, while neglecting and ignoring those who were genuinely needy).

In any case, Eliphaz clearly accused Job of sending away widows and crushing the strength of orphans. He showed no care or concern for their needs. Perhaps the point is even that Job took unfair advantage of these helpless people and took away what they did have to increase his own gain (as in verse 6). Job later denied having committed such a wrong (31:16ff).

22:10,11 – Eliphaz claimed Job suffered snares and dread because of the wrongs he had done.

These verses state as clearly as any the view of the friends that Job's problems were a consequence of his sins. He had sinned against other people (verses 5-7,9), so now he was suffering as a consequence. Snares surrounded him and fear troubled him. He was like a man overwhelmed by darkness, drowning in water. Doubtless Job felt like such snares and troubles surrounded him. What he denied was that it was a consequence of his sins.

Though he stated his conclusion so clearly and forcefully, yet Eliphaz offered no proof that Job was guilty of sin. The only "evidence" was that Job was suffering. That was enough to convince Eliphaz that Job was guilty of sin. And that view is what Job repeatedly refuted.

22:12-14 – Eliphaz accused Job of thinking that God would not see his sins.

Eliphaz affirmed that God was in the heaven, high above even the highest of stars. So Job claimed (according to Eliphaz) that God would not know about his sins. He would not see what Job did and therefore could not judge his conduct. God is covered by thick clouds so He cannot see, even though he walks about the circle of heaven.

The effect is that Eliphaz charged Job with denying the wisdom and knowledge of God. By claiming he was not suffering for his sins, Job was pretending God could not see his sins. But Eliphaz affirmed that Job actually had much sin to be seen. So did Job think God was so far distant or so weak he could not see and judge what Job did?

22:15,16 – Eliphaz charged Job with walking in the ways of wicked men.

His charge is made as a question, but appears to be a rhetorical question, since he has already repeatedly accused Job of sin. So Eliphaz asked Job if he intended to continue in the same old path that wicked men have trod in the past. He claimed that such men have been cut down before their time and all the things they trusted as a foundation were swept away as in a flood. (Could this be a reference to the flood of Noah's day?)

Here again Eliphaz stated his view that wicked men suffer in this life for their sins. Job was suffering, so he must be walking in the paths of the wicked. Would he continue to do so and continue suffering?

The question is very like the old loaded question, "Have you stopped beating your wife?" It assumes you have been guilty in the past. So Eliphaz assumed Job was already walking in the paths of wickedness and asked if he was willing to quit!

22:17-20 – Wicked people think God cannot harm them but the righteous know the wicked will be consumed.

Eliphaz continued his rebuke of Job. He said the wicked say (in effect) that they want God to leave them alone. They think He can do nothing to punish them. They should have known that God had given them the good things they had received, but instead they failed to give Him credit and just wanted Him to stay out of their lives.

He then said that he himself refused to accept the beliefs of the wicked (compare 21:16). And righteous people would laugh at the wicked. They would know that the wicked, whose lives made them enemies of the righteous, would be consumed by punishment. They would be cut down and those of them who remained would be consumed as by a fire. The righteous would see this to be the case and would rejoice at the downfall of the wicked.

22:21-23 – Eliphaz called on Job to repent, return to God, and learn His ways.

Instead of walking in the ways of the wicked, Job should learn the ways of God so He can be at peace with God. If he did so, good would come to him instead of all the harm he had been suffering.

So Eliphaz called on Job to listen to instruction and hold God's words in his heart. The solution to Job's problem would be to return to serving God. Then he would be built up instead of being overcome by God's punishments. He would remove sin far from his tents – i.e., from his life and his surroundings.

Eliphaz continued to make obvious the conclusion of the friends: Job suffered because he sinned and he would be restored to blessings if he would repent. It was as simple as that.

All this assumed, of course, that Job had not been listening to God's word nor had he been aware of the teaching God gave.

22:24-27 – Eliphaz promised wealth and divine favor if Job would repent.

As part of his return to God, Job would have to give up his desire for material wealth, so Eliphaz claimed. He would have to place his gold in the dust and his gold from Ophir (a place known for its gold) in the stones of his brooks. This is a bit confusing, but the point seems to be that Job should cease trusting in his wealth. He should put it away from him as though throwing it away (not necessarily literally but in the sense of ceasing to trust in wealth). Note that in 31:24,25 Job denied making gold his trust.

Having advised Job to repent, Eliphaz then promised good would come to Job instead of the problems he had been suffering. Especially, God Himself would be as gold and precious silver to Job. Job would have Divine favor. He would delight in God and be heard when he prayed to God. Whereas Job complained that God was not listening to his appeals, he could be sure to be heard if he would repent of his sins. He would then fulfill His vows or commitments made to God.

22:28-30 – Eliphaz promised Job would be delivered if he would humble himself before God.

Eliphaz closed his argument and his final speech by assuring Job that, if he would repent and return to God as Eliphaz had described, his word would be established. What he declared to be true would be proved to really be true. Perhaps this includes his claim to be right before God – he really would be right if he would repent.

Light would shine on his ways, instead of the deep darkness that Job felt surrounded him (19:8). This was doubtless symbolism for the joy and blessings Job would have instead of his suffering.

When Job felt downcast and rejected, as he had repeatedly said he did feel, he could be sure that exaltation was coming. God would save and care for him, if he would humble himself before God. God would deliver even those who have not been innocent, if they would repent. Then the purity of Job's hands would lead to deliverance. (An alternative view of these verses is that, if Job would repent and become pure, he could not only be free from hardship himself but could help other people overcome their difficulties.)

This chapter states as clearly as any other the view of the friends. Wicked people suffer in this life for their evil. Job was suffering, therefore he was evil. They were convinced he was guilty of all kinds of horrible crimes, despite the fact they had no proof of any specific evil. But he must be evil, since he was suffering so terribly. If he would just repent, his problems would be solved.

All this we know from the outset of the book to be false. Job did not know why he was suffering, but he continued to maintain that it was not for any guilt he had committed.

Job 23

Chapter 23 & 24 - Job Answers Eliphaz

23:1,2 – Job responded by maintaining his bitter complaint.

As always, Job refused to allow false accusations and false concepts to have the last say. So he responded to Eliphaz, but basically ignored most of what Eliphaz actually said.

He began by insisting that the reason for his bitter complaints was his suffering. His groaning because of his suffering made him listless. (Other translations indicate that the verse refers to God's hand, so that it was God's hand that caused Job to suffer so much that he had a right to groan.)

23:3-5 – Job sought opportunity to present his case before God and hear His response.

Job wished that he could know where to find God so he could speak to Him personally. He would present his case and speak multitudes of arguments before God, as before a great judge. Then he would seek for God to answer and explain to Him why Job was suffering as he was. Job had frequently expressed such a desire.

No doubt Job would have wanted such an opportunity. And who of us has not had a similar wish? How many times, when we face some troubling issue or difficult situation, have we wished we could have a "heart-to heart" talk with Jesus and have Him explain to us plainly exactly why things are happening as they are and especially what His will is and what He wants us to do in the situation we face? Yet we must learn to be satisfied with the revelation He has given us and find therein the truth we need to sustain us. Things not revealed are not for us to know (Deuteronomy 29:29).

23:6,7 – Job was convinced he could be vindicated before God if he could just reason with Him.

Job continued that, if he could present his case to God, God would understand, give heed to his case, and vindicate him. He did not believe God would contend with him – i.e., He would not disagree with Job's claim to be righteous. Rather, Job could reason with God, He would listen to Job's arguments, and in the end Job would be delivered – God would accept Job's evidence that he was upright and would cease causing him to suffer.

23:8,9 – But Job could not find God to talk with Him.

Job wished for an opportunity to present his case before God, convinced that God would vindicate him. But he did not know how to find God to be able to present his case. If he went forward or backward, God would not be there. If God was working on Job's left or to the right, still Job could not observe Him. These expressions may be equivalent to our "north, south, east, or west": the four points of the compass (see NIV). Job could not stand vindicated because he did not know how to locate God to speak to Him.

23:10-12 – But God still knew Job's conduct and in the end would vindicate him.

Though Job could not find God to speak with him, yet he was convinced that God could still see Job. He knew Job's way or manner of conduct; and in the end – after the completion of the period of testing – Job would come forth as gold. That is, just as fire separates gold from impurities, so this time of testing would prove that Job's conduct was pure like gold, not impure. Compare 1 Peter 1:6,7.

Job repeated again that he had kept the path that God wanted him to follow. He had maintained the proper steps and had not turned aside into sin. He had kept God's words as a treasure more valuable than food and so had followed God's commands without departing from them.

Completely contrary to Eliphaz' assertions, here again was Job's confident assertion that he did not deserve the suffering he was enduring. While he could not understand why he was suffering, he continued to be convinced that it was not a punishment for sin. And of course, in this he was correct.

23:13,14 – God was doing what He chose to do in His power.

Despite his suffering and his disappointment that he could not meet with God to present his case, Job knew God was God. He was not a man or an animal. He was different, He knew His own mind, and had the power to choose to do whatever He wanted to do. So how would man understand Him or compel Him to do differently? So Job expressed confidence that, what God was doing in Job's case, was simply what God had decided to do, and He often otherwise did such things.

These words come about as close as Job ever came (before God did speak with him) to stating the truth of the situation. God was doing what He chose to do, and no one had the power to change what He chose to do. Job still appeared to be blaming God for his suffering, but at this point he realized there was little he could do about it except to trust that God knew what He was doing.

23:15-17 – *Yet Job feared God, concluding that it was God's will to let him suffer.*

It terrified Job to know that God was able to do whatever He chose to do, and that was not what Job or any man might understand or expect (verses 13,14). If God would allow Job to suffer so much, for reasons that Job did not understand and could not change, that was cause for fear. It made Job faint or weak of heart, terrified of the Almighty.

Verse 17 is difficult, both in translation and in interpretation. Apparently the original language is difficult for translators to understand well enough to translate, so naturally it is hard for us to explain. Perhaps in some general way Job is describing the darkness that he felt in his suffering. Because God allowed Job to suffer such a dark time in his life, this contributed to the fear that Job felt toward God.

Job 24

(Job Continues His Answer to Eliphaz)

24:1-4 – Job wondered why good people do not see evil punished. Wicked people steal from others and mistreat the needy, poor, and widows.

Job continued his response to Eliphaz by pointing out that many people sin but are not punished for it in this life. He began by wondering, since God is able to observe the world and the "times," why those who know Him do not see His days (His judgments on the wicked?). ("Times" could refer to times for people like Job to ask their questions and receive answers – God knows people want such times). Job appeared unable to explain why it is this way, and almost implied that he thinks it should not be this way. Nevertheless, he affirmed it to be so. He then proceeded to give many examples of unpunished sin.

Some people remove landmarks. The landmarks identified the boundaries of people's properties. By moving them, the wicked would claim property for themselves that actually belong to adjoining neighbors (Deuteronomy 19:14; Proverbs 22:28; 23:10). People often did this but suffered no apparent consequence in this life.

Other people steal the flocks and herds of others, often even by violence. Then they feed on what they have stolen, enjoying the fruits of their evil. Yet often they are not punished in this life.

Such thieves may be so heartless that they even mistreat defenseless people like widows and orphans. They steal a donkey from one who is fatherless. They take an ox as a pledge (in a debt) from a widow. Then, apparently, without mercy they keep the ox and leave the widow without means to provide for herself.

Wicked men may push the needy off the road. They are bullies who take what they want, even from people who have little or nothing. They deny even basic justice and kindness. People whom they ought to help with compassion, they take advantage of. Perhaps the reference is to robbers who steal on the highways, or perhaps they simply do not allow poor people to travel in peace. As are result the poor are forced to hide, presumably for safety. In any case, the point is that innocent people do suffer!

The point of all the examples appears to be an effort to confirm Job's argument that people who do wrong often do not suffer the consequences of the wrong in this life. This is intended to refute the claims of the friends that the wicked suffer in this life as consequences of their sins.

24:5-8 – Job then described how the victims of evil people suffer the lack of food, clothing, and shelter.

The wicked cause their victims to be without even the basic necessities of life, so they must hide for safety (verses 3,4). Job then continued to describe the suffering of these victims (it appears to me that, rather than a further description of the wicked, Job has turned to further discuss the suffering caused by the wicked to their victims).

They wander without homes like wild donkeys in the wilderness. They must search for food for themselves and their families in the wilderness. They gather fodder in the field and glean in the vineyard of the wicked. The wicked have taken the property of the victims, leaving them no choice but to work for the wicked to obtain the necessities of life. The result puts these victims at the mercy of the very people who caused their problems.

Just as they have no home and struggle for food, so they lack even basic necessities of clothing. They are naked at night, having no clothing to protect them from the cold (naked may not mean totally unclothed, but the point here is they lack the clothing they need to keep warm on cold nights). When it rains, they are soaked and must seek places to hide in the rocks of the wilderness.

All this shows the great cruelty of the wicked to cause such suffering. But Job's point is that the wicked do not suffer for their evils. Rather, it is their innocent victims who suffer. So how can the friends be right when they argue that people suffer only as the consequences of their own sins?

24:9-12 – Job continued describing how the victims of wicked men suffer, yet God does not punish the wicked.

Some wicked people are so cruel as to take a fatherless child from one who would at least care for it, even from one who would have compassion enough to nurse a baby orphan. Perhaps the reference is to the mother who nurses her fatherless child. But the wicked do not care. They take the child away, such as to sell it as a slave to pay for the father's debts. The wicked would take a pledge from a poor man, knowing they may soon be able to foreclose and take what little the poor man has.

As a result the poor man goes naked without clothing (see verse 7). Yet the wicked takes away even the sheaves the poor man has, leaving him nothing to eat. The poor man presses out the oil from the olives and the juice from the grapes, yet he himself has nothing to eat or drink. Presumably this is because the wicked man takes away what the poor man has. Or perhaps the poor man is working for the wicked man (verse 6), so he can see the nourishing food as he does his work, but he himself is not allowed to partake of the benefits.

So the poor victims of the wicked men die groaning. Their souls cry out. Yet God does not charge with evil ("them" is added by the translators). Whom does He not charge? The verse does not say, but the point in context is that the wicked are not punished. So the reference here appears to be to the wicked men who cause all this suffering, yet Job often sees no sign that God seeks punishment of the wicked man in this life. This is his response to the friends' claims that wicked people suffer in this life for their sins.

24:13-17 – Wicked men hide in the dark to murder, steal, and commit adultery.

Job here began a lengthy discussion of the ways men hide their evil deeds, especially by acting in the dark. They rebel against light; they hardly know what it is like to act in the day, because they dislike acting where they can be seen.

Murderers often commit their evil at night, killing the poor and needy, just as thieves work in the dark (rising with the light may refer to rising as the light is leaving?).

Adulterers pursue their evils in the night, even disguising their faces, hoping no one will recognize them.

Thieves may watch houses during the day and mark them for victims, but they break into the houses to do their burglary at night in the dark. They don't know what it is like to act in the day.

Daylight is fearful to such people, because they are terrified that someone will recognize them; so they fear daylight like the approach of death.

Of course, all such conduct overlooks the fact that God sees everything we do. We cannot hide from God; He will reward us for all our conduct, even that which was hidden from men. See Ecclesiastes 12:13,14; Psalm 139:1-4,6-12; 147:4,5; John 16:30; Matthew 10:29-31; 6:8,32; 1 Kings 8:39. But Job's point appears to be that, in this life at least, such conduct often seems to succeed. The wicked often get away with hiding their evils; they are not punished in this life, contrary to the claims if the friends.

24:18-21 – Because of his evils, the wicked should be consumed, punished, and forgotten.

This is a difficult section for various reasons. As in the NKJV, verse 18 states that those who commit such evil should be cursed even on the earth. They should be punished, should have to flee as on a swift ship, and no one should turn into their vineyards. Apparently the translation here is very difficult. The ASV reads as though the wicked themselves should not be able to enjoy the fruit of their vineyards.

Job affirmed that the grave would consume these sinners just as surely as drought and heat consume snow. Such a man should be forgotten by the womb – as though even his own mother should not remember him with grief or respect. He should be the eaten by worms. Men should no longer remember him (as though to honor him). His wicked way of life should be brought to an end like a tree destroyed by a storm. This is what he deserves for the way he has preyed on innocent, helpless widows and orphans.

It is unclear whether Job is saying this is the way it ought to be but often is not (which would agree with his point in the previous verses). Or could it be (as implied by the ASV) that he is here quoting the friends' argument: this is the way they say it should be, but Job's observations in the earlier part of the chapter show that it is often not this way?

In any case, we see part of Job's problem. He agrees with the friends about how the wicked ought to suffer in this life, but he does not see it happening that way. This is what bothers him. Apparently, he fails to take into account the punishment of the wicked after this life.

24:22-24 – Men may prosper for a while but in the end will be brought low.

God by His power draws away the mighty man. Though man may rise up (to prosperity?), yet no man is sure of life. The meaning of "draw away" is unclear, but in any case the point is that no one is sure of life. Whether spoken of the wicked or the righteous, the same is true of both. No one knows what the future holds or how long he will continue here.

Men may dwell in security, because God has blessed them with security. So they come to rely on it – they think it will always be this way. But God watches over their ways. The result is that they are exalted for a while, but then they are gone. They are brought low or even brought to death, just like all people eventually are. Like a head of grain, they dry out – their prosperity ceases and eventually even life ceases.

It is difficult here to know whether Job still speaks of the wicked, or whether he speaks of the righteous who suffer at the hands of the wicked. Perhaps Job's point is that this is true of all men, good or bad. God does not make the distinction between the good and the evil in this life that the friends profess to see.

Job himself had prospered greatly and had come to rely on it as though it would continue. But it all ended in a day. The same may happen to wicked people. But the point is that justice is not done to the wicked in this life as distinguished from what happens to the righteous.

The wicked often do not suffer any more or even as much as do the righteous. How then can the friends be correct when they claim all suffering occurs as punishment on a man for his sins?

24:25 – Job concluded with a challenge to the friends to prove him wrong.

Job had at this point argued endlessly with the friends. They had argued repeatedly and incessantly that he was suffering because he had committed sins. Job has now argued, based on observation, that often people do not suffer for sin in this life. Good people suffer too in this life. It simply cannot be true that all who suffer are suffering for sins they committed. Job does not have the answer for why people suffer, but he cannot accept the friends' view.

So, having given his evidence, he closed by challenging the friends (or anyone else) to prove him wrong, if they can. In doing so, they would prove him a liar and make his speech worthless.

Bildad will respond with one last short speech, then the friends give up the debate. It is unlikely Job has convinced them they are wrong, but they seem to realize they cannot convince Job.

Job 25

Chapter 25 - Bildad's Third Speech

25:1 – Bildad began his third speech.
In this third and final round of speeches, only Eliphaz made a lengthy speech. Bildad's speech was very short, and Zophar did not respond at all. Apparently they had given up trying to convince Job that their view was correct.

25:2,3 – Bildad praised the greatness of God.
Bildad appealed to the greatness and might of God. Dominion and fear belong to God: He has power over all, and all should respect Him.

"He makes peace in His high places" is a difficult statement. What are the high places? Heaven? The stars in the Universe? God doubtless has power to make peace in all such places, but I am unsure what is meant here.

He has innumerable armies at His disposal. This expression seems similar to the common Old Testament expression that God is "Jehovah of hosts." He rules over the hosts of His angels and also over the hosts of the heavenly bodies (stars, etc.). Whichever is meant here, the point seems to be that He has strength or rules over all as a general over an innumerable army.

His power is evident everywhere, so that there is nowhere that His light does not rise (or shine). In other words, everything everywhere experiences the effects of His power.

So God has supreme power and greatness in the Universe. But what is the application in the context? Consider how Bildad attempts to apply it in the following verses.

25:4-6 – God is so great that no one can be righteous before Him.
If God is so great, Bildad asked who could be righteous before Him. How could any man, who is born of woman, stand pure before Him? He claims that, compared to God, even the moon is dim so that it does not shine. And compared to Him the stars are not pure. This must

be figurative, since the moon and stars have no wills and therefore no moral responsibilities. Their impurity must be physical.

But the application is that man, who is like a worm or maggot before God, cannot possibly be truly clean or upright before God. Of course, we are all created in the image of God, so we are truly great in His order in the universe (Genesis 1:26,27; Psa 8). But in a moral sense Bildad is correct. We do all sin and therefore are unworthy of God's favor.

What does this have to do with the discussion? It seems to me that the point is that Job cannot possibly be truly upright before God. Job has claimed to be upright and undeserving of His suffering. Bildad's argument would claim that no one is truly undeserving of suffering, for all are worthless compared to God.

Such an argument, however, seems to me to prove nothing. If that were true, then everyone should be suffering as bad as Job was and far more so. The book began by proving that Job was one of the most upright of men. If Bildad is arguing that even Job deserves to suffer, then the same would be even more so of the friends and all other people on earth. So the point still does not answer why Job was suffering while other people were not.

And above all, the argument does not take into account that men can be righteous before God by being forgiven of sin and dedicating themselves to his service. In this sense, Job was upright. We all deserve to be punished for our sins, true. But God in His mercy provides a way of forgiveness whereby we can escape punishment for our sins. Bildad's argument ignores this entirely.

Job 26

Chapter 26 - Job's Response to Bildad

26:1-3 – Job questioned the usefulness of the friends' speeches.

Job responded to Bildad by sarcastically praising the great help he had offered! He expressed awe at how much help Bildad had given one who needed power and how he had strengthened the arm of the one without strength. He offered great appreciation for the counsel and sound advice that had been offered to one who lacked wisdom.

Of course, all this was stated with tongue in cheek: he really meant the opposite of what he said. The comments Bildad had offered had, not only been without value as help, but had actually been discouraging and increased Job's distress. What help was it to a suffering man to accuse him of sin without proof or evidence? Such statements often begin speeches, and what Job said here directly to Bildad would also apply to the speeches of all the friends.

(An alternative view is that the friends had accused Job of neglecting the needy, so he is here asking them what they have done for the needy. If they have done no more than he has, why are they not suffering as he is, if that is why he is suffering?)

26:4 – Job challenged the source of Bildad's speech.

To whom was Bildad uttering his speech? It was supposed to be directed to Job, but Job's point is that it did not fit his case at all. So it was entirely misdirected.

And what was the source of Bildad's views? Whose spirit was he expressing? Job implied that the source was not what Bildad thought it was. The speech surely did not express the spirit of God. The views did not harmonize with anything God would teach.

So Job challenged and denied, not just what Bildad taught, but the same would apply to what all the friends had said.

26:5,6 – Job described the greatness of God in relation to the dead. God knows and sees all.

Job then began his own description of the greatness of God. He and the friends agreed about how great God was. They had expressed many great things about God, and Job does the same. Their differences of views about suffering did not come from different views about the greatness of God. Job viewed God as no less great than did the friends.

God has caused the dead to tremble, including the dead under the waters (this may simply be an expression for the location of Sheol – the place of departed souls). Why they tremble is not stated – suffering or fear of God's power. But Job's point is that God knows where they are and what happens to them. Even Sheol is open to His knowledge and the power of the destruction (of death) cannot hide people from him. You and I cannot see the dead or know what is beyond the grave, but God knows. Nothing can be hidden from Him. Compare Psalms 139:7-12.

26:7,8 – God stretches the north over empty space and hangs the earth on nothing. He binds up water in the clouds.

Job continued describing God's greatness by saying that He placed an empty space in the north and hangs the earth on nothing. These facts have been scientifically established as accurate in relatively recent times. We have even sent vehicles into space that have taken pictures of the earth and have substantiated that it hangs on nothing. But how did Job know these things thousands of years ago?

This would seem to indicate that Job was inspired. However, we have established that Job spoke as a man and made several errors in his speeches for which he later repented (see introduction). So that would indicate that he was not inspired or at least was not generally speaking by inspiration. Hailey denies that Job spoke this by inspiration but somehow observed it for himself, perhaps by observing that the sun and moon appear suspended in space with nothing under them.

However, it appears to me that God spoke to men, especially the heads of houses in the Patriarchal Age in a way different from how He afterward spoke to prophets. Abraham was called a prophet (Genesis 20:7), but no one else was so designated until Moses, even though God did speak to Adam, Noah, Isaac, Jacob, etc. In the end of this book God likewise spoke to Job, so perhaps He spoke to him previously as He spoke to the heads of households in the patriarchal age. Perhaps Job received this information in such a way.

Further, Job said that God binds the water in the thick clouds, but the clouds are not broken by it. A person could observe this without direct revelation, for it is obvious that rain comes from clouds. Yet it would seem strange that all that water could be in the clouds and yet it does not break the clouds open and flood out. God invented the way to do this, but it is doubtful that Job knew how. Today we have a better understanding of the concept of evaporation and condensation.

26:9,10 – God spreads a cloud over His throne and draws a horizon on the water.

Job mentioned other aspects of God's greatness. Specifically, he said that God covers the face of His throne and spreads a cloud over it. This seems to view God as dwelling in heaven (the sky), but we can't see Him because of the clouds. Of course, this is not literally true, and Job would know it because then on clear days we could see God. It appears to be just a poetic expression of God's greatness. Perhaps Job refers back to the fact that God would not reveal Himself to Job though Job called on Him to do so.

Then he said God drew a circular horizon on the face of the waters at the boundary of light and darkness. This appears to refer to the horizon that we see, especially when viewed on the sea. Over the horizon is the curve of the sky, so the horizon appears to serve as the boundary between light and darkness – that is, light and day are determined as the sun comes up over that horizon or goes down behind it.

26:11,12 – God has power over the pillars of heaven, the sea, and the storms.

Job continued saying that God's word causes the pillars of heaven to tremble and be astonished. Of course, he knew of no literal pillars of heaven. The idea seems to express God's power to shake the heavens as by thunder or a storm.

Likewise, God's power can stir up the sea, as by a storm. Then when He chooses, He breaks up the storm (KJV says "Rahab"). All these expressions appear to refer to God's power as manifested in weather and storms.

26:13,14 – The power of God's Spirit is seen in the heavens and among animals. It is beyond our understanding.

Job says further that God's power adorned the heavens. This may refer to the beauty of sky, clouds, sunshine, and perhaps even the stars, perhaps after the storm of verse 12 has passed. The sky is beautiful to observe and so demonstrates God's power.

His hand can pierce the fleeing serpent. This meaning is difficult. Of course, God can overpower any animal, no matter how it attempts to flee for safety. Yet the expression appears to have a more symbolic meaning. Perhaps it refers to some constellation, that God has power even over the stars.

Job concludes his description of God's greatness saying that he has been able only to touch the border and only a whisper of the great power of God. The reality is so much greater than any man could describe. In fact, the thunder of His power is so great that no man can really understand it, let alone describe it in words. All we can do is praise God for His greatness in our limited human way, but the reality is far beyond our comprehension.

Job has finished his answer to Bildad. It would now be Zophar's turn to speak. But he says nothing, apparently because he has given up attempting to convince Job. So Job continues to speak in the next chapter, since the friends have abandoned the discussion.

Job 27

Chapter 27 - Job's Speech Continues

27:1 – Job continued speaking.

After Job had responded to Bildad in chapter 26, it would have been Zophar's turn to speak to Job. But Bildad's speech had been short, then Zophar did not speak at all. This could mean that the friends realize they have been wrong, but the far more likely explanation is that they have simply given up trying to convince Job. They have all tried repeatedly to no avail. Nothing is being accomplished, they said what they came to say, so they dropped their part of the discussion. But Job had much more yet to say.

27:2-4 – Job repeated his conviction that he had spoken truth.

Job proceeded to insist that he would not speak wickedness or deceit. Just as surely as God is alive and so long as he had breath from God in his nostrils, he would persist to speak the truth.

Yet even as he says this, he casts complaints against God that God had taken justice from him and made his soul bitter. So, ironically, Job appealed to the greatness of God as proof he spoke the truth, even as he criticized how God had treated him. In a sense he showed faith that God did make him and God does live, despite his frustration with his suffering.

The friends had accused Job of sin and he had denied it. Here he repeated with emphasis that he had not and would not lie about it. He knew of no error that would explain his suffering.

27:5,6 – Job refused to admit that the friends were right or that he had done wrong that would explain his suffering.

Job became direct in responding to the friends' accusations that he was suffering because he had sinned. He stated flatly that agreeing with such a view was far from him. He would maintain his integrity and not deny it till he died. He would hold fast to his righteousness and not let it go. As long as he lived his heart would not accept the conclusion that he was guilty of wrongdoing.

This was an absolute rejection of the friends' view, because their view would require Job to deny his own righteousness. In this Job was correct, as we have learned from the beginning.

27:7-10 – Job began a description of the wicked implying that he has no hope and will not call upon God.

The friends had repeatedly described the wicked man, showing that he must suffer for his wrongdoing. Their application had been that Job fit the case they were describing, and his suffering was the punishment for his evil. Job here began his own description of the wicked. He too believed the wicked will be rejected by God and will suffer for his wrongdoing, but he did not believe they always suffer in this life for their sins.

He began by wishing that his enemy would be like the wicked and the unrighteous. This appears to be almost a curse on those who would oppose him. Some think it included those who would falsely accuse him of sin as the friends had done.

If a hypocrite prospers greatly in this life, what is the profit if in the end God takes his life (or "soul" – ASV)? Compare Matthew 16:26,27. Job's view of life and rewards after death is not clear, but here he seems to hint at such a concept. In any case, he is convinced that God may punish the wicked in the end.

Would such a wicked person delight in God and call on God when he is in need? The implication is that he would not; but even if he did, God would not hear his call. God would not answer his prayer.

This appears to describe some consequences that Job believed the wicked man would suffer, but it did not fit Job's case for he had diligently called on God.

27:11,12 – Job then said he would tell them what God's hand would do to the wicked.

The friends had expounded on their view of how God punishes the wicked in this life. Job here countered by say he would teach them the truth of the matter of what God's hand will do (the context shows that he referred to what God would do to the wicked). Job refused to conceal the truth, but he was surprised that the friends speak such nonsense about the matter when they should already have observed the truth for themselves.

27:13,14 – Job argued that the children of the wicked would suffer.

Job then began his own exposition of what God would do to the wicked man. This would be the heritage or portion (a long-term result, not necessarily a quick or short-term result) that those who wickedly oppressed others would receive from God.

If the wicked man has children, even many children, they will die in the end by the sword: some sort of violent death. And while they live they will not find their blessings to be satisfying. Like the friends, Job believed that the children of the wicked would suffer, but not necessarily right away. And his other statements showed that he believed there were exceptions to this in this life.

So, the consequences Job described here are ultimate consequences that will come eventually, and perhaps not at all in this life. That would mean either that they would suffer after this life or that their suffering would at least be postponed. Job appears to believe that punishment must come, but he did not seem sure when or how. Meanwhile they would not find their wealth and blessings to be satisfying.

27:15-17 – In the end, the wicked will die and others will benefit from their wealth.

Some of the wicked man's family may survive him, but in the end they too will die. Their family left behind (widows) will not grieve deeply or truly to see them go, apparently because those who died were not worthy of being grieved or missed.

The wicked may accumulate great wealth and clothing, heaped up like dust and dirt – Job acknowledged that obtaining it would be possible for the wicked. But the wicked himself in the end would not enjoy it, but those who are innocent and righteous would receive the ultimate benefit.

Again, Job appears to be describing long-term effects, not necessarily in the short run. Nor does he seem clear about when or how this would happen. But in the end the wicked would not enjoy the fruits of their evil. Rather, the righteous would rejoice in the end.

27:18,19 – The rich man's house will be a temporary joy but in the end he will be gone.

The wicked man may have a house, even as he has wealth, but he will not enjoy it in the end. It will be like a moth's house or like a booth or temporary shelter made by a watchman. It would be temporary but soon gone; that is, the wicked man would enjoy it only temporarily. In the end he will not enjoy the fruit of his evil.

Rather than enjoying his gain, the rich man will die: he will lie down and not get up. He will be no more. The translation here is apparently difficult, but the point is clear: the wicked man will not enjoy his riches in the end. Again, the issue with Job seems to be the end result that the wicked man faces.

27:20-23 – In the end the wicked man is swept away as by a tempest or wind.

Job had already said that the wicked man would lose his family, wealth, and home in the end. Here he added that he himself would be carried away by terrors like one overtaken by a storm and a flood and a mighty wind. The problems would hurl against him without mercy. He would attempt to escape the destruction, but in the end he would be swept away and be gone. Men would mock and ridicule him for they see his defeat.

This again appears to be the end result Job sees for the wicked man. He may not suffer so throughout his life, but sooner or later the terrors overtake him. Whether Job viewed this as an eternal punishment after death is not clear to me. But his other statements appear to express that men may get away with evil for a long time in life and may never suffer for their sins in the life. But in the end they will be punished.

Job 28

Chapter 28 - Job Discusses the Value and Source of Wisdom.

Since Job's friends no longer were replying to his speeches, Job continued speaking without interruption. In this chapter he discussed at length the source of wisdom and the value of it.

Hailey describes various views about this chapter, but I see no reason to consider it other than what it appears to be: a continuation of Job's speech from chapter 27, which then continues through chapter 31.

28:1-4 – Job described the efforts men make to obtain metal from mines.

Men in Job's day, as today, had devised ways to mine various valuable metals from the earth. God has placed the metals in the earth, but they generally do not just lie around easily available on the surface to be gathered up.

Silver and gold must be mined, then afterward they must be refined to purify them into a useful form. The same is true for iron and copper, which must be taken from the earth and then smelted or otherwise purified.

In order to obtain them, men must search the recesses of dark places. They must end the darkness, presumably by making artificial lights in the mines. The "shadow of death" may refer to the fact they dig in the earth, the very place where people normally would not go until they die and are buried. Or perhaps it refers to the danger that men face in order to obtain metal from mines. Throughout history mining for metal has been a notoriously dangerous task. (ASV says simply "obscurity" and "thick darkness.")

To obtain the metals, men dig shafts deep into the earth in places no people would otherwise think to walk. They travel up and down suspended today in elevators or similar means of going down into the mines, perhaps in those days by baskets suspended from ropes swinging back and forth till they reach the depths of the mine.

While some details here may be unclear, nevertheless the main point is clear: Men go to great lengths and dangers to obtain valuable metals. The metals are not easily found or obtained, but men consider them to be worth the effort. We will see Job's application of this as his proceeds.

The use of metal for men's purposes is mentioned as early as Genesis 4:22. Hailey gives historical evidence that people were mining metals and making metal products as early as 4000 BC, well before the time we are discussing.

28:5-8 – Men search the earth for precious metals in places no animal has gone.

Job said the earth itself can produce bread – i.e., grain from which food can be made for men. But the metals are found underneath the earth. The earth must be turned up as if by fire. The reference to fire is unclear, but seems to refer to the destruction of fire. Men turn over the earth to find metals, destroying the ground like a fire burns and destroys. Or perhaps the idea would be like a volcano that burns and destroys the ground, so men do to find metals.

In the earth are precious gems like sapphires and precious metals like gold. So the man works diligently to obtain them.

But animals don't bother with such things. No bird would care or bother. A falcon has incredible eyesight, but he can't see underground where the metals are that men dig for. A lion has great power and courage, but he walks on the surface of the earth without ever bothering to dig deep into the ground to find anything of value deep in its interior.

Again, Job will make application later, but the point is that men go to great lengths to obtain that which is of great value to them.

28:9-11 – To find valuables in the earth, men overturn rocks, mountains, and streams.

Job continued describing the work of men in mining valuables from the earth. They put their hands even to the hardest of rocks, such as flint, to move or cut through them. They overturn mountains even to their roots. They cut, not just ditches, but tunnels in the rocks to dig out the metals and jewels. They dam up streams so they can obtain valuables that were buried under the waters; to prevent the water from interfering with the mining process, the flow of water must often be redirected or otherwise controlled.

So men find every precious thing and bring everything hidden to light. They are determined to allow nothing to prevent them from finding what is valuable anywhere in the surface of the earth. That was the case in Job's day and is still the case today.

28:12,13 – But why do not people show a similar appreciation for wisdom and put forth similar effort to find it?

Having described the inexhaustible and unlimited efforts of men to dig up items of material value in the earth's surface, Job then compared this to the efforts of men to obtain wisdom. True wisdom is in the end of far greater value than physical metals or jewels that can be at most of temporary value. But do men seek for wisdom with the same commitment and diligence that they seek for precious metals?

Where is wisdom found? Where can men go to find the place where understanding can be obtained? Job states the general truth that men do not appreciate the value of wisdom; it cannot be found by searching the wisdom or resources of men on earth. And in general a true appreciation of its value is not found among men. Few would begin to put forth the effort to obtain wisdom that men put forth to obtain the precious metals from the earth.

28:14,15 – Yet wisdom is of greater value and harder to find than precious metals.

The depths of the sea (personified) do not claim to know where wisdom is. It cannot be found by searching the oceans. It cannot be purchased for gold or for the price of silver.

Despite the great efforts men expend to mine for precious metals or jewels, wisdom is more valuable and cannot be obtained by paying silver or gold. Yet what efforts do most men expend to obtain it?

28:16-19 – Wisdom is of greater value than any precious gem.

Job then listed other precious items that men find in the earth, but none of them is as valuable as wisdom. You cannot measure the value of wisdom in terms or gold or precious gems, not even onyx, sapphire, crystal, fine gold, or jewelry made from any of these. None of these are sufficient to buy wisdom. Neither coral, quartz, rubies, nor topaz can compare to it.

Wisdom is of greater value that all these, and none of them are sufficient to purchase wisdom. Men may go to great lengths to obtain these valuables, but wisdom is far greater in value.

28:20-22 – Wisdom is hidden so that men cannot find it.

Job then asked, if wisdom is of such great value and cannot be bought even for great treasures, then where is wisdom? Where do we go to obtain it? True wisdom, of the kind Job refers to, is hidden from all living creatures. Even the birds of the air, that travel all around and have sharp eyesight, cannot find it.

Destruction and Death (personified) say they have heard about it, but obviously do not know where to get it. Even those who have died and gone to the next world cannot tell us where to obtain it (though many like to think that wisdom unknown to us could be obtained by calling back those who have died). Note how this ties back to chapter 26.

In short, man by himself is incapable of determining true wisdom. We are inadequate to determine it. This is true specifically in the spiritual realm, which Job must here refer to. This principle is often taught elsewhere to remind us that we must accept Divine revelation, for we are not wise enough ourselves to discover spiritual truth apart from God's word. See Matthew 15:9,13; Galatians 1:8,9; 2 John 9-11; Colossians 3:17; Jeremiah 10:23; Proverbs 14:12; 3:5,6; Revelation 22:18,19; 1 Timothy 1:3; 2 Timothy 1:13; John 5:43.

28:23-26 – Only God understands true wisdom.

Since men do not understand how to obtain or where to find true wisdom, Job concluded that only God does understand. He knows its place and understands how to obtain it.

God has superior intelligence and power to man. He sees everywhere on earth, everything under heaven. His laws control the wind, the rain, the lightning, and the thunder. Man can do none of these things. If God created and controls the weather, surely He and only He is wise enough to know true wisdom. He can reveal to us that which we cannot obtain for ourselves.

28:27,28 – God revealed that true wisdom is found in fearing and serving the Lord.

Since man cannot find or discover wisdom and the only way to obtain it is for God to reveal it, Job concluded his description of wisdom by saying that we must turn to God for wisdom. God knows it; He searched it out and prepared it. Therefore, He is able to declare it to us.

His answer was that true wisdom consists of fearing the Lord and true understanding consists of departing from evil. This answer is also revealed elsewhere in Scriptures, especially in Proverbs (1:7; 9:10).

This may seem like an oversimplification, but only if one does not truly understand the significance of fearing God and departing from evil. To fear God is to truly believe in Him, respect Him, and determine to serve Him. If we then follow through and depart from evil, we will dedicate our lives to obeying and serving Him. This is the whole duty of man (Ecclesiastes 12:13).

Our materialistic world would not see this as true value. They would prefer the material advantages of this life. They would be the ones who would seek meaning in life by mining for the valuable metals and precious gems, as Job has described. But when people value eternal life, wholesome living, the true purpose of life, and a relationship with the Creator of the universe, they will realize that one can have a truly blessed and meaningful life by serving God even if one does not enjoy the material prosperity that many seek. They will see that true contentment in life and hope for life after death come from serving God, and that is true wisdom.

Job 29

Chapter 29 - Job Describes His Former Blessings.

In this discourse Job recalled the joy and blessings he experienced before the calamities that had befallen him.

29:1-3 – Job recalled the former days when God had taken care of him.

As Job continued speaking, he wished he could return to the past months when God had watched over him. He remembered how blessed he had been and how God had provided light to shine on Job and light to guide Job when he walked as through darkness.

The language is doubtless symbolic, but the point is clear. Job remembered that he had been greatly blessed by God, and he regretted the loss of these blessings. God had watched over Job perhaps like a parent watches for a child: he kept His eyes on Job to protect and provide for him. He showed Job how to proceed safely, like a person who has a lamp over him can see clearly how to proceed.

29:4-6 – Job recalled when he was in his prime, surrounded by his children.

God's counsel had been friendly and had protected Job's tent – his home and family – in the days of his prime. The Almighty God was with Job, and he still had his children (before they had been slain). His life was as though it was bathed in cream, rivers of oil poured for him from a rock.

Again, this highly symbolic language expressed how he felt when God blessed him. We have similar expressions: "They lived off the fat of the land." "Everything was peaches and cream." The purpose is to describe someone who is richly blessed.

29:7-10 – Job recalled his days as a respected leader of the community when people listened to him with respect.

Community leaders in those days often met at the open square at the gate of the city. There they conducted business, executed justice, made judicial decisions, etc. There Job, in his prime, had been greatly respected.

When Job came to take his seat, people showed great respect. The very young would step aside into the background, not detracting in any way from the respect being shown to Job. Those who were aged and themselves respected, nevertheless stood to show respect for Job. Princes and nobles ceased speaking, refusing to allow their tongue to speak, as they listened instead to Job's respected views (compare verses 21,22). In this way they showed respect for Job's wisdom when he sat and spoke. His views were so worthy of hearing that no one else would consider expressing a contrary view.

29:11-13 – People blessed Job because he helped those in need.

Those who heard about Job would pronounce a blessing on him; and those who saw him recognized him with approval, because they respected the kind of man he was.

They knew that he delivered those who were poor and cried out to him for help, including the orphans who had no one else to help them. Likewise, those who were perishing pronounced a blessing on Job, and widows would sing for joy because of the good that Job did for them.

In saying such things, Job as not so much bragging as simply recalling how joyful and blessed his life had been before his agony began. However, he is also answering the false charges of the friends who had accused him of being a terrible sinner. They had in fact said he was the opposite of all that he here affirmed (compare 22:5-11). He is denying their argument that he was suffering because of evil.

29:14-17 – Job continued describing how he helped the needy and opposed evil.

Job claimed that, contrary to the accusations of the friends, he was clothed with righteousness and justice like a robe and turban. He surrounded himself with good conduct and that is what people would see who looked at him.

In particular, he helped those who had needs. If someone was blind, Job would do what he could to be his eyes. If one could not walk, he would serve as his feet. Of course, this cannot be literally done. The point is that he would see that their needs were met so that the things they needed done would be done for them, even though they could not do them for themselves.

Job was a father to the poor. That is, if someone was in need due to poverty, Job would take him under his wing to care for him like a father would provide for his own needy child.

He would search out the case that he did not know. This refers to the justice that he sought to exercise toward others. If someone was accused of wrong, Job made sure he knew the full facts of the case before he determined to treat them as right or wrong. This may imply that he was a judge in the city or that at least he participated in judgments men had against one another.

He broke the fangs of the wicked and plucked his victim from his teeth. Again, the symbolic language pictures evil people as being like a lion or other vicious animal that attacked and devoured other people. But Job would break the power of the evil to do harm and would deliver his victims. He championed those who were mistreated by others. This would be part of the justice that he had described in the previous verse.

Again, Job at great length defended his uprightness in contrast to the friends' false accusations (compare 22:5-10). He also recalled the better times before his hardships.

29:18-20 – In his prior days Job had thought his good life would continue without interruption.

As Job looked back on the good life he lived before tragedy struck, he realized that he had thought all these blessings would continue indefinitely. He thought he would multiply his days like the sand. So Job thought his good life would continue for many days like grains of sand. He expected to die in his nest – nothing would disturb the joy of his home and family till life ended.

Like a tree that dwells by the water and spreads its roots wide, so Job had thought he would always be richly blessed with all that he needed. He would be like plants on which the dew settles and provides all their nourishment.

So Job felt that his glory was fresh. The honor that he experienced was always refreshed; it never seemed to cease or grow old. His bow was renewed in his hand. He always had the means to defend himself, perhaps not just against violence, but against whatever problems may attack him. (Compare 30:11).

He expected his rich blessings to just go on and on and never anticipated such suffering as he had come to endure. He believed that God would continue to bless him richly, because he had served God faithfully. This is how we naturally tend to feel in such good times, but Job's case proves it is not always so. And perhaps this is part of the reason why Job felt God had not treated him justly.

29:21-23 – Job's words had been highly respected.

Job returned to the thoughts of verses 9,10. When he spoke, men listened. The kept silence while he spoke; then after he had spoken they added or contradicted nothing.

Men respected his wisdom and judgment, so that his speech settled on them like dew on the flowers. They waited for him to speak like the earth waits for rain; then when he spoke, they took in all that he said like the earth takes in the rain in the spring.

People believed and respected his speech. They viewed his judgments as wise and helpful, so they listened carefully and did not imagine that any other views could improve on what he said.

Of course, no one experiences such extreme respect without some jealousy and contradictions. But Job idealized the past as he looked back with regret. And doubtless much of it was basically accurate.

29:24,25 – So Job had been like a chief or a king among his followers.

The NKJV says that people would not believe that he was mocking them. This could mean that they could not imagine him saying things to hurt them, or perhaps it means they knew he must be kidding and would not take offense? They enjoyed being in his presence so that they did not reject or avoid the blessing of being before his countenance.

However, the translation of this verse is difficult. The ASV translates it in such a way that its meaning is easier to explain. It simply says that he smiled on them when they had no confidence. That is, when they were troubled or concerned, his confidence would give them confidence. They would trust him to give them the guidance and care they needed.

So Job led the people, making decisions about what course of action the people should take. He sat among them as a chief or a king amidst his army. So he gave them comfort and strength as one who comforts mourners.

All this expressed how respected Job thought he had been among the people. He had not at all been the evil tyrant that his friends had claimed him to be. While Job may have somewhat exaggerated in his reminiscing or at least left out the negative aspects of his former life, nevertheless he had enjoyed a good life. And above all, he had done nothing to deserve such suffering as he had come to endure. Chapter one had already confirmed this to be true.

So Job finally answered emphatically and at length the false charges the friends had made against him.

Job 30

Chapter 30 - Job Describes His Suffering.

In the previous chapter Job had remembered the blessings he had enjoyed before his suffering began. This chapter contrasts to the previous chapter by expressing how terribly Job was suffering now that his troubles had begun. He contrasts "before" and "after."

30:1,2 – Job thought he was being mocked by those who formerly respected him.

Before his tragedies began, Job was so highly respected that even people who were highly respected refused to speak up to add to his words but would accept his views as best. Now, however, even people that were younger than Job (let alone highly respected men) would mock Job. They would not only disregard his words and his honor, but would even ridicule him and speak disrespectfully of him.

This was done by people whose lives demonstrated that they themselves deserved little respect. Their families were so lowly that Job would not have allowed the fathers who headed the families (let alone the younger sons) to be among Job's dogs.

Job considered these men to be so dishonorable or ineffective that they could be of no use to him. Their strength or vigor was gone. It is unclear exactly what Job means, or whether this was true during his former or present circumstances. In any case, the point is that these youths were from useless families, yet now these people looked down on Job!

30:3-5 – He was mocked by men who were outcasts of society, living in want.

The people Job referred to lived in poverty, gaunt from hunger, going out late to dwell desolately in the wilderness. They ate what they could scavenge in the wilderness: mallow from bushes and broom tree roots. The ASV says "salt-wort," instead of mallow. Hailey comments that this was valued so little as a food that only the poorest of people would eat it.

They were outcasts or even criminal types. Society treated them as thieves, so they were driven out. Yet such rejects of society, living in abject poverty, had come to view themselves as superior to Job so they looked down on him.

30:6-8 – These people were vile and the scourge of society.

They could not afford real homes, so they lived in any cave or refuge they could find in the lea of some rock in the wilderness. They would live like a wild donkey braying among the bushes of the wilderness (as looking for food), or they would rest under nettles – the most uncomfortable of resting places, which was available only because no one else wanted it.

They were known to be from families of people without good sense or good morals: vile, foolish men. They were the offscouring of society, rejected by all. Yet they considered themselves good enough to look down on Job. This is how far he had descended in the eyes of others because of his suffering.

30:9-11 – Such people now treated Job as an outcast.

These people, so totally rejected by all decent people, yet now taunted Job, singing songs of derision and mocking him. Where before the best of men respected Job and sought his company, now the lowest of men had come to hate him and refuse to associate with him. They avoided him, and would not mind spitting in his face.

This change in Job's well-being had occurred, he said, because of how God was treating him. The affliction Job thought God had placed upon him made Job like a man whose bow had a broken bowstring. What good was it? He would be defenseless against his enemies. So the people showed no respect for Job and did not in any way feel obligated to restrain themselves from any form of conduct they might wish to show against him. Yet he was defenseless to stop it.

30:12-15 – Job described these outcasts as though they attacked him.

Having described their disrespect for him, he then continued to say they actually sought his harm. Exactly how they specifically treated him is not clear; but he figuratively speaks of them as arising against him, raising ways of destruction against him, pushing away his feet (perhaps so as to make him stumble). They destroyed the path in which he was walking, so that he was severely hindered from going where he wanted. So they brought calamity upon him. "They have no helper" might mean they needed no one else to help them attack Job. Or it might mean they themselves were such reprobates that no one would help them with their needs, yet they were willing to attack one less fortunate even than themselves.

He compared them to broad waves, breakers blown against him by a ruinous storm. The ASV translates this as a wide breach, so the "break" would be a break in a wall of defense, and the illustration would refer to an invading army attacking Job. The result is that terror was upon him, seeking to destroy his honor like a strong wind destroying what lies before it. So Job's prosperity and well-being passed like a cloud going by overhead or perhaps a fog being blown away.

So dishonorable men who should have treated Job with great respect, now felt no compunction about harming or attacking him however they could. And all this had occurred because Job had lost his wealth, his family, and his health, so that he no longer had any status in the community.

30:16-18 – Job then described the affliction of his body.

Because days of affliction had come upon him, his soul was poured out (in grief) over his difficulties. At night he was attacked by gnawing pains that never let up, and his bones pierced him. This latter may mean his bones are pierced with pain. Pain in the bones is a common expression in the Bible and even today to express a deep pain that reaches to the depths of the body. When we are really in pain or tired we say our bones ache or we are cut to the bone. It is not just a surface suffering.

Apparently there are numerous attempted explanations about Job's reference to his garment. In some sense even his garment seemed to be against him, for it no longer assisted him as a garment should. Perhaps instead of giving him warmth, comfort, and good appearance, it was disfigured as a by a great force and simply hung from his neck as a collar. Or some suggest that he referred to his skin as hanging so loosely about him in his disease that it hung like a badly disfigured garment.

30:19-21 – Job again viewed God as the One causing his great suffering.

He said "He" (God) had cast him into the mud, so that he became like dust and ashes. In his pain he was sitting in ashes, but he felt as though he himself was reduced to something as low and worthless as dust and ashes.

He cried to God as for help or deliverance – as he had often done throughout the book – yet God did not answer or help him. His suffering continued despite his appeals to God. God regarded Job when he stood up – apparently he knew God saw his plight, but chose to do nothing about it. This charged God with indifference.

But Job went further. He viewed God as not just indifferent; he charged God with treating Job cruelly and opposing Job with the strength of His hand. Instead of using His power to help Job, as Job requested, God actually used His power against Job.

So again Job failed to understand the real source of his suffering and blamed God. He continued speaking against God as though God was mistreating him.

30:22-24 – Job charged God with ruining his success and bringing him to death.

Job continued expressing his grievances against God. He said God spoiled his success. Again he viewed God as responsible for the loss of his wealth and well-being. He said God lifted him up to the wind and caused him to ride on it. His own children had been destroyed by a great wind. Perhaps Job here pictured God as doing a similar thing figuratively to him. It was as though God threw Job to the power of the wind and let the wind blow him away like a leaf in the fall.

So Job's life was as good as over. He was convinced God would bring him to the point of death, which he knew is the appointed end of everyone's life. He felt his life was already as good as over in that he could accomplish nothing useful, so why not be dead and get it over with? He had expressed that desire from the beginning of the discussion (chapter 3). He was convinced God would eventually bring him to that end.

He said God would not use his great strength to destroy a heap of ruins if it cried to him for mercy. This would appear to carry the idea that God would not treat a heap of ruins as he had treated Job. But the translation here is apparently one of the most difficult in the book. The ASV translates as though referring to one who is falling and so reaches out his hand to catch himself or cries out for help in time of calamity. The meaning is obscure because the translation is so difficult.

30:25-28 – Job had helped others who called to him, but he himself found no help.

Job returned briefly to his earlier claims that he had treated other people properly (chapter 29). When others were grieved or in trouble, he wept for them. But when he himself was in trouble, no one helped him. Other people had turned against him (including his friends), and God opposed him instead of offering help. He sought for good, but evil came; he sought for light, but only darkness resulted.

So, he viewed his life as days of affliction confronting him with turmoil in his heart and no rest available to him. He spent his days in mourning instead of going abroad under the sun (the translation here is also uncertain). He cried for help among those assembled, but no help came.

Job here expressed a sense of absolute hopelessness for his case. It is hard to criticize him, knowing how terribly he suffered. Yet he really was failing to give God credit for caring for him.

30:29-31 – Job concluded his lament by expressing his loss of companionship, loss of health, and loss of joy.

Job viewed himself as a brother of jackals and companion of ostriches. These are animals that have little value among men. Jackals are wild dogs that live off refuse. No people want them around.

Ostriches live in the desert with no companionship to men. So Job felt that he was not just an outcast among people, but the only living things he could identify with would be animals that men had no use for. He felt as though men viewed him among the lowest of living things.

Then he described the horror of his skin. It is a wonder he has said so little about this, since he was covered with boils. He said his skin grew black and fell from him. This must have resulted from the sores. Then his bones burned with fever. As in verse 17, the pain went deep within him. The fever may have been the result of the boils or perhaps other ailment.

Finally, Job said he felt no joy but only grief. A harp and flute would be used to express joy and sing songs of happiness. But Job had no use for them except to express songs of mourning and weeping. Nothing he could think of could give him any cause for joy. Everywhere he looked in his life he saw only grief.

We may grieve with him over his incredible hardship. Yet even so he was not justified in his complaints against God.

Job 31

Chapter 31 - Job Concludes by Again Affirming His Innocence

Job had described his joy and blessings before his suffering began, then he described how terribly he had suffered. Now in this last section of his final speech, he defended his uprightness and integrity in the strongest of terms. In so doing, he ended his part of the debate by contradicting as strongly as he could the friends' claim that he was suffering as punishment for his sins.

Remember that, if Job did live in the Patriarchal Age, the laws God had revealed to him may be somewhat different from what we have today under the gospel.

31:1-4 – Job controlled his desires because God knows our deeds.

Job here began a lengthy statement of his innocence before God. He did not claim to have lived a sinless life, but he did claim that he had corrected the errors he knew about. Therefore he knew no reason why he should suffer as a punishment of sin.

Specifically, he said first that he controlled his desire for women. Even with young, attractive women he guarded his gaze so as to avoid lustful desires. Note that this was a commitment Job had made – a covenant with his eyes. He knew, as Jesus later taught, that looking lustfully at a woman is wrong of itself and can lead to adultery or other sinful acts (Matthew 5:28,29). This is a lesson many today need to learn. Note that Job mentions especially young women. The point is that some women more easily become a temptation, not necessarily because they are sinful in appearance but just because for various reasons some women are more attractive to a man than other women.

Job further described his reasons for such conduct. He described the allotment or inheritance God would give to men for their lives. If a man lives wickedly, God will bring destruction and disaster on him. One cannot hide from God to avoid such punishment, for God knows all about our lives. He sees our ways and counts our steps. This is true.

Job nowhere denied it. But it does not follow, as the friends argued, that this was always true in this life. The punishment may come later.

31:5,6 – *Job stated that, if honestly evaluated, he would be shown to have avoided falsehood.*

As Job affirmed his uprightness, he stated specifically that he had not walked in falsehood or deceit. He claimed, if he were honestly judged – weighed in honest scales – God would know that he walked in integrity.

Of course, the implication is that the friends were not judging him honestly. They were not judging righteous judgment (John 7:24), for they accused him of sin simply on the basis of the fact that he was severely suffering, though they had no real proof he was guilty of the things they accused him of.

31:7,8 – *Job affirmed he was willing to suffer if in fact he had departed from God's way.*

If Job had turned aside from proper conduct, he would not refuse to be punished for it. If he had followed his own eyes – i.e., his own desires or lusts instead of God's will – or if his hands were stained with spot or iniquity of sin, he would be willing to suffer.

Job then began a series of consequences or punishments he agreed he should suffer, if he was guilty of the errors he described and was accused of. Here he said he would be willing to lose his harvest, if he committed sin. Let others take his crops and eat them, so he would go hungry. Such statements amount to a form of curse, but in any case Job is affirming his willingness to suffer if he was guilty. But he denied guilt.

31:9-12 – *Job denied having committed adultery and acknowledged that would be worthy of suffering.*

Having already denied that he looked after young women (verse 1), Job here denied that he had committed adultery with a neighbor's wife. He had not allowed himself to be enticed by such, nor had he waited outside the door (as for a chance to meet with her).

He agreed, had he done such, that would be wickedness and iniquity worthy of punishment. He said that, if he was guilty, then let other men likewise have sexual relations with his wife (bowing over her and "grinding" with her). Of course, it would not justify her unfaithfulness, but he would be worthy of such a punishment. Such evil on his part would be like a consuming fire bringing destruction. He would deserve to lose his prosperity. Note how people need to learn this today.

Adultery has been forbidden in every age. Note that by referring to his "wife," Job implies that he was monogamous.

31:13-15 – Job affirmed further that he had treated his servants fairly.

He claimed that he had not been guilty of mistreating a servant, male or female. He had not despised them when they raised complaints to him. This does not mean, of course, that he always agreed with every complaint, but he was willing to listen and offer a fair judgment. He did not refuse to grant justice to their legitimate issues.

He explained that God had made the servants, just as surely as He had made Job. They were all equally human beings. The fact he was rich and they were poor did not change the fact they were made in the image of God (Genesis 1:26,27). So if he mistreated them, that would be acting as though he was worthy of better treatment than they were, just because he was rich. He asked how he could answer God if he had so acted. Note how the wealthy today need to learn this.

Note that Job affirmed his faith in God as the great Maker of all men.

31:16-18 – Job affirmed that he had helped the poor, widows, and orphans.

Job argued that he had not kept the poor from achieving their desires or having what they needed. He had not kept widows from obtaining what they saw and needed. Of course, such needy people might not achieve all they desire, but it would not be Job's fault. He did not contribute to their problems.

Instead, he had helped many. If he saw one who was fatherless, Job himself would not eat without sharing with the orphan. Instead, he acted as a father in caring for the orphan, and since he had been born he had given guidance to widows (to meet their need).

This contradicted the accusation the friends made against him in 22:9.

31:19-23 – Job had helped those who needed clothing and had not harmed the orphans.

Job likewise said he was willing to suffer if he had failed to help those who were perishing from cold or exposure because they lacked clothing. Instead, such people blessed him in their hearts, because they were warmed by the fleece of his sheep. That is, from his own sheep he had provided them with wool for clothing to warm them, so they honored him for his goodness. This contrasts to 22:6.

Nor had he raised a hand to harm an orphan when he saw he had help in the gate. The gate again appears to refer to the judges or city leaders who made judgments at the gates of the city. If Job saw that he could get a judgment in his favor from the judges (so he had "help in the gate"), he would not take advantage of it if the result would harm an orphan. Again, despite some vagueness, the point is clear: he would not take unfair advantage of those who were defenseless and needy.

If Job had failed to do right in such cases, then he agreed he ought to suffer. His arm should fall or be torn from his shoulder socket. Job claimed that he greatly feared punishment or destruction from God if he mistreated other people. He could not endure the magnificence of God – i.e., he could not stand to do such wrong things because he knew God's greatness and majesty. He was restrained, not just by his concern for others, but by his knowledge that such conduct would displease the great God whom he served and feared to alienate.

31:24,25 – Job had not trusted in wealth.

Though Job had been an extremely wealthy man, one of the greatest in that region, he here denied that he had placed his hope and confidence in gold. Nor had he rejoiced in his wealth and great gain. The point must be in contrast to trusting in God. He did not view his wealth as the source of his joy or meaning in life. Nor did he think he could do as he pleased, disregard what was right, and yet continue to prosper without suffering consequences because he was so rich.

Many rich people believe their wealth gives them special privileges so that they don't have to follow the rules other people follow or that they will not suffer consequences if they do wrong. Job tried to live despite his wealth by the same principles he would follow had he not been wealthy. See 1 Timothy 6:17-19. This also responded to an implication the friends had made in Job 22:23-25.

31:26-28 – Job had not worshiped the heavenly bodies.

Many people in that day worshiped the sun, moon, and stars. Many still practice astrology, which attributes to the stars and planets the power to control events on earth and predict the future – powers the Bible says belong only to God. But Job denied he was guilty.

When he saw the sun shine or the moon in its brightness, he did not allow this to entice him to secretly kiss his hand toward them as an act of worship. This would be similar to our idea of blowing a kiss, except that it would be done to honor the heavenly bodies as deities. Kissing an idol was a form of worship (compare Hosea 13:2). Some today kiss the toe or foot of a man or idol as a form of religious honor.

Job agreed that any who did such would be guilty of iniquity and deserving of judgment, for they would have effectively denied the true God who rules above all. So it is today when people worship idols or practice astrology or kiss the foot while bowing to religious leaders to honor them religiously.

31:29,30 – Job had not even cursed his enemies or rejoiced when they suffered.

Many people think they will gladly harm their enemies if they get the opportunity. Those who have a somewhat higher morality may realize they should not harm their enemies, yet they rejoice when someone else or some event of nature causes their enemies to suffer.

But Job followed the highest standard, which we too ought to follow, in that he did not even rejoice when those who hated him suffered evil or destruction. In fact, he would not even sin with his lips by pronouncing a curse upon an enemy, hoping for harm to befall him.

Nothing here means it is wrong to hope that those who wrong us will be punished by God or by proper authorities if they will not repent of their errors. God's people recognize such punishments are proper. But we should not seek to do personal vengeance, nor should we rejoice in things that are truly bad for such people. Rather, we would hope they would repent and avoid God's wrath.

31:31,32 – Job had been hospitable to strangers.

No traveler had been forced to spend the night in the street, for Job was willing to open his doors to lodge them. As a result the servants in Job's tent asked who had not eaten at Job's table. The implication is that everyone knew that Job was hospitable to strangers.

In the Patriarchal age and for some time afterward, travelers often had no place to stay at night. If people did not take them into their homes, they would have to stay in the streets, where there was danger from robbers, etc. (Genesis 18 & 19). So those who were hospitable like Job would take such people in for their good and protection. Job affirmed it was known that he practiced such hospitality.

31:33,34 – Job claimed he had not secretly tried to hide his sins.

Adam had tried to cover his sin by hiding from God (Genesis 3). Job denied that he had practiced hidden sin or tried to hide his iniquity as by covering something in his garment. He did not keep silence or practice sin secretly behind the door of his house out of fear of other people finding out about his error.

These verses are difficult. But again the general point is clear. The friends had accused Job of terrible sins. He here denied that he even had sins that he had hidden from others so they would not find him out. He is not denying that he ever committed sin. But what sins he had committed he had confessed and made right before God and those whom he had wronged. He did not try to avoid the consequences by hiding and denying his guilt.

31:35-37 – Job again wished for God to hear his case and answer him.

Job had repeatedly asked for a chance to present his case directly to God and let God explain to Job what he had done wrong, if anything. The implication is that Job is sure he would be vindicated in such a hearing. So again, here he wished for God to hear and answer him.

Verses 36,37 are difficult. But the idea seems to be that he wished God's charges against him were written down in a book. Then Job was convinced he would accept the verdict and carry it around on his shoulder or wear it like a crown. This seems to me to imply that he is sure the verdict would vindicate him and he would be glad for all to see it. He was convinced he could approach God like a prince and let God declare what steps Job had taken. The result would demonstrate to the friends and to all that Job was not suffering for sin.

31:38-40 – Job had not taken land or profited from it by mistreatment of others.

Job closed his speech by affirming that he had obtained land and grown crops without ever mistreating others. If his land and its plowed fields could speak, they would testify that he had not cheated anyone. He had not taken land or used it without properly paying those who had owned it. He had not eaten the fruit of the land without properly recompensing those to whom the land had previously belonged or those from whom he rented it or the workers who labored in his fields. To do any of those things would have been to eat the fruit of the land without properly paying for it.

Had he been guilty of such things, then he again agreed he deserved to suffer. The land should produce thistles and weeds instead of wheat and barley. The point, as repeatedly, in this chapter is that Job was not unwilling to suffer if he deserved it. Rather he had gone to great lengths to refute the friends' accusations against him. He knew of no reason why he deserved to suffer as he was.

This ended Job's speeches to the friends. He did not speak again until he faced God and God had answered him as Job had so repeatedly expressed a desire for him to do.

Job 32

Chapter 32-37 – Elihu's Speech

32:1-3 – Elihu began to speak because he was upset with Job and his friends.

Job's friends then ceased the debate. This does not mean Job had convinced them that he was right, but he did convince them that nothing they could say would change his mind that he was righteous. They had argued that he was suffering because he had sinned. He did not really know why he was suffering, but he was sure he had not sinned. So they ceased trying to respond.

Another man named Elihu had been present throughout the discussion. This makes us wonder how many other people may have been listening to the discussion but never spoke at all. Some people believe that a fairly large number of people had gathered to hear the discussion, though we are never told who was there. Nevertheless, we know that one man besides Job and his three friends was there, because he began to speak.

The record says that he was the son of Barachel the Buzite, of the family of Ram. Abraham's brother Nahor had a son named Buz (Genesis 22:20,21). I am not sure this refers to that same man, but if it is that would date Job as sometime after Abraham. Ram is unknown elsewhere. Yet still this tells us little about Elihu. Nothing else is mentioned about him in any other Scripture. We are not told why he was present nor why he had not earlier been mentioned.

In any case, he finally spoke up because he was angry with both Job and his friends. He did not believe either of them were correct. He believed Job was wrong because he justified himself at the cost of criticizing God. He believed the friends were wrong because they had accused Job of sin but could not prove it or answer Job's arguments.

Five views of Elihu's speech have been suggested:

(1) It does not fit the record but was added by uninspired men. Such a view impugns the integrity and inspiration of Scripture (2 Timothy 3:16,17).

(2) It simply continues and repeats the views of the friends. But it is the longest speech in the book. Why include it if it adds nothing new?

(3) It expresses a view closer to the truth than the friends had expressed and it properly corrects some of Job's errors, yet it still does not fully reach the truth.

(4) Elihu's speech prepares the way for God's speech. He is not right in all that he says, but he helps introduce some new and helpful ideas.

(5) Elihu has the truth so he properly and correctly resolves the issues that Job and his friends could not solve. But if this view is correct, why did God bother to speak? We will see that there are points Elihu states that are demonstrably incorrect.

In my view, only #3 and #4 of these points are reasonably close to being correct. Elihu did correctly disagree with both Job and Job's friends. He was right that Job had unjustly accused God in order to avoid admitting sin himself; God later accused Job of this (40:8). And he was right that the friends should not have condemned Job when they could not prove him to be guilty or answer his arguments. And whereas God did rebuke both Job and his friends, yet He never rebuked Elihu. And though Job disputed with the friends, he never responded to Elihu.

So some have concluded that Elihu was the only human speaker who was correct. However, it is also true that God never commended Elihu nor said he had spoken truth. He simply never mentioned him at all. And while Job never argued with Elihu, he also never agreed with him. He simply said nothing at all. Further, remember that Job's wife had spoken obvious error, yet God never rebuked her either.

It is possible that Elihu was as close to the truth as any of the speakers. Yet we will see that his view was in many ways similar to that of the friends. He made no wild accusations against Job based on alleged past errors; yet like Job and the friends, he appeared to think God was responsible for Job's suffering. Yet I am unable to find where he really states a better view of the reasons for Job's problems than Job had stated. Nevertheless, he must have had something worthwhile to contribute to the discussion, else God would not have inspired the writer to include six chapters of his message.

It appears to me that we are left to decide whether Elihu is right or wrong by making an honest evaluation of what he said in comparison to the facts. So let us consider and evaluate his views.

32:4-7 – Elihu had waited to speak because of his youth.

Elihu was much younger than Job and his friends, so he had not spoken earlier. He correctly thought that those who are younger should respect the wisdom of those who are older and should carefully consider their views before expressing a contrary view. This is an admirable attitude and worthy of imitation today. Note that Job was already old, yet lived another 140 years after these events (42:16).

However, when he saw that the three friends could not answer Job – even though he thought Job should be answered – he became angry and determined to speak.

32:8-12 – Men who are respected and aged do not always have better understanding in every situation.

Having waited for the older men to resolve Job's problems, Elihu concluded that it is not always true that older people are always right. Man is the result of Divine creation: man has a spirit (given by God) and likewise has understanding given by the breath of God. This seems to mean that everybody has some degree of intelligence given them by God to understand and judge for themselves what they observe, whether it is right or wrong. In this case, Elihu's understanding led him to conclude that these men, though older, had not presented proper reasoning.

He had paid close attention to what the older men had to say, and he had weighed their reasoning. But none of the friends could really answer Job's arguments, even though they said repeatedly that he was wrong. So Elihu determined that he had to speak. He could not sit quietly by when he was convinced Job needed to be answered, but the friends had failed.

32:13-16 – Elihu claimed he would use arguments different from those the friends had used.

Verse 13 is difficult for me. As punctuated in the NKJV, it appears to mean that the friends might say they had found wisdom – i.e., they had answered Job adequately, despite the fact that neither Job nor Elihu thought they had done so. But Elihu claimed that only God, not man, could defeat Job's reasoning. Perhaps the point is that the friends had depended on human reasoning and experience to try to answer Job (which was true) and had failed (which was also true). But it would take more than human wisdom to disprove Job's views. If this is correct, it may be that Elihu was claiming to have some Divine information superior to what the friends had.

Elihu had not been in the discussion up to this point. He did not intend to use the same arguments or reasoning that the friends had used unsuccessfully. And Job had not yet said anything in response to Elihu. This implied that he intended to start the discussion over from a different perspective than either Job or his friends had considered. He is right Job had made some errors and that the friends had failed to prove him wrong. So a fresh approach might be a good idea. But does he have a better solution? We will see.

The friends had tried to answer Job, and now words had failed them. They could think of nothing more to say, despite the fact they had not convinced Job. Elihu had listened, hoping they would come up with better arguments. But the friends had given up. The implication was, as stated in the following verses, that he did not intend to wait any longer. It was his turn to speak.

32:17-20 – So Elihu must speak or he would burst!

He had determined that the time had come for him to express his views. He would give his answers. He was full of things he thought needed to be said. His spirit compelled him to speak.

He compared himself to a wineskin that was about to burst. Perhaps the idea is that the grape juice had been sealed in a wineskin to keep it from fermenting. But somehow it had become contaminated and had begun to ferment, giving off gases that must be released. If there was no vent, it would burst. So he felt like he was about to burst, if he did not express his views. He had to speak to find relief.

Many of us at times have felt like this. And so far so good. But none of this proved that he really had the answer to Job's problems.

32:21,22 – He intended to speak without partiality or flattery.

Elihu affirmed that he did not intend to show partiality to either Job or to his friends. He would attempt to avoid being influenced by personal relationships, friendships, or anything other than simply who was right or wrong according to the facts. We do not know what ties he had to any of the men in the discussion, but he affirmed he would try to overlook such influences.

He also would try to avoid flattering anyone. He would not speak to gain favor from either Job or his friends. He did not want to please or displease anyone simply to gain their good will or for other personal advantage. He claimed he did not know how to do that, and if he had tried he would have displeased God.

This is a fine start to his speech. Most of what he said was true and/or admirable. However, the fact remains that he was uninspired just as surely as the three friends were. And neither God nor Job ever evaluate what he says. This makes it hard for us to evaluate his speech. We will observe whether or not he ever comes up with an approach to Job's suffering that agrees with the Scriptures we now have revealed to us.

Job 33

Chapter 33 - Elihu Continues His Speech

33:1-4 – *Elihu claimed to speak from no ulterior motive but to speak as a man like Job.*

Having introduced his speech with a lengthy statement of his motives and reasons for speaking, Elihu then turned to speak in response to things Job had said. He began by urging Job to listen, assuring him that he spoke from an upright heart and pure knowledge. This seems to mean that he believed his motives were pure, he had no ulterior motives.

He then stated that the Spirit of God had made him and God's breath had given him life (compare 32:8). This affirmed his faith in God as Creator. Perhaps it also expressed that Job did not need to fear him. He was a human being like Job. Job had expressed fear that God, being so great, would not listen to his reasoning, etc. But Job could reason with Elihu man to man.

33:5-7 – *He then urged Job to reason and discuss with him without fear.*

He claimed that he was willing to listen to Job's reasoning and his response, if Job would lay out his arguments before Elihu. He would act as a spokesman with God. He was formed of clay, a man like Job (compare Genesis 2:7). So Job did not need to be afraid to express his views to Elihu. He would not be forceful or overbearing in his approach (as perhaps the friends had been).

This all seems intended to assure Job that Elihu was trying to be reasonable and would consider what Job had to say. There was no reason for Job to fear to discuss with him.

The reference to a "spokesman" before God sounds like an offer to be the mediator that Job had hoped for (9:33). But other translations translate differently. The ASV says simply, "I am toward God, even as thou art." So perhaps, in context of the surrounding statements, the point is just that Elihu viewed himself as having a similar standing as Job in relationship to God and speaking to God. He would do his best in speaking as God would want him to speak.

33:8-11 – He cited Job's view that God was punishing him even though he was innocent.

He began by recounting statements from Job that he objected to. He would not make unproved accusations (as the friends had done), but would refer to statements he himself had heard Job make.

Job had claimed (Elihu said) that he was pure, innocent, without transgression or iniquity. Nevertheless, God counted him as an enemy, finding occasion to punish him (as by putting a criminal in stocks), watching his paths (as to find fault).

This is a basically accurate account of things Job had said and which we too have criticized as we have studied them. Job had repeatedly affirmed his innocence, and in this he was basically correct. But he had stated or implied that God was punishing him as though he was guilty, when really he was innocent. This too Job had said. He could explain his suffering only as unfair punishment from God that he did not deserve. See 10:7; 13:24,27; 16:9; 19:8; 30:21.

33:12,13 – Elihu claimed that Job should not have accused God because God is greater than man.

He said Job was not righteous in claiming that God was punishing him though he was innocent. He then said he would respond to Job's statements.

He stated that God is greater than man and, as such, does not have to give account or explain to us what He says or does or why He does it. So why should Job contend with Him or criticize Him?

This may explain why God did not respond to Job as Job had insisted that He should: God does not have to explain Himself to us. He is above us. We should accept His actions as right, simply because He is God, regardless of whether or not we understand why He so acts. This is similar to the explanation God Himself later gave to Job.

It may also be that we are not capable of understanding God's reasons if He did try to explain them. In any case, we have no right to demand an accounting or explanation. God may choose to explain some of His reasons, but He does not owe us an explanation. If we truly believe in His goodness and wisdom, we must learn to simply accept what He says as true.

Note that Elihu did not really resolve the issue Job had. He did not explain whether Job was wrong in claiming that he was innocent or whether he was wrong in blaming God for his problem. He simply seems to say that Job had to be wrong on one end or the other. Job's view could not be correct, because it blamed God for something that God would never do. This is a correct conclusion, though it still left Job with no real answer to his problem.

33:14-16 – Elihu said God may speak to man in various ways, including visions and dreams.

Job had demanded that God explain to him why He treated Job as He did. So Elihu tried to explain some ways that God may have given Job helpful information, but Job just did not realize God was doing so. God may speak in ways that men simply do not perceive or realize that He is speaking.

For example, God may speak to man by means of a dream or a vision during the night. As the man sleeps, God may open his ears and seal instruction to him.

This was one of the ways that Eliphaz had earlier claimed that God had revealed to him his view of suffering – 4:12-16. As in our notes on that passage, it is true that sometimes, before the Bible was completed, God did use dreams or visions to reveal His will. Examples would be Joseph, Nebuchadnezzar, Jacob, and others (Genesis 28:10-22; chapter 41; Daniel chapter 2,4; etc.). But not all dreams or visions came from God. Some are natural and prove nothing whatever. Some are nightmares that are best disregarded. And this is not a method God uses at all to reveal His will today. A dream or vision would require a direct revelation, which ceased with the ending of spiritual gifts (see 1 Corinthians 13:8-11).

33:17,18 – Dreams could turn people from perishing by the sword or the Pit.

The information received in a dream, might lead a person to realize that a course of action is wrong and may turn him so that he does not do evil or act from pride. The result may save the man's life or save him from the Pit (death, the grave).

Elihu seemed to be saying that maybe God had spoken to Job in such a way, and Job had simply not realized that this was a message from God. Maybe God had not ignored Job's request for information as Job thought that He had. Of course, Elihu had no proof that God had done this. He was just suggesting it as a possible explanation for why Job may have incorrectly thought that God had refused to speak to him.

33:19-22 – God may chasten a man with pain.

Another way that Elihu suggested that God may communicate with a man is by sending pain to chastise him. This may result in pain that he suffers in his bed, even strong pain in his bones. He may abhor to eat even the best food. His flesh may waste away so that his bones stick out. As a result he approaches death (the Pit) as one approaches an executioner.

This appears to be an obvious description of the kind of thing that Job was suffering. And surely it is true that God sometimes does bring such suffering on His people as a means of chastising them – see

Hebrews 12:5-11. But though Elihu seemed to imply this was Job's case, he never directly states it as a fact but lists it as a possibility. We know from the introduction of the book that it is not Job's case. His suffering was not a chastisement by God but an attempt by Satan to get a righteous man to sin. The fact that Elihu suggested something that so obviously appeared to fit Job's case implies in my view that he still did not know the cause of suffering that did fit Job's case – at least he never suggested the real cause.

33:23-25 – *A mediator or messenger may help the sufferer understand.*

This seems to continue the point of verses 19-22, in which Elihu described suffering as a means by which God may chastise a man (as Job was suffering). In such a case, a messenger or mediator may help the sufferer understand what is happening. Commentators discuss at length the nature of such a messenger. The term can refer to an angel or to an inspired human or simply to an uninspired human who possessed wisdom sufficient to help the sufferer understand. Such would be a very rare individual – one among a thousand.

Such a messenger may explain to the sufferer that God is truly upright and gracious, despite how the man suffers. If God then is willing to deliver the man from the Pit (compare verse 22), he may ransom the man. As a result, the man will be healed. His flesh will become like that of a child and he will return to health as in his youth.

Again, this did eventually happen to Job, but that does not prove that he was suffering for the reason Elihu described here. One wonders if Elihu considered himself to be the kind of mediator or messenger he described here. Did he think he could explain to Job what was happening and help him restore his relationship with God? If so, though there is some truth in what he said, he would be mistaken in failing to see the suffering as a temptation from Satan. Furthermore, Elihu did not state what the ransom would be that would solve Job's problems.

33:26-28 – *The man who has been chastised and instructed can solve his problems by repentance and confession.*

Having received chastisement and then instruction from a messenger who speaks God's word, as in the previous verses, the one who is suffering may pray to God. God will then delight in the man, rejoice in him (in his face), and restore righteousness to the man. The man who has suffered and been restored can then admit to other men that he sinned and perverted what was right, and found such a course of conduct to be unprofitable. God will then redeem his soul from the Pit, and he can see the light of life (compare verse 30).

Again, all this can be true in some cases. And Elihu does not directly accuse Job of suffering because he has sinned. But if that is not the point, then what is the point of the discussion? He began by addressing Job specifically, and the whole debate has been about why Job is suffering. So if the application is not that this is or may be the reason why Job is suffering, then why bring it up? To the extent that the context implies that this is why Job is suffering – and therefore the solution is for Job to repent and confess his sins, so God will restore him – to that extent Elihu too is as mistaken as the other friends. His accusations are not as definite or extreme, yet the implications are the same, it seems to me.

It is true that Job has said things in the discussion that he will eventually need to repent of, but this is not the cause that originated his suffering. Therefore, repentance and confession would not necessarily remove the cause of his suffering so that he would find relief. While it may be that Elihu has some insights to add, frankly I find it hard to avoid the conclusion that Elihu is also wrong about his view of why Job is suffering.

33:29,30 – In this way God may restore a man from the Pit two or three times.

The process by which God does this for a man may be repeated. It may not be just once that one suffers as chastisement for his sins and is relieved because he repents. It may happen more than once – Elihu suggests two or three times. God would, as a result, restore the man's soul from the Pit, thereby enlightening him with the light of life. This appears to refer to restoration of his spiritual well being, not just freedom from suffering.

33:31-33 – Elihu then challenged Job to respond to what he had said.

It appears at this point that Elihu asked Job for a response to what he had stated. He said Job should respond if he had anything to say, because Elihu did want to justify Job. But if Job had no response, he should continue to listen while Elihu spoke further. Apparently, Job had no response, since Elihu did continue in the following chapters. (I don't take this as proof Job was convinced, though he may have been considering Elihu's points further.)

As stated above on verses 26-28, Elihu still seemed to believe that Job was suffering because of sin and that the solution was repentance. So how did his statement differ from that of the three friends?

(1) He did not directly accuse Job of sin. He suggested it as a possibility, but did not definitely accuse him and did not make up a bunch of unfounded specific sins.

(2) He based his objections to Job's statements on things he himself had heard Job say in the debates, not on assumed guilt simply because Job was suffering. This was both true and helpful, as shown by

the fact this is exactly what God later said about Job. Job had sinned in his speech, though this was not the original cause of his suffering.

(3) His approach was gentler and more respectful. In particular, he seemed to really want to help Job, not just condemn him as the friends had done.

(4) His discussion of chastisement for sin is interesting, even though it did not fit Job's case. He showed that suffering can teach useful lessons; it is not just a punishment for sin.

Nevertheless, Elihu's approach still seems to me to assume that Job was suffering because of sins he had committed. This is not true, as chapter 1,2 showed.

Job 34

Chapter 34 - Elihu Continues His Speech

34:1-3 – Elihu called on wise men to test his words.

Elihu continued his speech by calling on men of wisdom and knowledge to listen carefully to his words. He said the ear tests words like the palate tastes foods. In other words, one can know whether or not something tastes good when he considers it with his tongue. So wise men can tell whether or not an idea is good or bad when they hear it. So he called on them to test the wisdom of what he was saying. (One wonders whom he addressed unless there was an audience that had gathered to hear the discussion.)

34:4-6 – He called on them to consider whether Job was correct in saying he was righteous but God had taken away his justice.

Elihu specifically called upon men to consider whether Job's speech was just or good. They should then know and choose what is right.

His specific accusation was that Job claimed to be righteous and would not deny being right, despite the incurable wounds he was suffering. He claimed that he was without transgression, yet God had taken away justice. In effect, he had accused God of injustice by punishing Job when he was innocent.

It appears that this was a fairly accurate assessment of Job's statements, for which we too have criticized Job. Job had made statements that he was convinced he was innocent (compare 13:18). And in this Job was correct; he was innocent as the first two chapters showed. However, Elihu does not appear to agree that Job is innocent (see verses 7-9).

And Job had appeared to say that God had been unjust by punishing Job when he was innocent (27:2). There is no doubt that he repeatedly said God was the one punishing him. To the extent that Job had said such ideas, to that extent he was wrong. And we have pointed out that much of his error is based on the fact that he was convinced God was punishing him, when that was not the case at all.

34:7-9 – Elihu charged Job with walking with wicked men because he said there was no profit in delighting in God.

Elihu accused Job of drinking scorn like water. In context this does not seem to mean that other people were scorning Job but that he was stating scorn or mockery of God. I.e., he was willing to accept into himself the practice of scorning God. Compare 15:16 where Eliphaz spoke of a man drinking iniquity like water – i.e., he accepted it into his life as easily and quickly as he would drink water. So here Elihu accused Job of being willing to make mockery of God a part of his life. In this Job was, Elihu said, putting himself in company or fellowship with men who work iniquity and wickedness.

Specifically, he accused Job of having said that there is no profit to a man in delighting in God. This was not really what Job said that I know of. It may have been Elihu's conclusion from what Job said. Job had said that men may suffer in this life even though they served God, so there may be no apparent benefit in this life of serving God. And that may be true in a physical sense. And Job had said that God was causing him to suffer as if he was a sinner; in this Job was incorrect. But it does not follow that Job meant there is no benefit at all in serving God. There may be – and in fact there are – many benefits in serving God that do not fall in the realm of physical blessings in this life. Job did not describe any of these, and it is possible that he did not think about them; but I am not aware that he denied them either.

So here it seems to me that Elihu went too far. He overstated his case even as the friends had, though he may not have been as extreme as they were. He seemed to base his case on things Job himself had said, rather than arguing (as the friends had) that people suffer in this life only because they are guilty of sin. Nevertheless, I am not aware that Job had scorned God, let alone doing it as easily as drinking water. Nor had he really said there was no benefit in serving God.

34:10-12 – Elihu argued that God would never do wickedly nor pervert justice.

Elihu then attempted to refute the views he had attributed to Job. Specifically, he argued (to those men of understanding that he had addressed in verse 2) that God does not do wickedness or commit iniquity. In particular, He would never pervert justice. These errors are so far from his character that they are impossible for Him to do. In this, we must agree with Elihu. And to the extent that Job had impugned God's justice, to that extent he deserved such a rebuke.

Elihu also added that God repays man according to his work, and makes man to find a reward according to his way. This too is true, and is evidence of God's justice. In fact this is almost a good definition of justice. But the point that Elihu failed to address is that the friends had argued that God gives this reward in the form of physical suffering or blessings in this life. Did Elihu agree with the friends in this? If so, he was as wrong as they were. If he did not agree with this view, then it appears to me that, given the context, he should have said so.

34:13-15 – *God has such control over the earth that it would perish if He ceased to sustain it.*

Elihu then praised God's power to sustain the earth. He asked who had given God charge or appointed Him to rule the world. The answer of course is that no one did, except God Himself. He took that role upon Himself as the Creator of the world and the Supreme Power of the universe.

Having created the world, God's Spirit must sustain it. If God decided to withdraw His Spirit, all flesh would perish and all people would return to dust. We continue to exist only by the sustaining power of God. This is absolute truth, taught in other passages, which no one in this discussion would have denied (Psalms 33:6; Colossians 1:16,17).

The point appears to be that no one should question the manner in which God rules. Especially none should accuse Him of injustice. He is the sovereign Ruler and should be respected, not criticized.

If this is the point, then it is surely true. Yet is does not resolve or even touch the issue between Job and the friends as to whether or not God physically punishes men for sin in this life, so that Job must have been suffering for his sins.

34:16,17 – *Is it proper to condemn a just ruler?*

Again, Elihu called upon those who have understanding to listen to his words. He then asked if government should be in the hands of one who hates justice. Of course, the obvious answer is that it should not be, though it often is among human rulers. But he then proceeded to ask if the most just Ruler of all – God Himself – should be condemned. Is it proper to accuse Him of injustice, as Elihu thought Job had done?

Again, Job had implied that God is unjust, and Elihu was right to call him to account for it. However, Job never said that God "hates" justice – only that he was not convinced that God had done justice in Job's case.

34:18-20 – *God is not partial to even the rich and powerful, for they all die.*

Elihu further argued that people should not insult rulers or nobles, as by saying they are worthless or wicked. The implication is that such is not appropriate for people to do (though we should say they have sinned when in fact it is true).

But God does not hesitate to call down princes or rich people. He has made them all, so why should He fear to rebuke even the mightiest of men? He is truly just and will not favor the rich over the poor. They die in a moment in the middle of the night; they are taken away without a hand (probably meaning without any human attack upon them, they die by unseen forces).

Elihu here seems to have continued making the point that God is just. He would never be unjust, as Job had implied. He shows partiality to no one, not even the greatest of men. So to call Him unjust is itself unfair and disrespectful.

34:21-23 – God sees all men so they cannot hide their sins.

Elihu further said that God sees everything people do. No sinner can hide from Him. His eyes are on men's ways, seeing all their steps. No darkness can hide them, not even death. God does not need to have a man stand before Him in any formal judgment in order for God to know about His life.

This is also true and is taught in many other passages. See Proverbs 3:19; Psalm 139:1-4,6-12; 147:4,5; John 16:30; Matthew 10:29-31; 6:8,32; 1 Kings 8:39; Romans 11:33,34; Isaiah 55:8,9.

If the point is that God is just in rewarding men for the conduct He sees in them, that is also true. But again, the rewards are not necessarily given during this life in the form of physical blessings or problems. Elihu still does not deal with that basic issue.

34:24,25 – God's knowledge of man may lead Him to punish them regardless of their power.

Seeing men's lives so they cannot hide (verses 21,22) enables God to know their works. On this basis he may break men down and set others in their places. He does not fear them; they cannot overpower Him. No matter how mighty they may be, He can punish them by overthrowing and crushing them, even in a night. "In the night" could mean that it can happen suddenly, without long drawn-out delay; or it could mean that not even the darkness can prevent Him from seeing and punishing (compare verse 22).

So Job should not accuse God of being unjust. But again, this often does not happen during this lifetime.

34:26-28 – God punishes wicked men for turning from Him and oppressing the poor.

Elihu continued defending God's justice by saying that God will strike or punish wicked men and will do so openly so that others may see. Such people, by their wickedness, have turned their back on God. Instead of repenting from their sins, they do not consider their ways. They do not examine their hearts and lives to see whether or not they are pleasing to Him, because they don't care.

Included in their conduct is mistreatment of the poor and afflicted. The cry of these mistreated people comes up before God and is one reason why God determines to punish these wicked men.

Yes, God sometimes does punish wicked men in a way that men see it. But He does not always do it openly. Often He waits till after this life is over. So He is just. Is Elihu saying this explains what has happened to Job, like the friends claimed? If so he is completely wrong;

nothing here explains anything about what happened in Job's case, for Job was not suffering for sin.

34:29,30 – God also gives quietness that none can change.

In the previous verses Elihu had described how God punishes the wicked. Here he stated that God also may give quietness or freedom from suffering to men. If God gives that, who can change it? Or if God turns away to hide His face from a nation or a man, who can change that and see Him anyway? The result is that the hypocrite or evil man cannot reign and ensnare people against God's will.

The point seems to be that, whether God punishes a man for evil or does not cause trouble, what can people do about it? Whichever God chooses, it is to prevent evil people from causing trouble for others.

And again there is some truth in what Elihu says. God sometimes causes hindrance and defeat to those who are wicked, and He sometimes is quiet and turns his face from people. But the fact remains that He often does not punish evil people in this life, and often the hypocrite does reign and ensnare the people with no apparent retribution in this life. And nothing here resolves the conflict between Job and the friends.

34:31-33 – Can a man determine the circumstances of God's reactions to his sins?

Elihu then asked if any man – specifically applying this to Job – would have the right to say to God that he has suffered enough for his sins. He has learned his lesson and will sin no more. Would that require or compel God to then deal with the man according to the man's terms? Can a man tell God that his punishment has been bad enough, he has learned his lesson, and then expect God to quit punishing him just because he disavows his error? He then calls upon Job to make a choice and give answer.

Of course, the answer is that no man has the right to tell God what punishment he should receive for his errors. We cannot say we are sorry and therefore He must stop punishing us. This is how children often act toward parents. They think, if they say "I'm sorry" for having done wrong, then the parents must not punish them. The point is that the one in charge – God in this case – must decide the punishment, not the offender.

At the risk of sounding like a broken record, I say again that these are true statements. But how do they apply to Job? The clear implication is that Job is suffering for his sin and is complaining that he is suffering too much so God should quit punishing him. But none of that is the fact. Job is not suffering for sin, so how do these statements help him? I fail to see how Elihu can be correct in his statements as applied to Job's case.

Note that, apparently, the translation of the Hebrew is difficult in these verses.

34:34-37 – Elihu then indicted Job for speaking like a wicked man and adding rebellion to his sins.

Elihu then again called on men who have wisdom and understanding to consider his statements. The conclusion, he said such men should reach, is that Job spoke without knowledge and without wisdom. That was surely correct, especially in Job's accusations that God had been unfair. And God later taught Job so that Job agreed he had spoken without wisdom (38:2; 40:3-5; 42:3-6).

Elihu then claimed that, if Job's conduct was thoroughly put to trial, the conclusion would be that Job had answered like a wicked man would answer. In addition to his other sins, Job had added the sin of rebellion, multiplying words against God. (Compare 35:16.)

But here again Elihu goes far beyond what the evidence dictates. Yes, Job said some things he should not have against God. But accusing Job of rebellion seems to harsh to me, especially considering all that Job had suffered and knowing that he did not deserve to suffer at all.

But above all, by saying Job "added" rebellion "to his sin," Elihu was clearly saying that Job had sinned in the first place and was just making it worse by his accusations against God. This is the sense in which Elihu thought Job answered like a "wicked man." But this just reaffirmed the friends' view. Elihu, like the friends, has concluded that Job had sinned to begin with and was now just making it worse by his arguments. Yes, his arguments at times were wrong, even sinful. But what "sin" was this adding to? There was no sin to begin with; God Himself said so. Elihu has gone too far and his view too is wrong at least in this regard.

Job 35

Chap 35 - Elihu's Speech Continued

35:1-3 – Elihu charged Job with saying he was more righteous than God and there was no profit in serving God.

Continuing his speech, Elihu asked Job if it was proper for him to say (by implication) that he was more righteous than God. How had Job said this? He had in essence accused God of being unjust, yet he had claimed that he himself had done no wrong. So he was not wrong, but God had done wrong. The result was an indirect claim that he was more righteous than God. (Hailey thinks the point is that Job has claimed he would be fair in the areas where God has been unjust. The point is the same.) Good point, so far as I can see, and something Job would have to consider.

He then accused Job of having asked God what advantage or profit he would receive by serving God above what profit he would have received by not serving God. That is, if he served God he suffered just the same as those who did not serve God, so where was the advantage in serving God?

Again, Job had indirectly asked this, but only as pertained to material advantages in this life. And it may well be that there is little or no material advantage in serving God. Faithful servants of God often suffer as much or more than the wicked, and the wicked often prosper as much or more than the righteous (compare the story of the rich man and Lazarus in Luke 16). But Job, the three friends, and Elihu all seemed to largely overlook the issue of possible rewards or punishments after life. So Job's question involved correct implications regarding this life, but it neglected life after death.

35:4-8 – Elihu asked what benefit or harm we can give God by being righteous or wicked.

Elihu claimed he could respond to the arguments that he had attributed to Job in verses 1-3. He first said that the clouds of the sky are much higher than are people like Job. They are essentially unattainable. God put them there.

The point seems to be: What can we do to benefit or harm the clouds? Likewise, God is above our ability to harm or benefit Him. If we do many evils, what harm comes to God as a result? If we do many righteous deeds, how is God benefited or profited? Of course, the answer is that we cannot ultimately either harm God or profit Him physically, though our sins grieve Him and our goodness pleases and honors Him. But Elihu says that what a man does may cause harm or benefit to another man (verse 8).

If we were to grant all this to be physically or materially true, what is Elihu's point? Is he saying, we should not expect benefit from God for our service, since nothing we do benefits God? If so, then why should we expect punishment from God when nothing we do harms Him? This would deny that God has reason to ever punish or reward anyone.

Or is he saying that the evil we do harms ourselves and others (not God), and the good we do benefits ourselves and others (not God), so that is the harm or benefit that follows from our conduct? Again, if that were the only effect that followed, then God Himself would neither punish nor reward the wicked; the only effects would be what we enjoy or suffer in this life.

The whole discussion appears to look only at the physical or material effects of our conduct. It ignores rewards after death, which perhaps these people did not yet understand. It seems to ignore the fact that, as our Creator who loves His creatures, God chooses out of His own goodness to reward us if we serve, and out of His justice to punish us if we sin.

In any case, I fail to see the validity of Elihu's argument as an answer to Job. Either I am missing the point, or he has not really answered Job's concerns.

35:9-12 – Men seek God's help but fail to appreciate His blessings and the exalted position He has given them.

Elihu then pointed out the inconsistency of crying out to God for help, as Job was doing, when we fail to give thanks for His blessings. When they suffer, men seek God's help. But when they have reason for singing God's praises (because of God's blessings), they do not seek to honor Him as Maker. God has taught us to be more understanding than brute beasts or birds of the heaven. We ought to understand and appreciate God's blessings more than do the animals.

But the implication is that men often do not appreciate God more than do the animals. So when such people cry out for help, God does not come to their aid, because they are so proud.

Again, I'm not sure I see the point. Perhaps Elihu was describing the pride and ingratitude of men who – as men often do – call upon God for help in trouble; but then when things go well, they don't praise or thank Him, but think they are doing just fine by themselves. They show no more understanding or gratitude to God than do brute beasts. This is pride and ingratitude. Why should God help such people when they do cry to Him?

People surely do often act this way. But if that is the point, then what is the application to Job? Is Elihu accusing Job of pride and ingratitude? Is God not delivering Job from trouble in answer to his prayers because Job had failed to appreciate the blessings God had give him before the troubles began? Many people do so act, but there is no evidence Job was guilty. He had diligently worshiped God according to chapter 1, both when things went well and when they went badly.

Or perhaps Elihu is not talking about Job so much as about other people who disregard God. Job seems to think that God had not justly punished such people as He should. He let them go on living without suffering, whereas he allowed Job to suffer. So, Job implied God was unjust. If this is the point, then Elihu's next words respond to it.

35:13-16 – God does not answer empty prayers; wait for His justice.

Elihu concluded that God does not hear or regard empty talk. Perhaps this referred to the cries of those who, as in verses 9-12, show pride and ingratitude so their prayers are empty. Elihu said that God may not have punished such people or taken notice of their folly. But He will do so. You may not have seen it yet, but God is just (despite Job's claims). Men must be patient and wait for God to deal with matters justly.

This too is true, though none of these men fully grasped it. The punishment of such people comes after death in eternity. We must patiently wait for God's judgment. But all of the men in this discussion appear to think the judgment should come in this life; Elihu seems to think they should just wait and eventually they would see the proud man get his due. Just because God has not done much yet, that does not mean He will never deal with it. Be patient and give Him time.

So Elihu claimed Job had failed to see this point, so he was in error. If this was the point, then it is true that Job had failed to see that God may yet produce justice. And God did eventually bring justice even during Job's lifetime. Yet none of the disputants seem to see the possibility of rewards and punishments after death.

Job 36

Chapter 36 - Elihu's Speech Continued

36:1-4 – *Elihu continued saying he would fetch knowledge from afar and speak on God's behalf.*

Elihu then continued speaking by asking them to bear with him (he does seem a bit long-winded). He claimed he would bring knowledge from afar, speak words on God's behalf, and ascribe righteousness to his Maker. Doubtless this was intended to contrast to Job's criticisms of God's justice. Elihu had properly rebuked Job for his harsh statements implying God had been unjust. He here appears to continue to seek to defend God's righteous judgments.

He affirmed that his words were true, not false. Then he stated that one who is perfect in knowledge was with them. This statement is connected to his claim that his words were true, and makes it sound like he is claiming perfect knowledge for himself. Such a claim would be incredibly egotistical. The word "perfect" may simply mean completely true. So perhaps he was simply claiming complete truth for his statements. Even so, it surely comes across as egotistical, especially in light of how he had humbly introduced his speech by expressing respect for the older men he was addressing.

However, as an alternative view, we note that he proceeded to describe the understanding of God in verses 5ff. So perhaps verse 4 is just an introduction to God's perfect knowledge.

36:5-7 – *Elihu said God is mighty, wise, and just. He cares for the afflicted and the righteous but does not preserve the wicked.*

In his defense of God's righteousness (verse 3), Elihu claimed that God, who is so mighty, is specifically mighty in understanding and does not despise anyone. This appears to contrast to Job's implications that God was punishing him without cause. Elihu argued that God would not be guilty of so despising anyone.

Elihu then proceeded to argue that God does do justly. He does not preserve the life of the wicked, but gives justice to the oppressed. This appears to mean that God will punish the wicked (or allow them to be punished) and will protect the oppressed.

Further, Elihu argued that God does not withdraw His eyes from the righteous – i.e., He keeps watch over them. He does see and know when they suffer. He cares for them. They are exalted to places of authority, such as kings or rulers.

I find it hard to see how this significantly differs from what the friends had argued. As with what the friends said, it is true that sometimes evil people suffer in this life and good people are protected or exalted to high position. But anyone with eyes can see that often it is simply not so in this life, and the Bible confirms that it often is not so. Evil people do often appear to prosper and come to rule and be exalted, where good people often do suffer and endure oppression. Job was not the only good man to have so suffered throughout history.

Job's problem is based entirely on the fact that he apparently believed things should be the way Elihu here describes them; but in fact they are not that way, neither in Job's life nor in the lives of others around them. If Elihu was describing ultimate destinies in eternity, we should wholeheartedly agree. But what he describes simply is not always true in this life.

36:8,9 – *When people suffer affliction, God is telling them about their sins.*

Elihu continued that, when people find themselves bound in fetters and held by the cords of affliction, God tells them that they have acted defiantly. He informs them about their transgressions.

Again, where does this differ from the view of the friends? He claimed that God informs those who suffer that they have sinned and been defiant. It almost sounds as though suffering is God's way of teaching people that they are guilty.

Surely it is true that suffering is ultimately here because people have sinned. But it does not follow that the person who is suffering is himself suffering the consequences of his own sin. It could be that he suffers as a result of someone else's sin or because of the sin of Adam and Eve that brought pain and suffering into the world. It could even be, as in the case of Job himself, that Satan is tempting the person to try to get him to suffer.

If Elihu was claiming, as it surely sounds as though he was, that people suffer because they have sinned, then his statement simply is not always true. And in the context of the conflict between Job and his friends, Elihu appears for all the world to have taken the friends' false view.

36:10-12 – If people will turn from sin, they will prosper; if they disobey, they will perish.

Elihu proceeded to further advocate the friends' view by saying that God used suffering to open the ears of men to hear His instruction. He was commanding them to turn from iniquity. If they heed and obey and serve God, then their lives will be spent in prosperity and pleasure. If they disobey, they will perish by the sword in their ignorance.

Yes, it is sometimes true that suffering leads people to humble themselves, repent, and devote themselves to God's service. If they do, they may receive blessings in this life. And it is sometimes true that those who will not obey God will suffer or even die as a result.

But the claim that this is generally true in a material or physical sense is nonsense! Many people do evil without suffering in this life as a result. If they suffer and don't repent, they do not always die or even continue to suffer. And if they choose to serve God, they surely do not always have prosperity and pleasure. Elihu has virtually argued for the gospel of health and wealth! It is simply not true as a generality.

The only sense these statements are true is if one views eternal rewards after this life. Yet nothing indicates that Elihu had any such idea in mind. To the extent that Elihu was attempting to explain Job's suffering or was applying his statement to Job, he was completely wrong.

36:13-15 – The hypocrite dies in wrath, but God delivers the poor.

Elihu continued by claiming that those who are hypocrites (especially those who disobey God despite suffering – verse 12) are storing up wrath. God binds them (with suffering), but they do not turn to Him for help. Instead, they continue in sin and as a result they die in youth among others who are perverted.

However, those who are poor and suffer affliction, God delivers them and opens their ears in (by means of?) their oppression. That is, if as a result of their suffering, they listen to the message God is trying to convey, then He delivers them from their suffering.

The obvious application in the context is that Job was suffering because of sin, just as the friends had claimed. If he continued to deny his guilt and refuse to repent, he would die in sin. But if he would heed the message of rebuke that God was sending through the suffering, then God would deliver him.

See the notes on verses 10-12 above. It all applies here.

36:16-18 – Elihu applied his argument saying Job was suffering the judgment due the wicked.

As translated in the NKJV, these verses appear to remove any doubt about whether or not Elihu intended to apply to Job the things he has been saying. He addresses "you," which in context can only refer to Job. However, apparently the original Hebrew is quite difficult to translate here. While the following comments are my conclusion, it is possible that alternate translations would weaken the conclusions.

Elihu said that God would have brought Job out of his dire distress and put him in a place with no restraints and with a table filled with richness. This appears to be a follow-up on his reference in verse 15 that God would deliver the poor from their affliction. So he would have delivered Job, if Job would have listened and repented (verse 11).

But instead, Job was filled with the judgment that was due to those who were wicked. Judgment and justice had taken hold of him, just as Elihu claimed would happen to those who did not obey or heed the lesson God intended to teach them by suffering (verses 12-14).

The reference to "wrath" in verse 18 could refer to Job's wrath or God's wrath. If it is Job's wrath, then the consequences Elihu described would come on Job because he had expressed anger at God's mistreatment of him. If it is God's wrath, then God brings wrath on the wicked. In any case, Job should beware lest God destroy him with one blow. No amount of money could ransom Job and help him avoid such a catastrophe in such a case.

To the extent that the above conclusions are correct, there can be little doubt that Elihu is defending the same basic view as the friends did. His claim was that Job's suffering would have been relieved had he repented. But he continued to suffer because he was receiving the consequences that are due to the wicked, and if he continued he would be completely destroyed.

36:19-21 – Elihu warned Job not to turn to iniquity because of his affliction.

Elihu here continued to address Job ("you"). As in verse 18, he continued saying that neither power nor riches – no matter how much Job possessed – could enable him to avoid distress. (The ASV uses "cry" instead of "riches," but the point is the same: no power Job had could prevent his suffering.)

He admonished Job not to seek or desire the night, since people there are cut off. This could mean Job should not try to hide from God (as in darkness) or hide the evils he committed. Or it could mean Job should not turn to evil and sin (as in verse 21). But perhaps it is a reference to such speeches as chapter 3, where Job had sought death. In that case, Elihu would be urging him not to seek such darkness, since it involves people being cut off.

He admonished Job not to turn to iniquity, for it appeared that Job had allowed his suffering to lead him to choose sin. I.e., rather than suffer his affliction patiently, he chose to sin in speech and attitude. This is true to some extent, as God later said. However, the implication that he had been guilty all along is simply not true.

36:22-26 – Since God is so exalted, who can teach Him or convict Him of wrong?

God is so highly exalted above men in power (including the power of understanding – verse 5), who could teach Him, tell Him what way to act (assign Him His way), or prove that God had done wrong. Instead, men should magnify or praise Him for His work, as men have sung about Him in the past.

All men see the evidence of God's power (as in creation). But we look from afar. This could mean we don't understand like He does, because we are not intimately involved in His decisions. We do not know all the facts or reasons why He acts as He does, as per verse 26. God is so great and exalted that we cannot really understand Him, just as we cannot discover how many years He has existed.

Here we can agree with Elihu, and Job had erred in this regard. He had tried to say God had mistreated him or been unjust, and if God would talk to him, he could show God He had done what Job did not deserve. Elihu's point, well taken, is that no one can prove God has done wrong. God is so high above us, He cannot do wrong. And how could mere men prove He had done wrong? Instead, we should praise and honor Him.

36:27-29 – God's greatness is demonstrated in rain and storms.

Elihu proceeded to give an illustration of God's power and exalted wisdom. He described how God draws water up into drops in the mist, from which it condenses as rain. The clouds come closer to earth as they become heavy with water, and they pour their rain on man. Elihu asked if anyone could really understand how this process works as the clouds spread out and from that canopy over us comes thunder.

Yes, men may know some about how all this works, but we don't understand it well enough to duplicate it or to control it. As has been said for generations, "Everybody talks about the weather, but no one does anything about it." Exactly. God created the forces that lead to storms. And He can use those forces for His purposes as He chooses. If we cannot understand them, what right do we have to question or dispute what He does in any other realm?

36:30-33 – Elihu then described lightning and thunder in the storm.

Elihu then described how God scattered light upon it (the canopy?), covering the depths of the sea. This could refer to the sun shining through the clouds, as it sometimes does. Or perhaps it may more likely refer to the lightning of verse 32.

God uses these forces of nature in the storms to bring judgments on people or to provide food. This is an interesting thought. Rain and storms provide the water so necessary for the growth of our food, yet the same process can become terribly destructive and bring great hardship on men. Elihu calls this a judgment, in harmony with his view that suffering is judgment from God (see earlier comments).

He then figuratively described God's hands as covered with lightning that He uses to strike where He wills. Likewise, He uses thunder to declare the coming of a storm to animals such as cattle. (V33 is apparently quite difficult of translation.)

The point throughout these last verses is to demonstrate God's great power, which is beyond man's ability to understand. It follows that we are not wise or powerful enough to question or doubt God's wisdom in any of His works. This was surely a lesson Job (and we) needed to learn. God Himself will make similar points to Job when He speaks.

Job 37

Chapter 37 - Elihu's Speech Concluded

37:1-3 – Elihu continued to describe how a storm reveals God's power.

Elihu had begun, in the previous chapter, to describe the power of God as demonstrated in the lightning and thunder. He continued in this chapter saying that such power caused his heart to tremble. So it does for most people today. Children are often frightened of storms; and when storms become truly fierce, as in tornadoes or hurricanes, all people of good judgment tremble.

He described how, when we listen, the thunder seems to rumble from the mouth of God, sent forth along with the lightning to the ends of the whole earth under heaven. There is probably no place on the face of the earth that can escape the power of storms; they occur in some form everywhere on earth. Of course, the thunder does not really come from God's mouth, but it does result from His power as demonstrated in His creation.

The point is simply that such power causes us to stand in awe. Surely men could not create such power. We can use the power God has created, as in the destructive power of an atomic bomb. But we are just harnessing power that God Himself created. We are yet unable to control the storms Elihu described.

37:4-6 – God sends the snow and rain, as well as the thunder.

Elihu continued describing the thunder that roars after the lightning. It sounds like the majestic voice of God when His voice is unrestrained. God also tells the snow to fall on the earth, or He sends either gentle rain or heavy rain. All this comes from God and demonstrates His power, not because He necessarily always directly chooses when, where, or how fiercely a storm will strike, but because His power created the laws that cause storms.

In short, Elihu said that God does great things we cannot comprehend. And this is the point of the whole description. Storms and many other forces of nature, being created by God, show how great His power is and how humble and weak people are by comparison. Who are we to question Him or argue with Him (as Job had done)?

37:7-10 – *God sends cold winds and ice, weather that hinders men and animals from their normal activities.*

The effect of such powerful storms is that men are able to observe God's work when they see their own hands are sealed. Animals also are compelled to seek refuge in dens or lairs; they cannot face the force of the storm to go about their daily activities. In a similar way, Hailey explains that sealing up man's hand refers to compelling man to close his hands so that he cannot work. No matter how important a man's work may be, there are times when he is restrained from it by the weather. Instead of going about our own work, we must sit back in awe as we observe God's work.

Whirlwinds (such as hurricanes) may come with storms from the south, and cold and ice come from the winds of the north, bringing ice, freezing even broad waters like lakes and wide rivers. This may appear to come on the wind as if from the breath of God; or perhaps Elihu meant that it occurs because God's voice commands it.

God's creatures are subject to God's laws and God's power. No matter how great a creature we may think we are, we must submit when God proves His power. We may consider ourselves to be above the wild animals, but we are no different from them in that we are all subject to God's power in a severe storm. We cannot ignore the impact of it and go boldly on with our work, unaffected by the weather.

37:11-13 – *God sends precipitation for His purposes.*

So Elihu had described that God saturated the clouds with moisture and scattered them for His purposes. They are turned by His guidance and do what He commands over the face of the whole earth. Again, this occurs according to the laws God established, though of course by His providence He can control the outcome to meet special purposes.

Elihu listed three reasons why God might cause such a storm to come at any given time or place. It may be for the benefit of the land – i.e., to provide the moisture the land needs to grow crops and plants. Or it may be for correction – i.e., some events of nature are a punishment upon sinners or a reminder of the power of God, so that men ought to see that power and repent of sin. Or it may be an act of mercy. In the case of a storm, the mercy might refer to providing needed rain to grow the food needed by men and animals.

Elihu did not state which of these he believed fit any particular case – specifically if a storm came in Job's case. We would have to agree that storms did accomplish these various purposes in that day and still would do so today. However, it may be that no one looking on would know which applied in any specific storm.

37:14-16 – Elihu asked if Job understood the works of God.

Here Elihu began to make application of his descriptions of God's power in the storm. He urged Job to listen and consider such works that God has done. He asked if Job knew when God would send or how He would cause light to shine of His cloud (lightning). Did he know how clouds are balanced and how God does these wondrous works, since He is perfect in knowledge? (I am not quite sure the significance of the reference to the balance of clouds, unless it simply means how they manage to float in the air.)

Here we see the point Elihu has been leading up to. God is perfect in knowledge and great in power, far beyond man. How can man understand such knowledge or power? If we cannot understand or begin to duplicate such works, why should we set our understanding in array against His as though we have the power to prove that He made a mistake?

37:17,18 – Elihu asked Job to explain a warm wind or the spreading of the skies.

Continuing his application from the previous verses, Elihu asked if Job can explain why a wind from the south brings heat making one's clothing hot and quieting the earth. This probably refers to an extremely hot wind, the Sirocco, which occurred in those areas causing people and animals to seek shelter and cease their work. Did Job understand why such extremely hot winds occur? We now may have some concept of what causes winds with heat convection and circulation, but the fact remains that we cannot control the wind or duplicate it in any degree even approaching what God can do. And what causes such extremely hot winds, what triggers them that they come at certain times? This is the thrust of Elihu's question.

Likewise, he asked if Job had spread out the skies along with God. He describes the sky as a strong metal mirror, which it may appear to be like on some hot days.

These are the very kind of questions that God Himself eventually asked Job. Did Job know how God did these things? Was He there when God formed these aspects of nature? In short, is it proper for Job to question God when God is obviously so far above him?

37:19,20 – Elihu called on Job to explain how a man could speak to God.

Job had claimed that he wanted to speak to God and present his case before Him. He implied that He could convince God that God's treatment of him was undeserved and perhaps even unjust. Elihu here appears to be applying his discussion of the storm and the power of nature to ask Job if he really thought he could speak to God in such a manner.

Could he tell other people what to say to Him? Darkness (lack of understanding?) leaves us unable to prepare to properly argue with God. Can we tell God our ideas (as though ours could improve upon His)? If we try to do so, we will be swallowed up – i.e., overwhelmed by God's obvious superior power and wisdom.

This is the point to which Elihu has been leading. Job was wrong to think he could criticize God's judgments. No one can win an argument with God!

37:21,22 – God is brighter in splendor than the sun in the sky.

Elihu compared God in His splendor to the sun in the brightness of the sky, when the wind has cleared away the storm clouds. Not only did the great storm demonstrate the power and wisdom of God, so does the brightness of the sun when the clouds have gone. Men cannot stand to even look at the sun on a clear bright day. (The ASV translates somewhat differently, but the point is similar.)

In the same way God's majesty is so awesome when He comes in splendor that we cannot possibly stand up to Him (coming from the north in golden splendor appears to be just an expression for His greatness). Why should any wise person challenge such a God to a debate or criticize His decisions?

37:23,24 – Elihu concluded that God is so great in power and justice that men should fear Him.

This is Elihu's conclusion. God is great or excellent in power and judgment and His justice is abundant. We cannot find Him ("find him out" – ASV), probably in the sense that we cannot understand Him or find out His reasons for what He does. Contrary to Job's complaints, God does not oppress men nor show partiality to men as though men were wise enough to deserve special treatment from Him. Instead, we ought to fear and respect Him.

Conclusions about Elihu's speech

Valid points

(1) Elihu was correct in rebuking Job for criticizing God's justice and for claiming that He could convince God if he could speak to Him. Elihu has correctly concluded that God is just, fair, and impartial. He has not mistreated Job. God has his reasons for what He does, but as illustrated by the storm, the sun, the sky, and God's other great creations, man simply is too weak and foolish to understand why God does what He does. This is exactly the point God Himself will soon make to Job.

(2) Unlike the friends, Elihu did not make up a list of sins that he imagined Job had committed, then accuse Job without proof.

Weaknesses or errors

Like Job and the friends, Elihu discussed at great length the reasons why Job was suffering. So it is fair to consider how accurate his views were.

(1) Elihu still appears to me to hold the view of the friends that God will punish wicked men in this life for their sins. Several times he implies this is the reason why Job is suffering. His main arguments are directed toward Job's views. At no point do I recall him criticizing the friends for believing suffering is the consequence of personal sins. Rather, his criticism of the friends appears to be that they failed to make good enough arguments for their case, whereas he thought he could make better arguments (32:3-5).

(2) At no point does Elihu acknowledge that the righteous do suffer in this life despite the fact they have no sin to be punished for. In particular, at no point does he acknowledge the truth that Job had been righteous and that his suffering was not caused by his sins. Job had stated repeatedly that this was the case, and he spoke the truth. Yet Elihu never acknowledged that Job was correct on this point.

(3) At no point did Elihu or any speaker suggest that Job's suffering may have been a temptation to get him to sin, rather than a punishment for his sins.

It follows that, while Elihu may have corrected some of Job's errors, I conclude that he did not yet come to the full truth and in fact was himself mistaken in some of his views. In any case, it is clear to me that Elihu too did not have the answer to why Job was suffering.

Job 38

Chapter 38-42 – God's Speech

Chapter 38 - God Begins His Speech

38:1-3 – God questioned Job calling on him to answer, saying Job spoke words without knowledge.

At this point the men had all expressed their views, so God then spoke to correct the errors that remained to be corrected. He first spoke to Job out of a whirlwind. This refers to a destructive tempest, not necessarily a tornado – Proverbs 1:27; Hosea 8:7 (compare Elihu's description?).

He challenged Job by asking who it was that was confusing the truth by speaking words without knowledge. Since He was here addressing Job, and considering Job's eventual response, it seems obvious that He was rebuking Job. Eventually He would rebuke the friends even more severely than He did Job, yet Job had said things that show lack of knowledge. We will note specifics as we proceed.

So God called on Job to answer some tough questions He had for Job. Job had called for an opportunity to present his case to God; he had called on God to answer his questions about the treatment he had received. But instead God first asked Job some questions. The court case Job had wanted was about to begin, but instead of Job calling God to account, God called Job to account. Before God was through, Job would learn that he should not have criticized God (9:34,35; 13:20-24).

God's speech appears to have one intent: He sought to show that He is infinitely superior to Job and to all men in wisdom and power. So, it is foolish for men to question what He does. No man could possibly understand what God does well enough to improve on it.

Job had apparently passed the test Satan had said he would fail. He had not renounced God but had maintained his determination to serve God. Nevertheless, he had questioned and even impugned God's treatment of him in a way that showed a lack of confidence in God's wisdom and justice. God intended to show that no one has the right to criticize Him, for no one has the wisdom to improve on anything He has done.

38:4-7 – *God asked where Job was when God began the foundations of the earth.*

He compared the work of creation to a man building a house. Men understand the concept of building a house, so God asked, in effect, if a man could build the earth! Note that everything God here describes is symbolic, not literal. Where was Job (or any of us) when God laid the foundation of the earth (it has no foundation in the sense of resting on anything, but its inner substance rests as a foundation for its surface)? Who measured it out, checked it with a plumb line to be sure it was built properly, secured its foundation, and laid its cornerstone? The stars of the morning sang at the creation and the sons of God (surely angels, since no man was present) shouted for joy. (It is unclear whether the stars of morning refer to actual stars that were made at creation or are simply another term for the angels.)

Obviously no man could build the earth. The whole point is that only God could do such a great work. Man can make some impressive structures, but compared to the earth, they are nothing. So, what right does man have to question how God has done anything? Seeing we cannot begin to make such things as He has made, how can we criticize His work and think we could improve it?

God's word has often used creation as proof of God's existence and power. We should remember this when we wonder whether God exists or when we begin to doubt how great He truly is. See Genesis chapter 1; Exodus 20:11; Psalm 33:6-9; 102:25; 89:11; 90:2; 104:5-9,24-28; 19:1; 24:1,2; 95:5; 146:6; 136:5-9; 8:3,6-8; 148:5; Jeremiah 10:12; 27:5; John 1:1-3; Acts 14:15; 17:24; Isaiah 42:5; 45:18; 40:26; Hebrews 1:10; 11:3.

38:8-11 – *Next God asked Job about the creation of the sea.*

He compared the forming of the sea to a birth. People can understand how an animal or person is born (though it is quite beyond us to create such a process, let alone fully understand all about it). But who gave birth to the mighty oceans? It is surrounded by clouds and darkness like the clothes of a baby when it has been born. The shores set its limit so that it can come only so far and no further. God claimed He did this. What man can do such a thing or question God's doing of it?

Men build mighty cities by the ocean, but how impressive are those cities compared to the sea itself? Who can stop the force of the ocean? At times it has overwhelmed cities, as in a typhoon or hurricane. What man at such a time can stop that raging force? But even the sea can overwhelm the land for only a time, then it must recede. God created the sea and has ultimate power over it. What right then has man, who can neither create nor control the sea, to question God?

38:12-15 – Next God asked Job if he possessed power over the sunrise.

Does man command the morning or have power over the sunrise? Would the sun obey our command to rise or to refuse to rise when we tell it to? The sun rises and sheds it light to the ends of the earth, causing the earth to appear to take shape where its shape was unclear before.

Yet Someone made the light and caused it to shine. If man cannot do it, then He who did it must be greater than we. Who are we to criticize Him?

The references to the wicked could mean that, as wicked men prefer to do evil at night, the sunlight catches them and reveals them. So, they are defeated in their evil plans, yet they themselves are not benefited by the light. (Compare 24:17.) They are like cockroaches or bugs you try to shake out of a rug.

38:16-18 – God asked whether Job understood the sea, death, and the size of the earth.

God then asked if man has power to enter the very depths of the sea and search out its depths? In Job's day, no one had gone deep into the sea at all; and even today we have not fully explored the greatest of its depths, nor will we ever fully understand. (Or perhaps God was asking if Job had investigated the origin of the sea. Did he know where the sea came from?)

God then asked about death. What man understands the real nature of death? Death is a mystery to man, always has been and always will be, simply because no one can come back to tell what is on the other side. We know things that cause death, but we do not know what is beyond those gates. In truth, we do not really understand what life is, so how can we really understand loss of life?

Can man really understand all there really is to know of the earth? The breadth of the earth could refer to its immense size. Job would have had no idea. Today, men have traveled around the earth, but even so who can really understand it greatness? And who can understand all about it?

God challenges Job to answer if, as a man, he can know all this. The answer of course is that we cannot. If not, what right have we to criticize the One who made it all?

38:19-21 – Then God asked Job about the dwelling of light and the paths of darkness.

What does man really know about the origin of light and darkness? Can we tell where or how it originated? Scientists have studied light for years, yet today our ideas of the nature of light are only theories. We can cause light to shine in a small way at times to light our work. But we surely cannot control the ultimate source of light. We do not know what caused it to begin, let alone do we have the power to make a sun. We can neither cause nor prevent sunrise or sunset.

God asked Job if he understood all this because He was there when light was created (Gen. 1). Of course, no man was alive when God made the light, so surely no one in Job's day (or our day) could be so old as to have witnessed it. If so, then who are we to doubt the One who did make it?

38:22-24 – God then asked Job about snow, hail, and wind.

Who has seen the source from which snow and hail come? Has Job or any man ever gone to the treasury where snow and hail are gathered to send them to earth? Of course, we know, and Job would have known, that snow and hail come from clouds. But he had never gone there to see them being formed. Today with airplanes we can go to the clouds, but that still does not answer God's real question. Furthermore, can man understand, let alone control, the sending of the light or of the wind?

The point is, what man can really understand the processes by which weather forms, let alone what man has the power to really control the formation of snow, hail, wind, and other forms of weather? We may understand some aspects of weather better than people did in Job's day, but we still cannot explain the ultimate origin of it. Compare Joshua 10.

It has repeatedly been said that man talks much about the weather, but no one ever **does** anything about it. We are powerless before it. But God can send it for His purposes whenever He chooses.

(The reference to trouble, battle, and war is difficult. The reference could be simply to times when men face hardship and difficulty, such that precipitation even as snow would be helpful. Or perhaps the idea is that God can use weather even to affect the outcome of wars and battles, if He so chooses.)

38:25-30 – God asked Job about thunderbolts, rain, ice, and frost.

He asked if Job (or any man) can control flooding or thunder. We may make minor provisions to use or somewhat control these. But they can overwhelm and defeat us at any time, and we surely do not cause them. We may understand some aspects of them, but we do not ultimately understand the origin of weather, let alone can we control it.

What about rain? Does man cause it to rain or to cease raining? Of course not. It even rains in places where there is no man present to cause it or to benefit from it. Yet God sends the rain to benefit the plants and animals. Is there a man who is the source of this, like a father to a son?

And what about ice and frost? Did a man create it or give birth to it? Water freezes hard as stone; even great bodies of water freeze over solidly. Can a man control the weather so as to cause that? If not, who does it? It must be one far greater than man. Does it make sense then for us to dispute with Him about what He does?

38:31-33 – Next God asked Job whether he understood stars and constellations.

Can man capture and tie up the heavenly bodies or constellations (Pleiades, Orion, Mazzaroth, the Great Bear), or cause them to appear in season, or tell them where to go? In other words, does man really understand what causes the heavenly bodies to move as they do? We observe their movements and can even predict them. But who can have power to control them? Surely not man, but only God. So, why should we dispute with Him?

38:34-38 – God asked Job if he was able to send lightning, thunder, and rain.

Who can call out to the clouds and make them give weather as we want it? Can we call for rain when we want it and expect obedience? Can we send out lightning and make it do our bidding? Jesus controlled the storms by a few words, proving God's power. This amazed His disciples, because men know we can do no such things.

By what source do we have even the wisdom we have? Have we wisdom to even count all the clouds and cause them to pour out their contents on earth, when the ground is hard and needs to be softened? Knowing we have no power over any of this, should we criticize God who made it all?

38:39-41 – God then asked if Job could provide food for animals.

Can we satisfy the hunger of wild animals or provide for the offspring of great animals of prey? They crouch and lurk in dens and lairs, lying in wait to capture their own food, but man cannot meet their needs.

What about birds? Can we feed them or provide for their hatchlings? God not only made them, He made the means for them to have their needs met. What could we do about this if He had not made it? To criticize Him is foolish.

Job 39

Chapter 39 - God Continues His Speech

39:1-4 – God questioned Job about how mountain goats and deer give birth.

God continued, as in chapter 38, questioning Job regarding his knowledge and power, compared to that of God. He asked if Job knew about the birth of wild goats or deer. Could he look at one and say when it will give birth? We don't even know precisely for humans!

Of course, it is not just a question of when they do these things. The point is: do these wild animals need men in order to reproduce their kind? Did men teach them how to do it and give them ability to do it? The truth is (verse 4) that they give birth to their young who then grow strong and healthy eating grain till they are able to leave their parents; and they do all this without either man's knowledge or help, let alone did man create them able to do such a thing.

Men sometimes help some domesticated animals to give birth and even to conceive, but these wild animals live apart from men on mountains and other inaccessible areas. And even domesticated animals came into existence and possess ability to reproduce, yet men did not create them with such ability. Who gave them this ability? It must have been God. If God did so, but we cannot, who are we to argue with God?

39:5-8 – God then asked about wild donkeys and onagers who live freely in the wilderness.

What about other wild animals such as wild donkeys, etc. (onagers are a form of wild ass)? Who gave them the power to be free and to live in wild, barren places, away from cities, refusing to be driven by men as domesticated animals? Some animals seem to prosper living with men and serving them. But others scorn areas where men live and refuse to be driven. They sustain themselves quite well living in the wild.

Did man make them and give them these abilities? Obviously not. Man cannot begin to make any such animal; and if he could make it, man would surely have made the animal to do service to man. But man does not control such animals, let alone did he make them. Obviously God made them.

39:9-12 – Could Job control or tame the wild ox?

While man may occasionally get some wild animals to do his bidding, wild oxen roam free to do as they please. They will not serve men or be fed by men. They will not serve to plow or do work for men. Though they are strong, they cannot be trusted to work for man like some domesticated animals.

This is not to say that men cannot tame some animals. Obviously many of them are quite tame and useful. But the point is that many animals cannot be made to be useful because of their nature. Where did such animals come from? Again, obviously man did not make them. The fact they exist, but man cannot make them, and they exist independently from man, proves there must be someone greater than man who made them. Why then criticize that One who is greater?

39:13-18 – The ostrich lacks wisdom, yet it laughs at men and horses.

Man may capture them and put them in zoos. But generally they are independent from men. They have wings that they wave proudly; but unlike other birds, they cannot use their wings for flying but only to help in running. They do some rather foolish things, such as leaving their eggs where they could be crushed by being stepped on. Then they are harsh to the young ones when they hatch, almost as if the offspring were not their own. They so act because God did not give them the wisdom to see the folly of their conduct.

Yet for all this apparent folly, they have advantages such as strength and speed sufficient to escape men when they try to capture her even on horseback. Man is not so great, therefore, as he thinks. Even the animals, that God made inferior to man in intelligence, yet have some superior abilities to man. And surely man cannot make them. Why then criticize Him who did make them?

39:19-25 – Did Job give strength to the horse that is mighty and valiant in battle?

The horse, unlike the animals previously considered, is often a domesticated animal. But such an animal! How could man have made him? Did we give him his strength, clothing his neck with thunder? He is stronger and braver than us! He can not be frightened off like an insect. He is a source of terror to others.

He is strong and brave, for example, in warfare. He does not fear to charge into battle, though weapons of all kinds surround him. Horses were often used in warfare in those days. They seemed at times to anticipate the coming of a battle from sounds and smells; yet instead of fleeing, they desire the battle!

Where did such an animal come from? Surely not from man. Only God could have made it.

39:26-30 – Did Job give the hawks and eagles their ability to see sharply and fly swiftly?

The hawk and eagle are great birds of prey. Did man give them the power and ability to fly? Can we teach them how to do so? Do they live as they do because man told them to so do? They dwell in high places in crags of rocks where men and other enemies can hardly reach them. From there they can see their prey with tremendous eyesight able to see afar off. They provide food for their young, where they can eat the flesh and blood of slain animals.

Could man claim the power to make such animals as these? If not, why criticize Him who did make them?

God's point throughout continued to be that Job (like all men) was weak and unlearned compared to God. He cannot do the great things God has done in creation, therefore man is vastly inferior in strength and wisdom. So why should we claim, as Job had, that we can sit in judgment on how God conducts the world?

Note also the great variety in the animals God has discussed. He has not made just one or a few that are similar, but many very different. All this shows His great power and wisdom.

Job 40

Chapter 40 - God Continues His Speech

40:1,2 – God rebuked Job for contending with Him.

God was obviously displeased with Job's comments about how God handled his problems. God has gone to great lengths to show His superiority to man: that man is totally unable to do the things God has done in nature. If God is so superior, man has no business trying to tell God how to do things or implying God has done it poorly. This is the real point of all of God's speech.

So God asked Job here if he still thought he has the right to rebuke God and contend with Him.

40:3-5 – Job responded humbly confessing that he would no longer speak as he had.

Job was beginning to learn what God was teaching. He saw his vile lowliness compared to God. He laid his hand over his mouth and made no attempt to respond to God. He admitted he had spoken, but here said he would say no more.

God would yet say more, and Job would speak yet even more humbly of himself than this. But at this point Job admitted that he had said things about God that he should not have.

We will see that God will strongly disagree with the friends. But at this point He was bringing Job to a fuller understanding of why he should not have been so critical of God. Note, however, that God did not explain to Job why he actually had to suffer so.

40:6-9 – God further asked if Job would condemn God to justify himself.

God spoke again to Job, this time from the whirlwind. He challenged Job to answer the questions God would put forth. Here God spoke most clearly His criticism of Job. He asked if Job would annul His judgment and condemn God that he may be justified. God asked if Job had an arm like God or could thunder like God: did he have the power of God? If not, how could he question God?

Job was not rebuked for defending his own integrity before God. He was correct when he claimed that he was not suffering as punishment for his sins, contrary to his friends arguments. The problem was that, in justifying himself, Job condemned God and spoke against God's judgment. He criticized God as though God had done wrong in His treatment of Job. This, in a simple statement, was God's problem with Job.

See some examples in 10:1-7; (16:11-14?);

40:10-14 – God challenged Job to show his own glory and punish the wicked.

God continued to call on Job to compare his power and wisdom to that of God. God was beginning again to describe what He had done, but He did so challenging whether Job could do the same.

He called on Job to adorn himself majestically (perhaps figuratively: show how great you really are). He called upon Job to see if he could right all the wrongs in the world. Would Job bring his wrath on all proud people and make them humble? Would he bring down the wicked? If so, then God said He would confess Job could deliver himself by his own hand.

Perhaps the point was that Job had complained that God allowed Job to suffer wrongfully, so God was not just in dealing with man. But Job himself did not have the power and wisdom to right all the wrongs in the world. If he did have that power and wisdom, then let him do so and deliver himself from the suffering he is enduring.

But if he did not have that power and wisdom, then why blame God for his problems? It must be that he recognized God does have the power to deal with these problems. But if God has that power and wisdom, but Job admits he himself does not, then wouldn't that mean God is greater than Job? And if so, why did Job criticize Him? God will someday correct all the wrongs of the world, but Job was correct that He is not doing so now. If we can accept the fact He is not doing it now, then He must have a good reason for this. So, why not in the same way accept the fact this means we must suffer at times now? Why not just admit that God is greater and we just do not understand what He is doing or why?

40:15-18 – God appealed to behemoth as proof of His power.

God continued describing His great power by considering great animals he has made, that man cannot make. In fact, man is afraid to deal with them, generally. The first is "behemoth." This term (and others used here for animals) are hard to determine by definition exactly what kind of animal was being referred to. All we can do is to try to compare the description to animals that we know about that might fit. In this way, some think the behemoth may refer to a hippopotamus or elephant. Others have thought the behemoth may even have been a dinosaur that is now extinct. If so, then this passage proves man co-existed with dinosaurs (note "which I made along with you.")

This behemoth was made by God just as surely as man was. He eats grass like an ox, and has great power in his hips and stomach muscles. His tail is strong and large like a cedar, and his thighs are powerful, his bones and ribs like bronze and iron. Such a description would fit a hippopotamus, except for the tail. It might fit an elephant, except that it does not eat grass like an ox. However, there are remains of dinosaurs that would fit quite well.

40:19-24 – The behemoth lies in shade and is not afraid. Who can capture him?

The behemoth is chief of God's ways (one of the greatest of God's creatures). Only the God who made him can come near him with a sword. Perhaps this means you cannot harm him with a sword — you would have to be great as God who made the animal to be able to do so. Others think the sword refers to behemoth's teeth or other dangerous defense.

He eats where he pleases, yet other animals can play nearby: apparently he is not a threat to them since he eats grass (verse 15). He lies in the shade by a brook. Yet even a raging river does not frighten him, even if it is a high up as his mouth. Though one try to capture him, he is wary and cannot be taken by a snare in the nose.

The point throughout is the greatness of this animal God has made. Can man make one like him? Man can hardly control this animal, in general. How could he ever have made him? God made him and can control him. If so, why try to question God's control of the universe or suggest it be done a better way?

Note: Whether or not behemoth was a dinosaur, the fact is Bible teaching requires that dinosaurs and men were made on the same day of creation (day 6). Therefore, they must have coexisted at that time. Evolution is wrong to say they became extinct before man existed. They **may** have become extinct before Job lived. But there is no Biblical proof that would deny dinosaurs could have existed in Job's day, and any "scientific" reason would contradict the Bible. No such evidence can properly be used to argue against behemoth and Leviathan having been dinosaurs.

Job 41

Chapter 41 - God Continues His Speech

41:1-7 – God then described Leviathan, asking if one can easily capture him or train him.

God has been describing his creatures that Job (and man in general) could never make, and in general cannot even control. The point is to prove that man is far inferior to God and therefore should not question God's control of the universe but trust Him. If God can make and control these great creatures, then He is the supreme power in the universe. Who are we to question Him?

Here he described Leviathan. As Hailey says, this is probably the most difficult chapter in the book to understand.

Some say this refers to a crocodile. Others think it is a large sea monster, perhaps even a dinosaur. The problem is that the description seems to be of a living creature that existed at Job's time, otherwise the argument has no force. But the description does not literally fit any known creature today. The only real difficulty lies in verses 18-21, referring to flame, smoke, etc. This sounds much like we would think of a dragon: a dinosaur-like reptile having powers that we cannot prove today.

The point being made by the Lord is valid whether or not we know exactly which animal is meant. However, if the description is of a dinosaur, it would prove that men and dinosaurs coexisted.

Do you catch such an animal with a fish-hook and pull him in as with a rod and reel? Or just grab him and tie him up with a cord, or a rope through his nose or a hook through his jaw?

Do you expect him to speak softly and plead with you ("I'll be good, just don't hurt me!")? Will you simply make a bargain with him that he will be your servant for life? Would you have him as a house pet like a bird for your children to play with? Such things can be done with some animals, but not with Leviathan!

Would you make traffic of him like fishermen do with fish they catch as with nets, or like merchants do with cloth or garments? Would you kill him with just harpoons or fishing spears? Now today we can kill almost any animal with a big enough gun. And even crocodiles have been hunted for their skins, etc. But in those days not so. And the point even so is the same: no ordinary means will suffice, but it takes something extraordinary. And this is to destroy the animal! The point is who made it and therefore who is really great in this universe?

Note: Some people doubt or deny that Leviathan ever existed because they think they have never seen or heard of one living today. Question: Do you believe dinosaurs existed? Have you ever seen one living today? I believe they existed, though I have never seen a live one. If we can believe dinosaurs existed because of the claims of scientists, though we have never seen one alive, why not likewise believe that Leviathan existed because of the testimony of Scripture? Why insist that it must exist today for us to believe in it? And why put more faith in the evidence of science than we do in the statements of God Himself in Scripture? Were the animals described in Job 39 literal? Then why doubt that behemoth and Leviathan were literal?

41:8-11 – Leviathan is exceedingly fierce and dangerous, so to try to touch him results in a great battle. This demonstrates the greatness of God who created him.

You don't just walk up and pet him, or catch him with your hands. If you tried, you would never forget the battle that followed. In fact, to hope to capture him is vain; it is overwhelming just to look at him. Nobody is so mighty than he can just go stir one up and not worry about the consequences.

This would not necessarily mean that one could not be captured. It simply means it would be such a terrible task that it would not be worth it, especially in those days. Again, the point is that man could never make such a creature. If man had made such an animal, he should be able also to handle him. The fact he has such difficulty handling him, proves man is inferior to the Maker.

If man cannot control the creature, how much more is he unable to stand against the Creator who made such a creature! Who has ever done anything for God that put God in his debt so that God owes him something? God owes nothing to anyone, but rather all things here are under His control. This is really the point of the whole discussion. If God can make such animals, then what is man compared to Him, and what man can control Him? Since we are clearly so inferior to Him, what right do we have to criticize Him?

41:12-17 – Leviathan is strong, having vicious teeth, and covered with strong scales.

His power is great, and yet he has a solid frame (ASV). Who can go to him, as one would with a horse, to put a bridle in his mouth? Who could shear him as one would a sheep? His jaws (doors of his face) are so terrible and enclose such terrible teeth that no one would try to open them. His body is covered with scales so tightly sealed that no air can pass between them and they cannot be separated.

Such a description could surely fit a crocodile, but could also fit a dinosaur.

41:18-21 – *Light, smoke, and fire come from his nose and mouth.*

Light flashes when he sneezes, and his eyes are bright like the morning. Light and sparks of fire shoot from his mouth and smoke from his nostrils like from a pot that boils and burns rushes. His breath is like coals that send a flame from his mouth.

I have been told that, for some reason, vapor does come from the lower jaw of a crocodile, appearing like smoke. However, that is not literal fire. Either this description is a symbolic description of the terrifying appearance of a crocodile, or else this is a reference to some other animal. So much of the rest of the description appears to be literal (or at least lets us know when it is symbolic), that this seems literal to me.

The passage does not say that flame shoots far from his mouth, but that he does breathe smoke and flame. While I cannot prove any dinosaur has ever done such a thing, yet ancient stories have told for years of dragons, just like dinosaurs, that do exactly what this describes. These stories come from many different cultures (China, England, Europe, etc.). Why should it be thought a thing impossible that such animals existed but have become extinct? A dragon would fit exactly what this chapter describes (but it would swim, not necessarily fly).

Before we reject as impossible the idea of flame coming from an animal's mouth, let us recall that we all know animals that do similar amazing things.

Fireflies produce light by means of chemicals within their body. Some kinds of fish in deeper areas of the ocean can make light. Why couldn't a dinosaur do something similar?

Note the following regarding electric eels, taken from Wikipedia:

> The electric eel generates its characteristic electrical pulse in a manner similar to a battery, in which stacked plates produce an electrical charge. In the electric eel, some 5,000 to 6,000 stacked electroplaques are capable of producing a shock at up to 500 volts and 1 ampere of current (500 watts). Such a shock could be deadly for an adult human.

If an eel can produce electricity powerful enough to kill a man, why be surprised if an animal could produce fire?

Bombardier beetles produce explosive chemical reactions. Note the following from Wikipedia:

Bombardier beetles are ground beetles (Carabidae) in the tribes Brachinini, Paussini, Ozaenini, or Metriini—more than 500 species altogether—that are most notable for the defense mechanism that gives them their name: When disturbed, the beetle ejects a noxious chemical spray in a rapid burst of pulses from special glands in its abdomen. The ejection is accompanied with a popping sound.

A bombardier beetle produces and stores two reactant chemical compounds, hydroquinone and hydrogen-peroxide in separate reservoirs in the rear tip of its abdomen. When threatened, the beetle contracts muscles that force the two reactants through valved tubes into a mixing chamber containing water and a mixture of catalytic enzymes. When combined, the reactants undergo a violent exothermic chemical reaction raising the temperature to near the boiling point of water. The corresponding pressure buildup forces the entrance valves from the reactant storage chambers to close, thus protecting the beetle's internal organs. The boiling, foul-smelling liquid partially becomes a gas (flash evaporation) and is expelled through an outlet valve into the atmosphere with a loud popping sound.

Why couldn't a similar process in an animal produce a flame? Why can't Leviathan refer to a dragon-like creature that has simply become extinct?

The remains of dinosaurs that we have found have mostly been bones. If any ancient dinosaur had been able to breathe fire, this would have been accomplished by soft parts of the body (glands, etc.), which would not likely survive for many years after the animal died. So we should not expect the remains of dinosaurs to show proof one way or the other if the dinosaur could breathe fire.

41:22-25 – *His neck, flesh, and heart are so strong they cause great fear.*

His neck is strong, and before him goes sorrow (i.e., he is so fearful that the coming of him produces sorrow). His flesh is strong and firm. His heart as hard as stone, a millstone — no sympathy or pity on others. (Note that this symbol is clearly described in the passage as being a symbol: "as hard as." This to me implies other descriptions, not identified as symbolic, are generally meant to be literal.)

When he rises, even mighty men are afraid. His violent actions and sounds cause men to be so fearful they are beside themselves. Again the point is he is so great a creature, men fear him. How could men have made him? Ought we not to fear much more Him who did make him?

41:26-29 – *All the common weapons of that day were useless against him.*

He could not be killed with sword, spear, dart, or javelin, or arrow, or slinging stones. He laughs at them. Iron and bronze are too weak to harm him (note again that symbols are clearly identified as such). Again, it is likely even in that day they could occasionally kill one, but it was extremely difficult (see notes on verses 6,9).

41:30-34 – *He is even strong on the underneath portions of his body, and makes a wake when he swims.*

His undersides are sharp like potsherds, leaving marks in the mud. The water boils around him as he thrashes, and in swimming he leaves a white wake behind him (note that he can swim well in the sea). Nothing else on earth is like him in fearlessness. He is king over all creatures (in these matters described). (Note again the identification of symbols as such.)

Again, the point is to show the greatness of God's creatures and so the greatness of God the Creator. The point is to exalt, not the creature, but the Creator by means of the creature. If God's creatures are so great, then surely man should exalt God and honor Him. He should not dispute what God does.

Job 42

Chapter 42 - God's Speech Concludes

42:1-3 – Job confessed that God can do all things and that Job himself had spoken things he did not understand.

Job had learned his lesson. He responded that God can do everything and no one can resist any purpose that He determines. He referred to God's earlier question regarding who had hidden counsel by speaking without knowledge (38:2). He confessed that he was guilty. He had said things he did not understand and talked about things so wonderful he did not understand them.

This had been Job's error. He was not wrong, as the friends believed, in defending his own integrity. He was correct in believing that his suffering was not a punishment for sin. He was wrong in saying things that implied God made mistakes in how he handled Job's case.

God is so great in wisdom and power that who among man can possibly be wiser? Who can possibly come up with a better way to do things? Who can correct Him or reprove Him for His errors? Instead of criticizing Him, we must accept that His ways are best, even if we don't understand them. We cannot possibly come up with a better way of doing anything, so why criticize?

42:4-6 – Job plainly admitted his error and confessed his repentance.

Job further referred to God's statement that He would question Job and see if Job could give good answers. But Job now realized that he had no answers. He could not approach God as an equal. (The ASV does not treat the second half of the verse as a quotation of God's statement, as in the NKJV.)

So he confessed that he had heard about God, but now his eye saw Him. This was not meant to be literal. The point was that, whereas he had heard some things about God in the past, he had come to fuller knowledge, comparable to the difference between just hearing about a thing and actually seeing it. Often a personal experience with a situation – especially a problem – will teach us important lessons that we would never have understood or at least not appreciated until we experience it ourselves.

God's words to Job, following all that Job had suffered, had brought Job to a much deeper appreciation of God's true nature. This is often true of suffering and is one of its benefits. It leads us to a fuller appreciation of God and His gifts to us. When people tell us about their problems, we may say, "I understand," but we really don't understand like those who have been in the situation. Actually experiencing problems leads us to personally understand and appreciate many aspects of God and His care for us that we do not really appreciate simply by hearing about them.

Job said he abhorred himself and repented in dust and ashes. He recognized and confessed his error in speaking against God. Note that in the Old Testament, as well as in the New Testament, sins were forgiven on the basis of repentance and confession. Then, as now, when God's children sin, we need to humbly acknowledge our sin before God and plead for His forgiveness. See Acts 8:22; Matthew 6:12; 21:28-32; 2 Corinthians 7:10; 1 John 1:8-10; Proverbs 28:13.

42:7-9 – God then strongly rebuked Job's friends and required them to offer sacrifice.

Then God dealt with the case of Job's friends. God expressly said that He was angry with Eliphaz and the other two friends because they had not spoken what is right regarding God as Job had. Therefore, they were required to offer sacrifices and have Job pray for them. (Contrast God's statements about the friends to Elihu's statements. If Elihu was right in his views, as some claim, why did he not strongly rebuke the friends like God did here?)

This made clear beyond question that the friends were wrong in accusing Job of sin. We knew this all along because of the introduction of the book. But of course the friends did not know what we knew, nor did Job. But still they were wrong. God accused them of "folly," He said His anger was aroused against them, and He twice said they had not spoken what was right.

No doubt it galled them to have to admit they had been wrong, and even more so to have to go to the one whom they had wronged and seek him to be their mediator before God. This would be especially difficult when they had repeatedly accused him of sin, but they themselves turned out to be the sinners. But when we wrong others, we must be humble enough to make it right with them as well as with God. (The fact they took the sacrifices to Job, instead of to the Levites at the tabernacle, is further evidence that these events occurred in the Patriarchal Age.)

Note further that God expected Job to pray for his friends. This would indicate his forgiveness of them. They had said some terrible things to him. Just as it would have been hard for them to confess and ask him to pray for them, so it would have been hard for him to forgive and pray for them. But this too was required of him, and we are likewise required to be willing to forgive and pray for those who sin against us.

The friends were wrong in their belief that all suffering is the result of sin, and that sin is always punished in this life. These are untrue premises. The case of Job, and this ensuing discussion and God's evaluation of it, prove for all time that such conclusions are not valid. There are other possible reasons for suffering. Some good people suffer because they are mistreated by evil people, just as Job had described in chapter 24. Other good people suffer like Job as a form of temptation from Satan. Good people often do suffer in this life, just as Job had affirmed

The friends were also wrong, not just in their beliefs, but also in the actions those beliefs had prompted. They had repeatedly and harshly accused a man of sin when they had no proof of it – and he was a deeply suffering man to whom they ought to have shown pity. Job asked them for their proof, but they had none. It is wrong to accuse one of sin when we have no evidence.

But it is interesting that God did not accuse them of having wronged Job (though of course they had terribly wronged him). He accused them twice of having spoken wrong regarding God. All wrongs against people are wrongs against God. But this sin was specifically wrong against God because it misstated God's conduct toward men. They had said that God punishes all sin in this life, and that all people who suffer are doing so because of what God had done. It is dangerous to accuse God of harming people when we do not know He is the one doing it. We often hear people do this today and may be guilty ourselves if we do not take care. Not only had they falsely accused Job of sin, they had also falsely accused God of severely harming Job when in fact God had done none of it. Job was an upright man. To accuse him of suffering for sin was to accuse God of doing vicious harm when they had no proof God was doing any such thing. This is impugning God's righteousness and justice.

42:10-17 – God then restored all Job's blessings, including his flocks, herds, and children.

The end of the story finally is told. The trial was over and Job had proved Satan wrong. He did not renounce God, but maintained his faith. True, he sinned in his speech, but even that was corrected. And he had prayed for his friends, indicating his forgiveness of them. Since the trials had accomplished their purpose, there was no reason for them to continue. So God caused them to end and gave Job more blessings than he had before.

Job had seven sons and three daughters as before. His daughters were the fairest in the land. Their names are given, each name signifying beauty, charm, grace, or other virtue attractive in women. He gave them inheritances along with his sons. He had exactly twice as much prosperity in flocks as he had before (compare 42:12 to 1:2).

In addition, his friends and relatives came bearing gifts in sympathy for his suffering. These are said to be his brothers and sisters, as well as acquaintances. One wonders where they were with these gifts and condolences when he was still suffering. They are strange friends and relatives who are nowhere to be found when a man is deeply suffering but come to his "aid" when the problems are over and he is again prospering. As Hailey said, they should not just have come back to him, they should have come "crawling back" to him!

Job then lived to a very old age, seeing four generations of children and grandchildren (which implies he lived in the patriarchal age).

These blessings served to prove to Job, his friends, and all who knew Job, that he had been righteous before God and had not deserved his troubles. However, we should not conclude that God will always bless the righteous in this life, any more than we should conclude that He will always punish the wicked in this life. The ultimate reward for our lives comes after death.

Yet what did God tell Job about the reason why he had suffered?

One wonders, as we conclude, at the fact that *God never did explain to Job the real reason for his suffering.* We were told the reason in the very beginning of the book, yet the record nowhere states that God ever told Job. Over and over Job and his friends disputed the reason why Job was suffering. This one issue was the major theme of the book till God spoke. Yet the book ends without Job or his friends ever learning the answer! This used to really frustrate me. It almost appears that God missed the point of the discussion – that He never even discussed the real issue. But of course, we must never think God makes a mistake – that would be similar to the error Job committed. So why did God not answer Job's questions?

Note what God did do. God did not explain to Job why he had suffered, because that is not the main lesson Job needed to learn. Instead, Job needed to learn a bigger lesson. What God did was to teach Job what He really needed to learn: that God is in charge and knows what He is doing! Like Job, when we suffer, we too will often have no way to know the specific reason why we suffer each specific trouble. God has told us why Job suffered, but there are other reasons for suffering. How do we know in our case what the reason is? The answer is that we often will not know in this life or at least not at the time, just as Job did not know. Yes, we do need to know that there *are* reasons for suffering, so God does reveal to us why Job suffered. But in any specific situation, we will often never know why we suffered that specific problem.

So, what God did was to teach Job the real lesson and the most important lesson for every sufferer to understand. We may never know why we suffer, but the main lesson we need to learn is that *we must trust God to take care of us and to do what is right at all times, including when events don't seem to make sense to us according to our human wisdom*. We are not wise enough to be in charge of this universe. God is the only One wise enough and powerful enough to be in charge. We must trust Him to do right, even when we don't understand. That is the real point God made to Job. God has proved He is the only one wise enough to handle all this.

Applications of the lesson God taught Job

And the same lesson applies in many other areas besides suffering. Lots of people have the same problem Job had, just regarding other issues. Often people doubt or question God's wisdom: why does God do what He does or give us the commands that He gives? Often these doubts lead people to criticize God's word or to refuse to obey it.

* Why did God let my loved one die? I just can't believe in a God who ...

* Why doesn't God answer my prayer? I asked him for ... and never received it. Why should I believe in a God who ....

* Why does God require baptism as a necessary condition to salvation? I just can't believe...

* These good people believe in God and they are sincere and conscientious. Why isn't that good enough? I just can't believe all these good people will be lost.

* Why must we have the Lord's Supper every Sunday? Why can't we have it on weekdays or once a month or once a year?

* Why would God say the man should be the head of the family? I can't believe in a God ...

* Why is fornication the only acceptable reason for divorce? Why can't a woman get a divorce if her husband is a drunken, worthless bum? I just can't believe that God would require someone to leave a spouse just because he divorced a former spouse for some reason other than fornication.

* Why wouldn't God want instrumental music in worship? They sound good and we can use our talents for God. I just can't believe ...

* Why can't women be preachers and elders? What kind of God ....

* I just can't believe in a God who would send people to hell.

I have heard people say virtually all these things. And we can go on and on.

We may or may not be able to give reasons for these commands that would satisfy the human reasoning of people. And we should show people exactly what the Bible says for each subject the question. But many people will still reject the truth because God didn't say what they want or expected Him to say. Like Job, they want God to explain and justify His decisions to their satisfaction. If it doesn't make sense to their way of thinking, they will criticize what God says in His word or refuse to believe it or completely reject God.

What is the answer to people who have such issues and criticisms?

Must God tell us why He made all these choices and gave all these commands? Must He reason with us on our level till we understand, and do we have the right to criticize His choices if we don't understand? He may choose to answer and give His reasons. But He is not required to answer, and in many cases we would never understand no matter how hard He tried to explain (Deuteronomy 29:29).

The answer to all such issues is the same one God gave to Job:
Did you make those stars in the sky?
Do you make the sun rise and set every day?
Did you make the earth, the mountains, and the sea?
Do you make the lightning, thunder, and rain?
Did you make all the animals and plants?

In short, who made the universe and who is in charge here? If we do not have the power and wisdom to make these things or to control them, who are we to criticize the wisdom and decisions of the one who did?

In short, when we question or doubt God's decisions, the main issue is **authority – dominion – sovereignty – preeminence.** Who is in charge here? Who is on the throne and who must bow before the throne? That is the ultimate issue. God's answer to Job was exactly the right answer, and it is the same answer we need to be given when we begin to doubt and criticize the sovereignty of God and His right to do what He chooses to do in the world that He made.

Illustration of the rug maker

The story is told of a Persian rug maker who views his rug being made suspended on a rack. Behind the rug are his assistants who must place each thread in place as he instructs them. From their side, the rug does not look beautiful. In fact, they may often question why the master instructs them as he does. They may think it does not make sense. That is because their knowledge is too limited. They do not see the whole picture from the view of the master who knows what is best. And even if he tried to explain it to them, they would not understand, because they simply cannot see from their perspective what he is trying to do. Their job is to follow instructions and trust the master that he knows what he is doing, so that the end product will be good if they just do what he says. And someday they will be able to move to the same side as the master and will see the real beauty of what they have made.

So God instructs us how to live our lives. From our earthly viewpoint as finite humans with our limited knowledge, we often do not see how the things that happen in our lives can be good for us or others. But that is only because we cannot see things from the viewpoint of the all-wise God who sees the whole picture from His infinite wisdom. And even if He tried to explain it, much of it we could never understand till the end product is complete. So we must not doubt God's wisdom or dispute His will. Instead, we must trust Him that He knows what He is doing. Our job is to just follow His instructions, whether or not they seem to make sense at the time. But if we believe Him and obey, someday we will be with Him in eternity where we can see things from His viewpoint. Then we will understand the beauty of what He has done with our lives.

Job and his friends argued on and on with endless repetition about the reason why Job was suffering. The reasons why men suffer are worthwhile considering. But God showed Job and his friends that there was a greater question. ***When we suffer, we do not need to know why we suffer so much as we need to put our trust in the One who is in charge. He knows why we suffer, but more important He can care for us, help us through our troubles, and ultimately reward us with eternal life in a land where no one suffers. Faith does not need to know all the whys and wherefores. It is enough to know God is in charge and He is wise enough to handle it properly. Do not doubt. Just obey Him in faith. That is the lesson of the book of Job.*** Have we learned the lesson? We will probably spend our entire lives learning it.

Sources Frequently Cited in These Notes

Hailey, Homer, *A Commentary on Job*; Religious Supply, Inc., 1994

Horne, Thomas, *Introduction to the Critical Study and Knowledge of the Holy Scriptures*, 4 volumes; T. Cadwell, Strand, London, 1828 (public domain)

Keil, C. F. and Franz Delitzsch, *Commentary on the Old Testament;* originally published by T. and T. Clark, Edinburgh, 1866-1891

Pfeiffer, Charles F., *Baker's Bible Atlas*, Baker Book House, Grand Rapids, MI, 1961

Waldron, Bob and Sandra, *Give Us a King, The United Kingdom and the Wisdom Literature;* Bob Waldron, Athens, Alabama, 1994

Printed books, booklets, and tracts available at
www.gospelway.com/sales
Free Bible study articles online at
www.gospelway.com
Free Bible courses online at
www.biblestudylessons.com
Free class books at
www.biblestudylessons.com/classbooks
Free commentaries on Bible books at
www.biblestudylessons.com/commentary
Contact the author at
www.gospelway.com/comments
Free e-mail Bible study newsletter –
www.gospelway.com/update_subscribe.htm

Printed in Great Britain
by Amazon